The Uncommon Case of Daniel Brown

TRUE CRIME HISTORY

Twilight of Innocence: The Disappearance of Beverly Potts · James Jessen Badal
Tracks to Murder · Jonathan Goodman
Terrorism for Self-Glorification: The Herostratos Syndrome · Albert Borowitz
Ripperology: A Study of the World's First Serial Killer and a Literary Phenomenon · Robin Odell
The Good-bye Door: The Incredible True Story of America's First Female Serial Killer to Die in the Chair · Diana Britt Franklin
Murder on Several Occasions · Jonathan Goodman
The Murder of Mary Bean and Other Stories · Elizabeth A. De Wolfe
Lethal Witness: Sir Bernard Spilsbury, Honorary Pathologist · Andrew Rose
Murder of a Journalist: The True Story of the Death of Donald Ring Mellett · Thomas Crowl
Musical Mysteries: From Mozart to John Lennon · Albert Borowitz
The Adventuress: Murder, Blackmail, and Confidence Games in the Gilded Age · Virginia A. McConnell
Queen Victoria's Stalker: The Strange Case of the Boy Jones · Jan Bondeson
Born to Lose: Stanley B. Hoss and the Crime Spree That Gripped a Nation · James G. Hollock
Murder and Martial Justice: Spying and Retribution in World War II America · Meredith Lentz Adams
The Christmas Murders: Classic Stories of True Crime · Jonathan Goodman
The Supernatural Murders: Classic Stories of True Crime · Jonathan Goodman
Guilty by Popular Demand: A True Story of Small-Town Injustice · Bill Osinski
Nameless Indignities: Unraveling the Mystery of One of Illinois's Most Infamous Crimes · Susan Elmore
Hauptmann's Ladder: A Step-by-Step Analysis of the Lindbergh Kidnapping · Richard T. Cahill Jr.
The Lincoln Assassination Riddle: Revisiting the Crime of the Nineteenth Century · Edited by Frank J. Williams and Michael Burkhimer
Death of an Assassin: The True Story of the German Murderer Who Died Defending Robert E. Lee · Ann Marie Ackermann
The Insanity Defense and the Mad Murderess of Shaker Heights: Examining the Trial of Mariann Colby · William L. Tabac
The Belle of Bedford Avenue: The Sensational Brooks-Burns Murder in Turn-of-the-Century New York · Virginia A. McConnell
Six Capsules: The Gilded Age Murder of Helen Potts · George R. Dekle Sr.
A Woman Condemned: The Tragic Case of Anna Antonio · James M. Greiner
Bigamy and Bloodshed: The Scandal of Emma Molloy and the Murder of Sarah Graham · Larry E. Wood
The Beauty Defense: Femmes Fatales on Trial · Laura James
The Potato Masher Murder: Death at the Hands of a Jealous Husband · Gary Sosniecki
I Have Struck Mrs. Cochran with a Stake: Sleepwalking, Insanity, and the Trial of Abraham Prescott · Leslie Lambert Rounds
The Uncommon Case of Daniel Brown: How a White Police Officer Was Convicted of Killing a Black Citizen, Baltimore, 1875 · Gordon H. Shufelt

The Uncommon Case *of* Daniel Brown

How a White Police Officer Was Convicted of Killing a Black Citizen, Baltimore, 1875

Gordon H. Shufelt

The Kent State University Press KENT, OHIO

ISBN 978-1-60635-412-4
Manufactured in the United States of America

Portions of the text have been published elsewhere: Gordon Shufelt, "Elusive Justice in Baltimore: The Conviction of a White Policeman for Killing a Black Man in 1875," *Journal of Southern History* 83, no. 4 (Nov. 2017): 773–814.

Cataloging information for this title is available at the Library of Congress.

25 24 23 22 21 5 4 3 2 1

For Susan—after more than fifty years, still my girlfriend

Contents

Acknowledgments

Nobody writes a history book without help and encouragement from many sources. Teachers, librarians, archivists, editors, friends, and family all help, and I have been fortunate in every category. The American University History Department has been a source of encouragement for a long time. Many in the history department have extended support, and I cannot mention all of them. But two stand out: Professor Alan M. Kraut and the late Professor Terence R. Murphy. When I first considered making Baltimore a subject of my research, I benefited from Professor Kraut's extensive knowledge of US history, as well as from his wisdom, patience, and kindness. He is the model of what a history professor should be: a first-rate scholar and writer, an energetic supporter of his profession and his university, and a gifted classroom teacher. At the beginning of my studies at AU, Professor Murphy showed me how intellectually challenging and exciting history could be, as he brought insight, humanity, and even a little humor to the classroom. I regret that I never thanked him enough. During a period of study at the University of Colorado, I was fortunate to have guidance from Professor James B. Wolf. Like Professors Kraut and Murphy, he brought to teaching and counseling all the qualities a student could hope for: knowledge, wisdom, an ability to make difficult ideas clear, and a humane appreciation for the subjects of our studies. Indirectly, and sometimes directly, these scholars have influenced my book.

Libraries, archives, and museums hold the secrets of history, and I am grateful to have had access to many of them. The Bender Library at American University has provided a home base and starting place for me for many years. Librarians and archivists at the Library of Congress; the Maryland State Archives in Annapolis; the Maryland Historical Society in Baltimore; the Baltimore City Archives; the National Archives and Records Administration in College Park, Maryland; and the Maryland Room in the Hornbake Library at the University of Maryland have been especially helpful. Among the archivists, special notes of gratitude go to Senior Archivist Joseph Leizear at the Maryland State Archives and the staff at the Maryland Room at the University of Maryland.

Editors at *The Journal of Southern History* encouraged me in the early stages of this project, and their skill and efficiency were instrumental in producing an earlier version of Daniel and Keziah Brown's story. Managing Editor Bethany L. Johnson delivered helpful guidance from early in the process, and the anonymous readers she brought to the project helped me think through my material and put it in better order. At Kent State University Press, the encouragement and guidance I have received from Director Susan Wadsworth-Booth, Managing Editor Mary Young, Design and Production Manager Christine Brooks, and Marketing Manager Richard Fugini have been helpful; and, once again, anonymous readers provided useful suggestions. Copy Editor Valerie Ahwee has helped with her efficient work and willingness to answer many questions. The work of these editors and staff members at Kent State has gone forward smoothly and efficiently despite this year's difficult circumstances.

Teachers, librarians, archivists, and editors make direct contributions to the writing of history, but family and friends indirectly provide support and inspiration that are equally essential. On the dedication page is the name of my wife, Susan, and, in view of the love, support, and inspiration she has given me for more than fifty years, the dedication page could not be otherwise. Her suggestions have greatly improved the manuscript's clarity, and she has been heroically patient in rescuing me from struggles with my computer. No day passes in which I do not turn for inspiration to memories of the love and support so selflessly provided me by my Italian immigrant grandparents, Antonio Gianfrancesco and Teresa Melocco Gianfrancesco, and by their Italian American children, Frances Gianfrancesco Shufelt, Mary Gianfrancesco O'Brien, Michael Gianfrancesco, and Florence Gianfrancesco Contadino. Love, inspiration, and support come also from my brothers, Frank Shufelt and John Shufelt, and my sister Linda Ansbach. Each is exceptional and talented in his or her own way, and, best of all, each one is thoughtful and humane. John has read portions of the work and offered wise suggestions. Friends teach and inspire, too. Over long lunches and in rambling conversations, Jean and Bill Randolph have taught me a great deal about politics, social issues, and life in general; and even when they didn't know they were doing it, by sharing their insights, they were helping me write about Daniel and Keziah Brown. Similarly, I am grateful for time spent with Roberta and Allen Schectel—thoughtful and generous friends who have shared their insights about local government and education.

Introduction

Late on a midsummer night in 1875, Daniel Brown stood in the doorway of his home facing Officer Patrick McDonald, an Irish-born Baltimore policeman. Officer McDonald had been directed to Brown's house by a neighbor complaining of laughter and singing coming from a party there. The interaction between Brown, a proud African American, and McDonald, an inexperienced policeman with expectations of deference from black citizens, suddenly turned violent. But the violence was one-sided. Brown had no weapons; the policeman had a club and a pistol, and he used both, inflicting a bruise on one side of Brown's head and a bullet wound on the other. In less than an hour after Officer McDonald had first rapped his club on Daniel Brown's door, Brown bled to death on the floor inside his own home.

Very little is known about Daniel Brown's life. His death certificate reveals only that he was born on Maryland's Eastern Shore. The coroner filled in no town, city, or county. Apparently Brown was born between 1838 and 1844: his marriage certificate suggests he was twenty-four years old in 1868, but 1870 census records show his age as thirty, and his death certificate indicates he died at the age of thirty-seven in 1875.[1] Some newspaper accounts of the events surrounding his death describe him as a "light mulatto," while others say he was a "dark mulatto." Available records fail to disclose whether or not he began life in slavery. Newspaper accounts provide some hints that allow for speculation about his character and personal life. Probably he was a strong man and a good worker, and probably he was serious and proud. Most likely he was frugal, and it seems that he enjoyed socializing with friends and neighbors, although he rarely, if ever, consumed alcohol. His critics could say no worse of him than he was "a little strong on the Civil Rights questions."

Despite the obscurity in which he lived, his violent death rendered him almost famous for a few months in 1875, at least in Baltimore, where the major daily newspapers reported, and sometimes sensationalized, the details of the killing and its aftermath. In the four months after Daniel Brown died, a coroner's inquest established that Officer McDonald's actions caused Brown's death, a grand jury indicted McDonald, a panel of Baltimore citizens convicted McDonald of manslaughter, and a Baltimore Criminal Court judge sentenced him to five years in the city jail.[2] An appellate court ruling, however, resulted in his release less than a year after his sentence began.

Even with the questionable abbreviation of the jail sentence, the response of law enforcement authorities to McDonald's use of lethal force against an African American more than 140 years ago seems surprising. In recent years, Baltimore's conviction rate in cases of police killings has been below 2 percent. From 2006 to April 2015, Baltimore policemen killed sixty-seven people, and prosecutors brought charges in two cases. One officer was acquitted, and one was convicted. The officer who was convicted was not on duty at the time of the killing. Following Freddy Gray's death in Baltimore in April 2015, prosecutors brought charges against six Baltimore officers, but none of them was convicted. And Baltimore's recent record is not out of line with a persistent trend in US law enforcement. In turn-of-the-century Chicago, prosecutors secured convictions in only 1 percent of cases in which policemen killed suspects.[3] A century later, national statistics reflected a similar rate of convictions. According to the *Washington Post,* law enforcement officers killed thousands of suspects in the decade preceding 2015, and only fifty-six of the officers faced charges.[4]

Undoubtedly, police officers sometimes face dangers that make the use of deadly force justifiable. But the high rate of exonerations suggests that some officers escape punishment when they use deadly force maliciously or carelessly, especially when the force is directed at minorities. And again, the statistics reflect patterns that have persisted for decades.[5] More than half of the 319 persons killed by police in Los Angeles from 1947 to 1966 were members of minority groups.[6] In cases in which the victims are African Americans, the evidence indicating police misconduct goes beyond suggestive statistics. Protesters, many of whom base their charges on personal experiences, contend that police officers in some cities have a long history of routinely abusing black citizens; and in recent years, video devices have sometimes provided evidence to corroborate their charges.[7]

Allegations of police violence against African Americans are not new. The troubled relationship between African Americans and police forces has deep roots in US history. Although Daniel Brown died well over a century ago, the circumstances surrounding his death and the conviction of Officer McDonald illuminate many of the social, political, and cultural factors that come into play when the justice system addresses cases of police violence against African Americans. Daniel Brown's case is unusual in that agents of the criminal justice system responded promptly and stayed with the process through all the steps necessary to get the charges before a jury. A thorough review of cases of police violence requires attention to all the steps in the criminal justice system. Although trials are more thoroughly documented than pretrial practices, the quality of justice in cases of alleged police misconduct is best understood by examining the first responses to violent encounters, especially in police magistrates' hearings and, in cases of homicides, in coroners' inquests.[8] In the Daniel Brown case, the social setting of the crime gave the incident an unusual significance in the city, and the social and cultural characteristics of the people involved in the case before the trial—those involved in the arrest and in the coroner's inquest—made a difference in the procedures leading to the conviction of Officer McDonald.

The location of Brown's death is significant for the student of policing in the United States. A recent study of nineteenth-century Baltimore has brought attention to the city's importance as a location for the study of professionalized policing. In his examination of rising rates of incarceration of African Americans, historian Adam Malka, in *The Men of Mobtown,* explains how Baltimore's modernized police force merged with a tradition of white vigilantism to perpetuate the subordination of African Americans and institutionalize a belief in black criminality.[9] For the most part, however, historians have overlooked Baltimore in studies of the development of uniformed, armed, full-time police forces. Beginning in 1967 with Roger Lane's study of Boston, historians focused on northern cities when they studied the role of police in municipal responses to social conflict in the nineteenth century. Following Lane's lead, historians produced studies of police and policing in New York, Philadelphia, Buffalo, Chicago, Detroit, and Columbus, Ohio.[10] After the initial flurry of studies of northern cities, students of the history of police and policing turned their attention to southern cities, and, continuing to overlook Baltimore, historians turned their attention to more typically southern cities—cities such as Charleston, South Carolina, and New Orleans, which, unlike Baltimore, left the Union, suffered defeat in the Civil War, and experienced Reconstruction.[11] Thus, with the exception of Professor Malka's recent work, researchers have overlooked

Baltimore as a representative city for their work, and no major study of the early development of the Baltimore police force has been published.

Baltimore has been similarly neglected in nationally focused works. In a study of nineteenth- and early twentieth-century policing, for example, Eric H. Monkkonen includes an appendix illustrating the significance of city size in relation to when uniformed police appeared in major cities. Although the data demonstrate Baltimore's significance based on these criteria, Monkkonen's main text barely touches on policing in Baltimore.[12]

Historians' neglect of Baltimore is unfortunate because the city's distinctive characteristics make it a good setting for studies of the history of policing. In 1860, Baltimore ranked third in population among US cities (fourth if New York and Brooklyn are counted separately). And mid-nineteenth-century Baltimore was an industrializing city that replaced its centuries-old night watch and constable system in 1857, making it one of the earliest US cities to establish a unified metropolitan police force. At the same time, as a result of southern influences in Baltimore's politics and culture, the city offers opportunities to examine issues from some unique perspectives; Baltimore retained cultural elements of a slavery-era society long after emancipation, and the city's post–Civil War political conflicts reflected Maryland's ambivalence toward African Americans and toward the Union.

Baltimore's social structure was always complex, and mid-nineteenth-century political and economic upheavals magnified old distinctions and added new ones. Social distinctions and political differences in both Baltimore's black population and white population mattered in the criminal prosecution of patrolman McDonald. African American activist businessmen responded to the killing of Daniel Brown more militantly than did black ministers. And the social standing of Daniel Brown and the black guests in his home on the night of the homicide set them apart from casual laborers and former field slaves. Many of the African American witnesses to the killing worked in the homes of wealthy white Baltimore families—a fact that mattered a great deal in responses to the killing. Among the white residents of Baltimore, political and ideological differences also played a major role in the outcome of the case. The divisive and embittering consequences of the Civil War weighed especially heavily on Maryland, where an estimated sixty thousand residents of the state had fought on the Union side and twenty-five thousand had fought for the Confederacy.[13] Rifts between those who had chosen opposing sides in the Civil War continued to plague the city in the 1870s.

These social, cultural, and political factors contributed to the outcome of Daniel Brown's case in two ways. First, the killing occurred in a social setting that reflected the lingering personal, paternalistic relationships of slavery-era Baltimore. Unlike most cases in which white law enforcement officers killed black men and women in nineteenth-century Baltimore, in the matter of Daniel Brown, the African American witnesses to the killing were not socially isolated from the white authorities who controlled the justice system. And second, mistrust of police was exacerbated by rifts within the white population because factions in the divided city used the city's police force against their opponents. As political control shifted from one faction to the other, white citizens on each side in turn felt the sting of police tactics perceived as arbitrary and oppressive.

In more specific terms, the individuals who interacted on Daniel Brown's doorstep on the night of the killing exemplified important elements of Baltimore's mid-nineteenth-century social structure. Brown and McDonald represented factions that came into conflict in the city in a period of rapid social, cultural, and political transitions. For both men, the hardships of their early years made a difference when they came face to face.

Daniel Brown began life in rural Maryland in the waning years of slavery, an era and a place in which the state's black code was enforced with heightened intensity against slaves as well as against the increasing number of ostensibly free blacks in the region.[14] In the same period, famine, disease, and economic stagnation drove men and women from Ireland in a mass migration that was at its worst in the very years McDonald and his family emigrated.[15] In Baltimore, each man found some relief from difficult times. For Brown, the anonymity and diversity of the city attenuated some of the most oppressive aspects of white intrusions into the private lives of black men and women. And, in the years in which Brown is known with certainty to have resided in Baltimore, 1868 to 1875, federal actions offered black Marylanders a hopeful, if meager, share in the civic life of their city. For McDonald, Baltimore provided a place in the world that was not haunted by immediate prospects of starvation and deadly fevers, and, at the same time, introduced Irish migrants to a social order in which the majority community in most instances relegated blacks rather than Irish men and women to the lowest stratum of a racial caste system.

Yet for each man some of the troubles of the past followed him to Baltimore; and for each man the foe he faced in the doorway on the midsummer night in 1875 was an embodiment of the forms of oppression he dreaded most. Baltimore was not the antebellum Eastern Shore, but white officials still authorized policemen to monitor assemblies of African Americans in private homes. Nor was Baltimore Ireland. But McDonald found that many Anglo-Americans disparaged the lowly Irish, and at least in some cases insinuated that Irish Americans should rank on a par with blacks in the economic and social order—a stinging expression of nativism that reminded Irish migrants of their caste status under English colonialism.

The story of Daniel Brown's death and its aftermath provides a framework in which to examine the social, political, and cultural characteristics that define the quality of justice in cases of police violence. Daniel Brown's case in some ways resembled other cases of police violence in this pivotal period of US history. But the case differed in some ways, too, and the differences—even more than the similarities—reveal the factors that influence the adjudication of cases of police violence. In exploring the events surrounding the case, it is important to note that no one factor accounts for the unusual outcome of the Daniel Brown case. The crime was obviously egregious and disturbing to white as well as black Baltimoreans. But the brutality of the attack on Daniel Brown does not by itself explain the manslaughter conviction. Brutal crimes against black men and women went unpunished in many other cases. The social setting of the crime and the white Baltimoreans' attitudes toward the police must be taken into account to understand the final resolution of the case. The setting of the crime illustrates why criminal justice authorities pursued the matter. The police department's entanglement in internecine political struggles helps to explain why there was sufficient support for prosecutors to see the matter through to a verdict. And posttrial proceedings reflect the ambivalence of a majority community confronting white-on-black police violence. In order to demonstrate the ways all these factors influenced the case, this book includes biographical sketches of Daniel Brown and Officer Patrick McDonald, an examination of the Baltimore police force's complicity in the rough electoral tactics of the era, a description of the functions of the coroner's office, an account of the trial of Officer McDonald, and a review of the posttrial legal proceedings.

CHAPTER 1

The Black Man in the Doorway

Whether or not Daniel Brown was born into slavery is unknown, but he began life in a place where the harsh realities of life in a slave-holding society weighed heavily on all African Americans, whether slave or ostensibly free. During Daniel Brown's childhood, life for African Americans on Maryland's Eastern Shore was grim enough to darken their perceptions of the world around them. An observer untroubled by an oppressive social order might have considered the region a picturesque place with "deeply indented inlets," an "immense navigable waterfront," and easy access to transportation on the Chesapeake Bay.[1] And the region's boosters might have described the farmland beyond the picturesque coastline as a place where melons and sweet potatoes flourished to "perfection" in the sandy soil.[2] But for African Americans, it mattered very little whether they labored along the waterways or on the sandy inland farms. For most of them, painful experiences overshadowed the Eastern Shore's assets. Frederick Douglass, who fled from Maryland at about the time Daniel Brown was born, recalled that on the region's remote farms, whites could whip, beat, and even murder African Americans without fear of the law because "killing a slave, or any colored person, was not treated as a crime, either by the courts or the community."[3] After his escape from slavery, Douglass's memories of the place reflected his bitterness: Talbot County, located in the heart of the Eastern Shore, as Douglass recalled it, was "remarkable for nothing . . . more than the worn-out, sandy, desertlike appearance of its soil, the general dilapidation of its farms and fences, the indigent spiritless character of its inhabitants, and the prevalence of ague and fever."[4] Daniel Brown, born in this place where he was vulnerable to the kinds of abuses Douglass described, might well have carried with him into adulthood memories that strengthened his resolve to resist an affront he perceived as rude or condescending, especially in a confrontation at the threshold of his home.

Slavery shaped the society that made life dangerous for young African Americans like Frederick Douglass and Daniel Brown, but the violence Douglass described occurred at the very time slavery was declining in Maryland. In the century before the Civil War, a combination of circumstances, some economic and some ideological, undermined slavery in Maryland.[5] One factor was market conditions, which eroded the economic basis for slavery in the state. At the same time, ethical and religious concerns weakened Marylanders' commitment to the institution. Slave labor could be exploited to the slaveholder's advantage in Maryland's tobacco-growing regions because the tasks required for tobacco production kept workers active throughout the year. As early as the mid-eighteenth century, however, market conditions turned against Maryland's tobacco growers, and Eastern Shore farmers began to reduce tobacco production in favor of wheat, fruit, and vegetables—crops that called for periods of inactivity during their growing cycles.[6] Then from the Revolutionary era to the Civil War, the political ideals of the new American republic, along with the theology and ethics of Quakers and Methodists, established an ideological foundation for manumissions.[7] Manumissions increased, and by the middle of the nineteenth century, the mix of slave and free in the black population gave Maryland's Eastern Shore a distinctive social and demographic configuration. In 1790, slaves outnumbered free blacks in the Eastern Shore counties by 38,591 to 3,907.[8] By 1850, however, slaves barely constituted a majority within the Eastern Shore's African American population, and by 1860—at about the time Daniel Brown reached maturity—free blacks in the region outnumbered slaves by a margin of 28,277 to 24,957.[9]

But manumissions did not make Maryland's African Americans free. White prejudices and fears continued to shape the state's social and political order. Accustomed to the enforcement of black subservience in a slave society, whites proved unable or unwilling to accept a social order in which black men and women shared equally in the rights and responsibilities of citizenship. Throughout the first half of the nineteenth century, as the number of African Americans living outside the direct control of slaveholders grew, white anxieties intensified. The fear generated by the increasing population of free blacks reached its highest levels in the regions of Maryland where tobacco plantations and slavery had flourished—the Eastern Shore and the southern counties on the Western Shore along the Potomac River and the Chesapeake Bay. With thousands of free black men and women living in close proximity to thousands of slaves, whites in these areas felt especially threatened by the possibility of concerted actions by slave and free blacks, and their fears only grew worse over the next three decades as the national crisis over slavery intensified. Observing life in the 1850s, Leonidas Dodson, a white Eastern Shore farmer, noted his white neighbors' obsession with the presence of free blacks. Dodson complained of his neighbors' paranoid ruminations about slave intrigues and expressed exasperation at the frequency of emergency assemblies conducted by "a certain portion of the community" in their excitement about "what this girl heard" or what "that lady overheard."[10]

Even whites who showed some humanitarian concerns for African Americans found it difficult to see their black servants and laborers as anything other than members of a lowly caste who could be productive only when supervised by whites. Dodson, for example, was a devout Methodist with some sympathy for the condition of African Americans, but he believed free blacks had no rightful place in the region's rural economy other than as workers who performed the same tasks as slaves, and who, like slaves, worked under the control of whites. Although Dodson criticized his white Eastern Shore neighbors for their prejudices and paranoid fears, he found no fault with white farmers who used judicial authority to compel free blacks to accept working conditions that differed very little from slavery.[11]

Driven by these anxieties, the Maryland General assembly enacted a series of oppressive measures aimed at controlling African Americans. Paranoid anxieties about black insurrections peaked after incidents such as Nat Turner's uprising, fugitive slave controversies, and John Brown's raid.[12] But even when immediate reactions to these episodes quieted down, the Maryland legislature continued to supplement and strengthen the body of laws that became known as the black code, an extensive statutory collection of oppressive measures that made everyday life hard for Maryland's African Americans, both slave and ostensibly free.[13] Antebellum Maryland's black code not only limited the rights of blacks and subjected them to intrusive methods of surveillance, but also rendered blacks defenseless when accused by a white person of violating the code's restrictions: Maryland's laws of evidence barred all blacks, "whether free or slave," from testifying in legal matters concerning white persons.[14]

The black code applied to blacks in all regions of Maryland, but white authorities and slaveholders applied it more aggressively in the tobacco-growing areas, including the eight sparsely settled counties of the Eastern Shore.[15] On the eve of the Civil War, Frederick Douglass said of Maryland that "No state had a more barbarous slave code, and in her remote districts a more rigorous bondage."[16] Like Douglass, Daniel Brown had roots on the Eastern Shore, and even if he moved on to Baltimore as early as the 1850s, he felt the constraints of the oppressive black code measures, and he knew that black men and women on his native Eastern Shore lived with an extra measure of intrusive white authority.

Free African Americans as well as slaves suffered indignities and lived with chronic insecurity under the black codes. In its fully developed form the code included ninety-four sections, with more than forty devoted to the control of ostensibly free African Americans.[17] Some provisions called for policing behavior in the petty details of everyday life in especially humiliating ways. It was illegal, for example, for a free African American to sell "any bacon, pork, beef, mutton, corn, wheat, tobacco, rye, or oats" without showing a certificate from a justice of the peace or three "respectable persons" to prove the seller came by the product honestly.[18]

Corrupt enforcement of black code provisions rendered all black men and women vulnerable not only to humiliation but also to arbitrary arrests. In 1854, the editors of an Eastern Shore newspaper, the *Cecil Whig,* complained of a recent incident in which two white men, one of whom was a constable, arrested a black woman and a black man and accused them of entering Maryland in violation of an 1839 statute restricting black migration into the state. The men making the arrests hoped to pocket the twenty-dollar fines the arrestees might be required to pay, but both black victims in the case reported in the *Whig* proved to be legal residents of Maryland. Nonetheless, the black woman and man had to be lodged in the county jail at public expense before they were cleared. The *Whig*'s editors expressed little concern for the injustice to the African Americans, but they worried about the cost to the public. They complained that "This thing of arresting niggers may be fine sport for Tom McCreary and Larry Simmons who have everything to gain and nothing to lose," but, the editors concluded, if men like McCreary and Simmons wanted to go about arresting "every strange nigger they see," they ought to do it at their own expense.[19]

Especially noteworthy in view of the circumstances of Daniel Brown's death is the fact that the code's provisions legalized intrusions into the churches and homes of African Americans. In Maryland's code, the white presumption of authority over the private lives of African American men and women was spelled out in regulations of "tumultuous assemblages" and in measures to suppress "incendiary publications." The provisions regarding tumultuous assemblages, which explicitly applied to both free blacks and slaves, restricted gatherings claimed to be for religious purposes. Such gatherings could proceed only if conducted by a white licensed or ordained preacher or, alternatively, by "some respectable white person" approved by a white licensed or ordained preacher. To ensure diligent enforcement, the law imposed fines on constables who failed to disperse unlawful assemblies.[20] Under other code sections, African American camp meetings and "all other outdoor protracted negro meetings" were declared to be "unlawful and tumultuous meetings" with two exceptions. First, such meetings could be held if a slaveholder or white employer granted permission to servants to hold prayer or religious services; and second, blacks could hold such meetings in Baltimore or Annapolis, provided they obtained written permission from a white licensed or ordained minister and the meetings concluded before ten o'clock at night. The law required constables to check "suspected places" of such gatherings once a month or more frequently if informed of such places.[21]

The code provision addressing "Incendiary Publications" authorized especially offensive intrusions into free blacks' homes. The applicable section required citizens to make an oath before a justice of the peace if they had "good reason to believe that any free negro" was concealing abolition papers or furnishing free papers to slaves. The provision further required that, upon receiving such an oath, the justice should issue a warrant authorizing a constable to "summon not less than three respectable citizens, and with their aid and assistance . . . search and examine the houses and premises of such free negro for abolition papers or free papers, using as little violence to the feelings of such free negro as is compatible with a faithful and diligent search."[22]

Available records do not reveal whether Daniel Brown lived on the Eastern Shore during the years when unscrupulous men like McCreary and Simmons preyed on black men and women and raided their homes. It is clear, however, that Daniel Brown had migrated from the Eastern Shore to Baltimore by the late 1860s. The first documentation of Brown's residence in Baltimore dates from December 28, 1868, when he married Keziah Chew.[23] The Browns probably remained in Baltimore from 1868 to 1870. Beginning in 1871, the record is more certain. In June 1871, Daniel and Keziah lived in a rented house on Sarah Ann Street, then sometime after June 1871, they moved to a house at 41 Tyson Street.[24] Even in those years in Baltimore, however, the Eastern Shore's slavery-era legacy of bitterness and conflict undoubtedly colored Daniel Brown's view of the world around him. As Dennis Halpin notes in his recent study of the legacy of Reconstruction in Baltimore, "Maryland's antebellum era cast a long shadow over the rest of the nineteenth century."[25]

But it is also true that during the 1860s and 1870s, Daniel and Keziah Brown lived in a place and in an era that differed significantly from Maryland's antebellum Eastern Shore. Nineteenth-century Baltimore was always a little safer than the Eastern Shore, and the war and its aftermath had transformed society in the entire nation. In Maryland emancipation arrived in November 1864, and the General Assembly repealed the state's black code in March 1865. Because Maryland had not seceded from the Union, federal troops did not oversee Reconstruction measures in the state, but Reconstruction-era laws altered life in all states, especially in former slave states. The Thirteenth Amendment to the US Constitution ended slavery throughout the nation in December 1865; the Fourteenth Amendment held out the promise of full citizenship for African Americans in 1868; and the Fifteenth Amendment granted voting rights to all citizens without regard to "race, color, or previous condition of servitude" in 1870. With a basis for African American citizenship in place, Republicans in Washington made some legislative attempts to address the enduring problems of discrimination and white supremacists' resistance to African Americans' claims to equality.

In Baltimore Daniel and Keziah experienced hopes and disappointments: Reconstruction-era laws promised progress toward black equality, but manifestations of the slavery era persisted. Black citizens opposed vestiges of the black code, discrimination, and segregation, but the struggle was never easy, and progress was erratic.[26] In the day-to-day lives of the Browns, lingering manifestations of the slavery era were obvious. Constraints that had been imposed on African Americans over a period of several decades limited the range of choices of employment and housing available to them.

In antebellum Baltimore, slaves and free African Americans worked in a variety of occupations, especially around the harbor and in the central business district. Free blacks and slaves drove wagons, unloaded ships, harvested oysters, dug ditches, and made bricks.[27] Most of all, African Americans held a wide variety of unskilled jobs in which they were simply described as laborers. In an 1850 sampling of twenty-seven hundred black workers, about eight hundred of them were classified as "laborers."[28] African American women had far fewer choices for paid employment; probably as many as nine out of ten black wage-earning women washed and ironed laundry.[29]A minority of African American men filled positions that required more skill, commanded better pay, and provided more security. In barbering, and especially in ship caulking, black men even dominated the trade.[30]

But antebellum demographic trends led to a contraction of the range of black workers' employment opportunities. In the three decades preceding the

Civil War, an expanding labor pool intensified employment competition. The workforce of the city grew as result of increases in the numbers of European immigrants as well as growth of the African American population. Beginning in the 1830s, massive immigration from Europe brought a new wave of workers into the city's labor force. German and Irish immigrants arrived in seemingly ever-increasing numbers in the 1840s and 1850s. By 1850 more than 50,000 European immigrants lived in Baltimore, including 25,000 from Germany and 20,000 from Ireland.[31] The African American population of the city grew as well. At the opening of the nineteenth century, 2,843 slaves and 2,771 free blacks lived Baltimore; by 1860, the slave population had declined to 2,218, but the number of free blacks had grown to 25,680.[32]

In an environment of increasing competition for employment, economic downturns had dire consequences for black workers. In competitions for jobs, European immigrants and native-born white workers had not only an advantage in numbers, but also the benefit of assistance from government officials and police.[33] Even before 1830, African Americans' choices of work were becoming increasingly limited, but the trend accelerated after 1830, especially during the panics of 1837 and 1857. In periods of heightened competition for work, gangs of whites drove blacks off work sites.[34] The process was ongoing, but the panic of 1857 brought increasing violence with especially harsh consequences for black workers.[35]

Work and patterns of racial residential distribution were closely bound together in the Browns' world. Pressures from white workers forced increasing numbers of black workers into the least desirable and lowest paying service jobs.[36] As the range of jobs open to African American men and women constricted after 1840, the concentration of slaves and free blacks in service occupations increased. In need of housing near their places of employment, black servants moved into prosperous white neighborhoods, where some resided in white households as live-in servants, while others found homes behind the street-front houses of white employers. In the neighborhoods of wealthy white elites, the presence of black servants in the alleys and backstreets was not a recent development. But the intracity migrations increased crowding and lowered living standards.

The resulting pattern of racial residential distribution differed from patterns found in the Deep South. Baltimore's border-region characteristics altered the usual southern configuration of black and white housing. Because southern slaveholders controlled their slaves' movements by limiting egress from the backs of their properties, slaveholders in Deep South cities preferred to house slaves in compounds and enclosures behind the residences of whites. Whenever feasible, whites in cities such as Charleston, Savannah, and Atlanta eliminated alleys or lanes that might allow slaves unregulated movement and permit them to congregate beyond the surveillance of white authorities.[37] In Baltimore, however, free African Americans outnumbered slaves by a wide margin, and the city plan included a grid of wide avenues interspersed with a maze of cut-throughs in the form of narrow backstreets, alleys, lanes, and courts.[38] As a result, many of Baltimore's African Americans lived near white residences, but in Baltimore African Americans lived in small houses in the city's many alleys and lanes rather than in compounds at the rear of street-front properties.[39]

The city's antebellum pattern of racial residential distribution remained common throughout the period of Daniel and Keziah Brown's marriage and beyond. In 1880 clusters of African Americans still lived in all quadrants of the city.[40] Hints of a more segregated future could be found. In Ward Thirteen, northwest of the center of the city, there were concentrations of black residents, many of whom worked in occupations that did not depend on employment by the prosperous residents of the Park Avenue and Cathedral Street neighborhood. To the southwest of the central business district near the Camden Station and rail yards, the beginnings of an isolated African American pattern were discernible.[41] But in the 1870s black residents made up more than 20 percent of the population in sixteen of the city's twenty wards. Despite the fact that east Baltimore contained three of the four city wards with black populations of less than 10 percent, several examples of the typical pattern of clustered black residences appear in the census data for that side of the city. The area near the northwest corner of Patterson Park, for example, included wide avenues and streets, such as Baltimore Street, Lombard Street, Pratt Street, and Patterson Park Avenue, as well as several alleys and backstreets. In 1880, along Baltimore Street in the first three blocks west of Patterson Park, seventy-one households of white shopkeepers and professionals—including butchers, tailors, lawyers, and sea captains—lived in solid, three- and four-story brick houses. Not a single African American family occupied a house in this section of Baltimore Street, but within the seventy-one white households, thirty-three African Americans found employment as live-in servants. The live-in servants in these households also included white women, usually German or Irish immigrants, but the African American servants far outnumbered the European servants.[42] On Lombard and Pratt Streets immediately west of Patterson Park, the white homeowners appear to have been less prosperous than the professionals and merchants of East Baltimore Street. Nonetheless, the pattern of racial residential distribution there resembled the pattern found on Baltimore Street. The dressmakers, boot makers, and laborers on these streets provided work for African American live-in cooks, servants, and nurses, but, as was the case on Baltimore Street, no African American families maintained their own residences along these wide streets.[43] Although no African American families maintained households in these sections of Baltimore Street, Lombard Street, and Pratt Street, these wide thoroughfares formed large blocks that enclosed narrow cut-throughs, such as Bohemia Court, Jones Court, Chapel Street, and Duncan Alley, all of which provided living space for African American laundresses, servants, waiters, wagon drivers, and laborers.[44]

These workplace and residential changes did not come without conflict, and again events that began in the antebellum city continued in postwar Baltimore. Frederick Douglass, who worked in the shipyards in his youth, remembered that beginning in the 1830s, white workers resorted to coercion—sometimes they collectively pressured white employers to ban black workers, but at other times they attacked individual black workers. Angry white workers once beat Douglass so severely that his master removed him from the shipyard.[45] Black workers resisted white coercion, often under the leadership of caulkers. The caulking trade was especially important to black workers in antebellum Baltimore. In the early nineteenth century, African Americans, both slaves and free workers, dominated the trade.[46] With a limited supply of skilled laborers in that period, shipyard owners and white authorities accepted the presence of black workers in skilled trades. Before 1840, white employers even favored African American workers for the trade, and Orphan's Courts commonly placed young African Americans in apprenticeships to learn caulking.[47] The importance of black caulkers in the work of shipyards made it possible for them to exercise some control over their working conditions. In 1838 black activists formed the Caulkers Association, and throughout the labor conflicts of the following decades, it was often the caulkers who led efforts to maintain the position of black workers in the shipyards. Some shipyard owners complained of the power of the Caulkers Association. One owner claimed that black caulkers compelled him to pay $1.75 a day, or fifty cents a day more than a white replacement worker commanded. Another employer complained that he was "entirely at the mercy of the colored association." Despite the complaints of some employers, others conceded that the black workers worked with greater skill and efficiency than the whites.[48] Although skilled black workers made concerted efforts to resist displacement, they steadily lost ground throughout the period. With an economic boom in the late 1840s, violence subsided, but the economic downturn in the mid-1850s led to renewed conflicts.[49] Caulkers held on longer than most black skilled workers, but those who remained in the shipyards had to fight for their jobs as competition with white workers continued to spark violence in the 1860s.

The war and emancipation brought changes that increased and intensified employment competition. The number of blacks in the city's labor force increased as African American men and women from southern Maryland and the Eastern Shore abandoned farmlands in favor of the city. From 1860 to 1870, the African American population of Baltimore grew from 27,898 to 39,558.[50] At the same time, the demise of slavery inspired black workers to stand up for their rights. Oyster shuckers struck for higher wages in December 1864 and again in 1865.[51] Black caulkers and stevedores continued to fight to hold their places in the dry docks and on the wharves. In perhaps the most dramatic episode of African American activism of the 1860s, Isaac Myers, a caulker, brought together several black businessmen in a campaign to raise enough capital to purchase a dry dock.[52] Myers and his associates advertised their purpose as "to give employment to colored men throughout the state."[53] Determined to create an enterprise in which they could practice their trades, African American caulkers, carpenters, and mechanics rallied behind the project, and in February 1866, they completed the purchase of the Chesapeake Marine Railway and Drydock Company. As inspiring as the successful new enterprise was, however, a single dry dock could not provide enough opportunities to maintain a corps of black skilled workers. By 1870, black workers had been almost completely excluded from skilled trades.[54]

During the six and a half years of Daniel and Keziah Brown's marriage, the consequences of these ongoing conflicts made a difference in their daily lives. Constraints inherent in the urban geography of racism limited their choices as they looked for work and living space. They worked hard for low pay, and although their home was a little better than the homes most African Americans occupied, the house was modest and it was not on one of the wide avenues. Living in a backstreet dwelling, with Daniel working as a laborer and Keziah taking in laundry, the Browns had to be aware of the limits a racist social order imposed on them. Emancipation and federal Reconstruction-era laws brought hope. Daniel and Keziah Brown were probably among the tens of thousands of Baltimore citizens who joined in celebrations to mark the Fifteenth Amendment's ratification with a parade and an address by Maryland's most illustrious former slave, Frederick Douglass.[55] But hope was necessarily tempered, not only by the Browns' immediate circumstances, but also by their perceptions of obstacles to equal rights that arose in Maryland and in the nation. It is not difficult to imagine that by the summer of 1875, accumulated disappointments with black Americans' setbacks had instilled in Daniel Brown an extra measure of determination to stand firm in the face of affronts to his dignity. His particular thoughts and emotions, of course, cannot be known, but public issues as well as his personal circumstances provide clues as to what might have motivated a man in his time and place.

The fact that Maryland was not directly subjected to federal Reconstruction measures had consequences for blacks. During the war, the federal presence had suppressed proslavery and states' rights elements of the Maryland Democratic Party. But federal forces departed at war's end, and conservative Democrats "redeemed" Maryland by 1867, a decade earlier than white supremacists and states' rights Democrats made full recoveries in the states of the former Confederacy. With the revival of the Democratic Party, old elites, some of whom favored aggressive opposition to African American rights and some of whom adhered to a more genteel, paternalistic racism, perpetuated the city's antebellum characteristics. From 1867 to 1876, while African Americans held political offices and gained access to public employment in states of the former Confederacy, Baltimore excluded blacks from public offices, and the state withheld voting rights from black Marylanders until the Fifteenth Amendment mandated a change.[56]

Opponents of black equality did not hesitate to make their intentions clear in Maryland. Through laws and symbolic gestures Democrats in the General Assembly promoted white supremacist policies. Under Democratic Party control, the state, in 1867, adopted a new constitution that limited voting rights to white males.[57] In January 1867 the legislature took the symbolic step of planning the transfer of the remains of Chief Justice Roger B. Taney, author of the *Dred Scott* decision, from Frederick, Maryland, to the state capital building, or to some suitable place on its grounds, where a monument to him would mark his resting place. As it turned out, Taney's family objected to the transfer of the chief justice's remains, but a committee headed by Severn Teakle Wallis, one of Baltimore's most respected citizens, carried out the will of the legislature as to the monument, which was dedicated in Annapolis on December 10, 1872.[58] The *Baltimore Sun*'s account of the ceremonies reflected the veneration many in Maryland held for Taney, describing the day as a "brilliant occasion," with attendance "much larger than could have been expected considering the extreme severity of the cold weather."[59]

In the same period, some of Maryland's most powerful citizens ardently promoted racist views and opposed measures to promote black equality at the national level. US Senator Reverdy Johnson, who had provided legal counsel for slaveholder John Sanford in the *Dred Scott* case, continued to speak out in favor of white supremacy and states' rights. Johnson professed his admiration for Chief Justice Taney and defended Taney's role in authoring the *Dred Scott* decision. In the US Senate, Johnson served on Congress's Joint Committee on Reconstruction, a position he used to voice opposition to Republican plans to seek ratification of the Fourteenth and Fifteenth amendments—amendments that were ratified without Maryland's support.[60] At other times, Senator Johnson expressed sympathy for white citizens in the South who, in Johnson's opinion, were being subjected to "the dominion of an ignorant African race."[61] In the winter of 1871–72, Johnson left Maryland to join the legal defense team of Ku Klux Klan members who faced charges of interfering with African Americans' voting rights in South Carolina.[62]

And the ideas promoted by conservative Democrats in Annapolis and Washington had consequences in the daily lives of African Americans in Baltimore. In March 1875, just a few months before Daniel Brown died, whites in Maryland responded to federal civil rights legislation with obstructive actions. Fearing they would have to admit blacks to their theaters on an equal basis with whites, managers of the Front Street Theater and Ford's Grand Opera House made plans to share expenses in their efforts to "resist the enforcement of the law in a legal way."[63] Some Baltimore hotels published statements claiming they were actually boardinghouses and therefore not subject to the public accommodations provisions of the federal law.[64]

At the flashpoint of conflict between Brown and McDonald, however, it was probably a city ordinance and its echo of black code regulations that most immediately moved Daniel Brown to forego a show of deference. Given the extreme violence of Officer McDonald's attack, and the intense anger the policeman expressed, even a deferential response from Daniel Brown might not have defused the conflict. But Officer McDonald made unwarranted assertions that the Browns' party was subject to a Baltimore ordinance authorizing policemen to regulate social gatherings. And as Daniel Brown probably knew, Baltimore policemen enforced the ordinance selectively. The policeman's repeated referrals to the ordinance may well have provoked Brown and precluded any possibility that he might respond diplomatically.

Although white intrusions into the private lives of blacks appeared in their most aggressive form in the antebellum black code, the threat of intrusive police power did not end with the repeal of the black code. Baltimore officials perpetuated the intrusive practices through ordinances. Long after the demise of the state's black code, Baltimore police enforced ordinances that required citizens to obtain licenses for social events, including those in private homes.[65] A Baltimore ordinance approved in 1858 regulated "musical parties" for which admission fees were charged and required the hosts of such parties to pay a tax or license ranging from one to five dollars per night.[66] The ordinance applied to all Baltimore residents, not only African Americans, but the long history of legally authorized intrusions into the private lives of African Americans, along with the possibility of selective enforcement by an all-white police force, led to friction between black citizens and enforcement officials. To make matters worse, at the very time the ordinance went into effect, a reorganization of Baltimore's police force increased the law enforcement presence on Baltimore's streets and introduced new possibilities for arbitrary and capricious applications of discretionary power. In 1853, the Maryland General Assembly authorized the Baltimore mayor and city council to replace the city's ancient constable-and-watch security organization with a modern police force. The city administration took a few years to implement the plan, but an enlarged force of armed, uniformed police officers began patrolling Baltimore in 1857.[67]

Conflicts erupted almost immediately after the city's ordinance regulating musical parties went into effect. In September 1858, an African American man named Davidge went to city hall to acquire a permit for a paid entertainment. Someone referred him to a janitor instead of the appropriate representative of the police force. The janitor filled in the blanks on the form for Davidge and told him no further approval was required. Perhaps the mishandling of the application was merely incompetence, but the details of the case raise suspicions of a setup. On the night of the entertainment, a policeman arrived at Davidge's home and demanded to inspect Davidge's permit. Davidge produced the permit, but because the permit had no endorsement from the district police captain, Davidge and his guests were arrested. Davidge spent a night in jail and paid a fine of thirty dollars, but he retaliated with a lawsuit against the city, and he won. Although he received no compensation for his night in jail, he was awarded reimbursement of his thirty-dollar fine.[68] In other instances, police raided African American balls based on complaints of disorderly behavior. After neighbors complained of noise and fighting at a dance in May 1859, a police lieutenant and a posse of twelve officers raided a dance hall and arrested thirty-three African American men and women, along with the proprietor of the hall, described as a white man named Thomas Bond. In the *Baltimore Daily Exchange,* the persons at the ball were described as "degraded and dissolute negroes of both sexes." A police magistrate committed at least seventeen of the arrested black men and women to jail, although Thomas Bond, who was charged with keeping a disorderly house, was released on bail.[69] In another instance, at about three in the morning "a large posse of police" raided a house where a "colored ball" was in progress and arrested thirty-six party guests, eighteen of whom were jailed.[70]

In contrast to the forceful responses to allegedly boisterous African American parties, dances, and balls, the police force apparently tolerated a high level of unruly behavior—even violence—at balls attended by white citizens. At a white ball at the Maryland Institute in 1858, for example, a man punched police captain T. W. Sparklin in the face, and several other men joined the attack. In the skirmish that followed, Sparklin was knocked down and kicked before friends of the assailants escorted them from the ball and restored order. Despite the reported assault and battery against Captain Sparklin, the police made no arrests.[71]

White citizens' preoccupation with black social gatherings persisted into the 1870s. In the aftermath of the killing of Daniel Brown, a Baltimore newspaper, the *Gazette,* attempted to compare McDonald's conflict with Brown to a recent instance in which a black man fired shots at a policeman when the policeman entered a "negro dance house" to quiet a disturbance. Comparing the Browns' home to the dance house was inaccurate. But the *Gazette*'s distortions of the facts surrounding the incident made it worse. The account of the alleged dance house shooting reveals more about the white journalist's preoccupation with the desire to control African Americans than it reveals about black violence. According to the *Gazette*'s account, Jacob Hock, a policeman assigned to the western district, entered the "negro dance house" shortly after midnight, and a black man, Charles H. Thompson, fired five shots at the policeman.[72] Other accounts of the incident, however, indicate that the supposedly recent event actually occurred more than five years before Daniel Brown was killed and, furthermore, the confrontation between Thompson and Officer Hock occurred on the street, not in a dance house. According to a report in the *Baltimore Sun* dated five years before the *Gazette*'s account, the shooting occurred after Patrolman Jacob Hock of the western police district approached Charles H. Thompson, who "was standing on Orchard street in an intoxicated condition and conducting himself in a disorderly manner."[73] The *Gazette*'s editors apparently either imagined—or wished their readers to imagine—that unrestrained dancing and carousing by gatherings of African Americans was causing an ongoing hazard for policemen.

The ordinance regulating musical entertainments, with a minor amendment in 1864, was still in effect in 1875.[74] Throughout the period of Brown's young adulthood, and until the night Officer McDonald killed Daniel Brown, African Americans remained vulnerable to arbitrary intrusions into their residences by agents of state and local government. The Baltimore ordinance of 1858 was less obviously racist than the black code provisions; on its face, the ordinance applied to white and black events. But the ordinance left blacks susceptible to abusive law enforcement measures and kept alive black consciousness of the need to remain on guard against unreasonable official interference in their private affairs.[75] And testimony at a coroner's inquest, as well as in the criminal trial of Officer McDonald, leave little doubt that McDonald's unjustified assertion of authority under the 1858 ordinance triggered the conflict that ended with Daniel Brown's death. When blacks in Baltimore gathered to protest Brown's killing, they voiced strong objections to a persistent pattern of warrantless police incursions into black homes.[76]

This social setting, with Baltimore's ongoing racial conflicts and the ebb and flow of hope and disappointment for African Americans, provided the context in which Daniel Brown confronted Officer McDonald. But Daniel Brown's individual response to a situation he perceived as an affront to his dignity as a freeman and the proprietor of his home played a role in the tragedy. Despite the limited documentation of most aspects of Daniel Brown's life, it is possible to discern some of the aspects of his personality and character. The evidence shows that in his daily life Daniel Brown was in the habit of standing up for his rights with enough self-assurance to get the attention of his white acquaintances. In comments about his character in the days following his death, acquaintances noted that he was assertive about his opinions and felt strongly about civil rights issues.[77] Based on statements attributed to Brown's landlord and his employer, Daniel Brown was a responsible citizen—a man who worked hard to maintain a stable household and who remained alert to infringements of his rights. And details of his life in Baltimore reinforce these statements about his character and personality.

One indication of his character is the purposeful way he and his wife planned their living arrangements. In the six and a half years of their marriage, the Browns appear to have tried to arrange their lives in a way that would relieve Keziah of the burden of working as a laundress, an occupation that was exceptionally demanding in an era in which indoor plumbing was rare in poor neighborhoods. As late as the turn of the century, in alley districts in west Baltimore, about one-third of the residents shared outdoor hydrants or sinks with neighbors, and even many of those fortunate enough to have a water source to themselves nonetheless had to haul in water from a fixture in the yard.[78] The need to haul water made the tasks of laundresses not only strenuous and time consuming but also distressingly uncomfortable in summer heat or winter cold. Conditions may have been slightly better in the area of Tyson Street, but even if an indoor sink was available, hand washing piles of laundry was a demanding job that paid poorly.[79] In the first few years of the Browns' marriage, Keziah endured these discomforts and contributed hours of her labor to providing clean laundry for other families. By 1873, however, Keziah apparently stopped taking in laundry. As is the case with so many details of the Browns' lives, facts cannot be established with certainty. But the city directories show that she removed her listing as a laundress after 1873.[80]

The Browns apparently employed two strategies to make it possible for Keziah to devote her energies to the Browns' own household. First, they rented houses that were big enough to provide rooms for lodgers. As a result of poverty, discrimination, and housing shortages, many African Americans in nineteenth-century Baltimore shared living spaces. But it appears that from the beginning of their marriage, Daniel and Keziah were the proprietors in the houses they rented; they were the ones who took the initiative in making the arrangements. In 1870 Daniel and Keziah shared their residence on Sarah Ann Street in west Baltimore with Minor Henderson, a hod carrier, and his wife Anna.[81] A few years later, when they moved to Tyson Street, they chose a three-story row house. Although the house was a small backstreet dwelling, the three levels provided the capacity to sublet upstairs rooms to John Gresham, his wife Minnie, and two or three other individuals.[82]

Second, Daniel Brown took jobs that were dangerous or especially strenuous, but which benefited the Browns' household by yielding wages slightly higher than the wages of casual laborers. Early in the Browns' marriage, Daniel worked as a hod carrier, a job that required him to put in ten-hour workdays hauling masonry materials in loads as great as 125 pounds. As described by the Maryland Bureau of Industrial Statistics, the hod carrier's occupation was "laborious" and one in which a man's wages were "well earned."[83] At the time he died, Daniel Brown worked in a sugar refinery. Laboring in sugar refineries was demanding and dangerous, in part because workers carried out the complex refining processes in multistory factories with open shafts that exposed them to the dangers of falls and falling equipment.[84] Daniel Brown's earnings in these jobs averaged from $1.65 to $2.50 per day as compared to casual laborers' wages of $1.25 per day. Probably as a result of this employment together with the income received from lodgers, Keziah Brown was able to remove her listing as a laundress from the city directory.[85]

Daniel Brown's literacy provides another clue to his character. The evidence for Brown's literacy is not entirely conclusive, but it is convincing. On the 1870 manuscript census reports, the census taker was instructed to check a blank reporting "cannot read" and another for "cannot write," where applicable. The information is not completely trustworthy; respondents reported on themselves, and the census taker's work was susceptible to careless oversights. However, the census taker's notations were neatly and carefully marked on the page, including the entries for the Browns. The markings indicate that several of the Browns' neighbors could not read or write, but the markings indicating illiteracy were absent from the lines on which the Browns' names were recorded.[86] The census report is reinforced by newspaper accounts referring to Daniel Brown as "quite intelligent"—statements attributed to white acquaintances who were willing to concede Brown's intelligence, although they were irritated by his tendency to be "strong in urging his own way."[87] There is no way to assess the level of Brown's literacy, but the evidence suggests he could read well enough to keep himself informed of civic affairs.

Brown's literacy demonstrates a determination to overcome obstacles. A black man born in the 1840s in Maryland had very few opportunities to learn to read and write. As was the case everywhere in the South, slaveholders in Maryland almost universally discouraged and even punished slaves' attempts to acquire literacy.[88] Frederick Douglass contended that during his youth on the Eastern Shore, he was the only slave in the region who could read and write.[89]

While it was more difficult to withhold opportunities from free African Americans, many whites responded to educational projects for blacks, whether slave or free, with hostility and even violence. In antebellum Maryland, a few whites—usually motivated by religious beliefs—taught reading and writing to black children despite the disapproval of white friends and neighbors. On the Eastern Shore in 1855, for example, a young Methodist woman, Mary Bradbury, arranged to provide lessons for black children on Sunday afternoons, but she had to draw strength from her Christian faith to carry out her plans. When she revealed her project to a friend, she wrote, almost hesitantly, "I feel a little uneasy for fear this Sabbath business will not meet with approbation, but I feel sure the Lord smiles upon my efforts, and that is enough."[90] By the 1860s, emancipation stirred hopeful blacks to seek education for themselves and their children, but many whites responded violently, especially on the Eastern Shore, where mobs stoned children and teachers, and arsonists burned churches and schoolhouses in Kent, Cecil, Queen Anne's, and Somerset Counties.[91]

If Daniel Brown learned to read and write in Baltimore, he faced somewhat less resistance than Eastern Shore blacks. When Frederick Douglass tried to improve his literacy in Baltimore, the response, while not encouraging, was not as hostile as the response he had encountered when he made similar efforts on the Eastern Shore.[92] Other ambitious African Americans observed that higher levels of literacy could be found among their people in Baltimore than in rural areas. An African American minister, Noah Davis, for example, noted a sharp contrast in the level of literacy between blacks in Baltimore and blacks in rural Virginia. As a young slave working as a shoemaker's apprentice, Davis learned to write by watching his employer record customers' names inside boots. Then, after he had become a Baptist minister, he traveled to Baltimore, where he felt intimidated by the level of literacy he observed among black ministers in the city.[93] Even with the advantages he might have found in Baltimore, however, Daniel Brown had to overcome obstacles to learn to read and write. He had passed his twentieth birthday by the time Maryland took the initial steps toward the establishment of public schools for African American children, and as of 1870, fewer than half of Maryland's black residents could write—a level of literacy that required simply printing out one's name.[94]

Thus, the man who stood face to face with Patrick McDonald was self-assured, proud of his status as a homeowner, literate, and inclined to be outspoken about his rights. For this proud, assertive man standing in the doorway of his own home, the presence of a gruff policeman may well have evoked memories of the black code that made life so insecure on the Eastern Shore of his youth. It is even more likely that he knew of the abusive practices and selective enforcement that marked the behavior of some of Baltimore's policemen under the city's ordinances. And it is fair to assume that on the night he died, Daniel Brown was well aware of how precarious his rights as a citizen and proprietor of his own home were. He had observed throughout his adult life the rhythm of advances and setbacks that marked the lives of Baltimore's African Americans. The black man who stood in his own doorway facing a policeman in July 1875 understood the need to remain vigilant against attempts to curtail his rights. And he was not likely to respond with unquestioning deference when confronted with a presence he perceived as threatening to his civil rights, his dignity, and the security of his home.

CHAPTER 2

The Irish Policeman on the Doorstep

The man Daniel Brown faced in his doorway on the night of his death also began life in a place where hardships were likely to color his view of the world. Like Daniel Brown, Patrick McDonald lived in humble circumstances, and his personal history was not well documented. But newspaper accounts and census records reveal enough to establish that his youth was contemporaneous with a catastrophic famine during which his native land lost one-third of its population. According to reports of his trial, he was born in Ireland between 1837 and 1845.[1] In the autumn of 1845, blight (*Phytophthora infestans*) appeared in Irish potato crops, and then increased in severity, resulting in the partial or complete loss of the nation's primary food source for several years.[2] Even before the onset of the Great Famine of 1845–55, Irish men and women had been migrating to the United States in increasing numbers as their nation's economy faltered and employment opportunities expanded in North America. But the onset of crop failures added famine and epidemics of typhoid fever and dysentery to Ireland's troubles, and the rate of emigration doubled. In the worst years of the Great Famine, nearly two million migrants left the island, and roughly one million Irish men, women, and children died of disease and starvation.[3]

In its magnitude and gruesome details, the catastrophe that overwhelmed Ireland in the first two decades of McDonald's life had a premodern aura—a quality that, as one writer has suggested, disorients historians because memories of the tragedy resonate like recollections of a medieval plague rather than recollections of a calamity that might seem imaginable to those accustomed to the industrialized world.[4] Other writers have observed that the Great Famine was the most acute social crisis to occur in Europe's modern era, and that the catastrophe "seems to have killed a higher proportion of the Irish national population than any other national catastrophe anywhere over the past three centuries."[5]

Inevitably, the catastrophe left lasting images in the minds of nineteenth-century Irish men and women, whether they emigrated or stayed home. The misery and terror that swept through Ireland during the famine is expressed vividly in contemporary accounts, which are filled with horrifying scenes of social disorganization.[6] From one end of the island to the other, observers reported the breakdown of cultural norms associated with funerals and burials. From observers in Armagh and Cavan in the north came reports of the dead left unburied for days and reports of the pace of deaths outrunning the coroner's ability to keep up with his duties.[7] In the west, Quaker relief workers arriving in the town of Clifden were told that on the previous night, a woman had crawled into an outhouse, where she had died and her corpse had been partly devoured by dogs.[8] Skibbereen in the south lived on for years in Irish memory as the "very nucleus of famine and disease."[9] From there came reports of mass graves and reports that residents patched together makeshift coffins for their children and buried them with no accompanying mourners because such burials were an "hourly occurrence."[10]

Faced with the destruction of the crop that provided most of the nourishment available to the rural poor, officials stumbled in their efforts to offer effective assistance, leaving many of the Irish who migrated embittered and convinced they had been driven into exile by the British. Jeremiah O'Donovan, an Irish migrant traveling in the United States in the 1860s, could not contain his rage when stating his views of the British administration of his homeland: "Millions, not thousands, of my countrymen were either starved, hanged, or decapitated by remorseless villains who were sent across the channel by the most rapacious, unfeeling, ungodly and cruel government that has been established in any civilized or savage country under the canopy of Heaven . . . ."[11] O'Donovan may have been excessive in his imagery, but his views nonetheless encapsulated the themes of oppression and exile shared by many Irish nationalists.

In some cases, the inadequacies in relief efforts that so embittered the Irish resulted from administrators' ideological or theological preconceptions.[12] Charles Trevelyan, assistant secretary of the treasury and director of government relief, for example, attributed Ireland's problems to an act of divine providence. Ultimately, in Trevelyan's view, the disaster would bring benefits to Ireland because it would purge the Irish of their dependence on the potato and "restore the energy and the vast industrial capabilities of the country."[13] In fact, however, administrators, whether sympathetic to the Irish or not, faced an overwhelming task.

Even harsh critics of the British presence in Ireland sometimes conceded that the emergency was unprecedented and one for which "no machinery existed extensive enough to neutralize its effects."[14] When initial efforts to provide assistance fell short, hunger and malnutrition rendered tens of thousands of Irish men, women, and children vulnerable to disease, and when weak and starving people crowded into relief centers, typhoid fever and dysentery spread throughout the island. As causes of death, the direct consequences of starvation could not be easily distinguished from diseases, but most historians of the tragedy conclude that the majority of deaths resulted from typhoid fever and dysentery.[15]

With massive numbers of the island's residents desperately ill or dying, local commerce came to a halt. Small landholders could not pay their rents, and tens of thousands of the rural poor could no longer make the purchases that generated revenues for artisans and shopkeepers.[16] Visitors to Skibbereen in 1847 reported that commerce had come to a halt in the once-prosperous town, and "shop-keepers from lack of customers stood idle at their doors."[17] The poorest smallholders and landless laborers, lacking even the means to feed themselves, could not afford passage to North America, but for those a little above the level of desperate poverty, emigration provided a means to escape from epidemics and a collapsing economy. Because shopkeepers and artisans as well as peasants fell into despair, many of the migrants who came to North America in the era in which Patrick McDonald's family migrated to Baltimore worked in trades or small businesses in their homeland. But many more lacked skills or capital, and as nearly all the migrants were limited by unfamiliarity with American work practices and hindered by nativist hostility, even those with skills usually entered the workforce at the lowest level, most often as laborers on canals, railroads, and docks.[18] Patrick McDonald and his family apparently fit the typical pattern of Great Famine–era migrants: Patrick worked on the Northern Central Railway for a period, and then took laboring jobs in Baltimore before he joined the police force.[19]

Census records and accounts of Patrick McDonald's arrest and trial establish that he arrived in Maryland in the 1860s at the very latest. A neighbor testified at McDonald's trial that he had known McDonald as early as 1860. All three of Patrick McDonald's children were born in Maryland, and the oldest was born in 1867 or 1868.[20] Thus, McDonald probably was living in Baltimore by the time he was a teenager. Possibly he never witnessed mass burials in Ireland, but in any case, it is likely he heard the adults around him speak of the worst times in the old country. Among the Great Famine Irish, horror stories circulated regularly—tales, for example, of the horrifying days when famine and disease killed off Irish men, women, and children at such a pace that undertakers resorted to "trap coffins," or hinged-bottom devices that could be reused.[21]

When they arrived in Baltimore, Great Famine–era immigrants found that their fellow countrymen had already established a presence in the city. Irish men and women had, in fact, lived in Maryland from the earliest days of English settlement. Founded by George Calvert, a Catholic, the proprietors, recognizing that Catholics would eventually be outnumbered by Protestants, established a policy of religious tolerance. Protestants quickly gained majority status, as the mix of immigrants arriving from England reflected the home country's population, but the colony in its earliest days also welcomed Irish Catholics. In the seventeenth century, Maryland's Catholics practiced their faith with little interference, and some Irish Catholics prospered. Charles Carroll, an Irish immigrant, held positions of influence in the colony's administration, and ultimately became one of the wealthiest men in Maryland.[22] Around the beginning of the eighteenth century, however, the Protestant majority began to suppress religious minorities, especially Quakers and Catholics. In 1706 the colony instituted poll taxes on "negroes and Irish papists."[23] Within a few years, new policies excluded Catholics from office, and in 1718 the assembly and governor acted to deny Catholics the vote.[24] Throughout the eighteenth century, fewer Irish Catholics migrated to Maryland, but even with the slower rate of immigration, the colony's Catholic population remained around 12 percent.[25] Many of the Irish migrants arrived involuntarily. From 1700 to 1775, English authorities deported an estimated ten thousand Irish convicts to Maryland and Virginia.[26]

Despite discrimination in the colonial years, the Irish population grew, and Catholics, including some Irishmen, prospered. By the last decade of the eighteenth century, the Maryland Catholic community included within its number an influential and wealthy minority. Nine Marylanders held 150 or more slaves in 1790, and five of them were Catholics. Charles Carroll of Carrollton held 316 black men, women, and children in bondage on his estate. But not all of Maryland's prosperous Catholics lived on great estates in the countryside. Some wealthy Catholics migrated from the plantations to the city. With the rapid growth of Baltimore after the Revolution, Catholic professionals and businessmen moved into the city's finer townhouses, and several Irishmen found places in this new urban "Catholic aristocracy."[27] In the same period, recognition from Rome greatly enhanced the status of Baltimore as a center of Catholic life in the United States. In 1789, the Vatican named John Carroll of Baltimore as the first bishop in the first diocese of the United States, making Baltimore in effect the most important locus of Roman Catholic authority in the nation.[28]

The presence of this influential community of Catholics, especially the Irish among them, ameliorated some of the suffering of the Great Famine–era Irish. By the opening decades of the nineteenth century, Baltimore had several churches and civic associations that could address some of the immediate social and economic consequences of the Great Famine. Roman Catholics established parishes that served Irish immigrants as early as the 1790s. Near Fells Point, St. Patrick's began ministering to newcomers in 1792. German immigrants attended masses there at first, but the church served many Irish parishioners by the time a new building was constructed for the growing congregation in 1806.[29] In time, under the guidance of Father James Dolan, St. Patrick's became Baltimore's most active Irish parish.[30] When ships carrying Great Famine–era immigrants began unloading their passengers at Fells Point, the church's location, just a few blocks from the wharves, provided a strategic site for relief activities. Irish civic leaders organized the Maryland Hibernian Society in 1816.[31] And in 1823, an Irish philanthropist left a portion of his fortune to the Hibernian Society for the purpose of founding a school for Irish children. John Oliver, born in Ireland and an ardent supporter of the Hibernian Society, left a bequest of $20,000 in his will to the Hibernians to be used for the education of Baltimore's poor children. The will provided that the school should be for "children of both sexes, one at least of whose parents must be Irish," and further that "no distinction is ever to be made in the school as to the religious tenets of those who may apply for admission."[32] The Irish Social and Benevolent Society was organized with aid to "the poor emigrant" as its first priority.[33]

Religious and social organizations such as these pitched in to aid immigrants in the Irish crisis years of the late 1840s. Members of the Hibernian Society and other businessmen and sympathizers responded to the crisis by forming an Irish Relief Committee. Committee members recruited Baltimore Mayor Jacob Davies to assist in the effort, and in February 1847, the committee was able to channel funds through Quaker organizations to help ease suffering in Ireland.[34] Through these efforts, Baltimore's committee contributed meal, flour, corn, and clothing to the relief effort.[35] On their own side of the Atlantic, Baltimore Catholic congregations tried to meet the most urgent needs of new arrivals. Father Dolan of St. Patrick's came to the relief of immigrants suffering not only from famine, but also from diseases that went unchecked aboard crowded ships. In 1847 a ship that had suffered a high fatality rate on the voyage from Ireland arrived at Fells Point with forty children whose parents had expired during the journey. Father Dolan assumed responsibility for the children and eventually raised money for an orphanage to be established under the direction of the Hibernian Society.[36] The Irish Social and Benevolent Society helped new arrivals find work.[37]

Poverty and memories of Ireland's tragedies influenced the outlook of McDonald and other Great Famine–era migrants in Baltimore, but social tensions and trends in Maryland politics had more direct and practical effects on their prospects in the economic and civic affairs of their new land. The responses of Anglo-Americans were not always friendly. Nativism was ascendant throughout the United States in the years preceding the Irish Famine, and Baltimore's immigrants encountered not only defenders like the Hibernians, but also detractors and anti-immigrant activists. In 1835, Rev. Robert J. Breckinridge of the Second Presbyterian Church of Baltimore assembled an association of ministers "to defend against the inroads of popery." Under Breckinridge's editorship, the association published the *Baltimore Literary and Religious Magazine*, a publication Catholics viewed as nothing more than a vehicle for baseless rumors and tales of "popish crimes and plots."[38] But opponents of nativism also made their voices heard in Baltimore. When anti-Catholic rioters attacked a convent in Boston in 1837, prominent Baltimore citizens rallied in defense of the rights of their "adopted fellow citizens." Joshua Vansant, whose career would later include terms in Congress and as Baltimore's mayor, served as secretary to the assembly. John Pendleton Kennedy, a novelist and future secretary of the navy under President Fillmore, attended the assembly along with dozens of other civic and business leaders. In its resolutions, the assembly noted that "there is a wild proscription stalking abroad . . . marking for its victims the generous and confiding, and more particularly the emigrants of Ireland."[39] Two years later, Baltimore would have its own problem with nativist disturbances in response to rumors of misconduct in a convent, but the mayor and police deflected an angry anti-Catholic crowd and prevented a full-blown riot.[40]

It was clearly a volatile era. Once settled in Baltimore, McDonald's family and other Irish immigrants found relief from starvation and an escape from the immediate threats of exposure to typhoid fever and dysentery. But as the mixed responses of Baltimoreans to nativist outbursts in 1830s demonstrated, Great Famine–era Irish immigrants could not count on friendly and sympathetic responses. The city had a long-standing reputation as a rough place with recurrent riots, especially during political campaigns. Great Famine–era Irish arrived in the city in a period of increasing tensions and violence, and Irish immigrants frequently became involved in episodes of street violence, both as victims and as perpetrators.[41]

Much of the violence arose out of the extended national crisis in the United States preceding the Civil War. In the 1850s, just when Irish immigration surged, the sectional crisis over slavery reached a level of intensity that threatened national unity. At the same time, in an economy shifting from craftsmanship to wage labor, the frustration and anger of US-born workingmen added to American anxieties.[42] The combination of an unprecedented increase in the foreign-born population and a highly charged political environment gave rise to the American Party (the so-called Know-Nothing Party), which successfully challenged the Democratic Party for control of Maryland from 1855 to 1859. Then during the Civil War, a coalition of Unionists took control of the state. Baltimore's Irish immigrants, well aware of the nativist rants of the Know-Nothings, inevitably became zealous Democrats. With considerable help from Baltimore's Irish community, the Democratic Party survived these crises and forged a solid, enduring majority by the end of 1866.[43]

By fighting side by side with Baltimore's Democrats during the party's struggles from 1855 to 1866, the city's Irish community contributed to the party's success and won a place within the coalition that dominated Maryland politics through most of the second half of the nineteenth century. Once aligned with the Democrats, Baltimore's Irish community proved its importance at the very time the party was most in need of loyalty.[44] In the local elections of 1855, only two Baltimore wards maintained their level of support for Democrats, the heavily Irish Ward Eight and the heavily German Ward Two. Subsequently, the Ward Two Germans shifted toward the Know-Nothings, but the Irish never faltered.[45]

In contests between Democrats and Know-Nothings, both sides resorted to violence. Know-Nothings succeeded in the elections in part because they had the support of gangs of thugs who intimidated immigrant voters. Know-Nothing gangs were notorious for tactics such as wounding their foes with shoemakers' awls and soaking the heads of political opponents in vats of pigs' blood.[46] At the height of the Know-Nothing era, gangs adopted the awl as a symbol of their movement.[47] On the other hand, Know-Nothings complained that Irish partisans aided the Democrats not only with votes but also with acts of intimidation. Know-Nothing congressman Henry Winter Davis charged that Baltimore's Irish ward was "a vast arsenal" from which Irishmen launched attacks on neighboring precincts.[48] According to Davis, Know-Nothings did not take to the streets to engage in violence, but to suppress the violence of their opponents.[49] Regardless of which side instigated the violence, the experiences of the Irish as comrades of the Democrats in street fighting undoubtedly solidified their adherence to the party.

By the eve of the Civil War, Baltimore's Irish community had established a solid alliance with the Democratic Party, a party that included among its guiding principles a commitment to white supremacy.[50] As a result, political tensions inflamed relations between Maryland's Irish Democratic Party supporters and African Americans. Chance encounters between groups of blacks and Irish men could easily devolve into name-calling, stone throwing, or fistfights. During the national election campaign of 1856, for example, a group of African Americans returning to Baltimore from a picnic in the country shouted cheers for Republican candidate John C. Frémont when they came upon a liberty pole erected by Irish Democrats, and a brawl erupted.[51]

In Baltimore, Irish immigrants and African Americans could not avoid each other. The Irish gravitated toward a core community in the city's Ward Eight, a neighborhood of brick row houses packed along a grid of streets north of the central business district. Irish families headed by laborers filled many of the row houses, often alongside households headed by widowed or unmarried Irish women who worked as laundresses or servants. A few tradesmen, especially stonecutters and stonemasons, also lived nearby.[52] But in 1860, Ward Eight's residents were neither uniformly poor nor invariably Irish. John McDonald, an Irish-born drayman, owned personal property valued at $400; if the census records are to be believed, this was a sum representing more property than most Baltimore workers had.[53] Hugh O'Brien provides another example. He, his wife, and four children lived among the ward's laborers, but O'Brien earned his living as a bailiff. At age thirty-eight, he had accumulated personal property valued at $200, considerably more than the zero to $40 amounts reported for most workers.[54] The ward's non-Irish residents included not only other European immigrants, but also African Americans. Usually the black residents of the ward were not interspersed among other residents, but rather clustered in a few adjacent households. In one block, nine African American families lived in adjacent buildings, with only one Irish family in their immediate vicinity—the family of John McDonald, the relatively prosperous drayman referenced above.[55] And, of course, neither Irish immigrants nor African Americans were confined to Ward Eight. Near Fells Point, in Ward Two, Germans predominated, but Irish and black families also lived there while they competed for work on the nearby wharves.[56] Even after Irish and blacks had established a history of troubled relations, poverty could throw Irish and black workers together. The 1880 census reports reveal a few cases in which Irish and African American residents lived side by side in the backstreets without separating into clusters. Nearly equal numbers of African American and Irish immigrant families lived together in a block of Duncan Alley between Pratt and Lombard, where they shared not only living space, but hard times, too; the residents included Irish widows, who lived on washerwomen's wages, as well as many black and white laborers, most of whom had endured extended periods of unemployment in the preceding year.[57]

Irish conflicts with native-born Americans arose most obviously in clashes with Know-Nothings, but it is noteworthy that nativism in Maryland differed somewhat from nativism in northern cities. Know-Nothings in Maryland, unlike northern Know-Nothings, did not object to the Irish primarily because most Irish immigrants were Catholics, but rather because Know-Nothings questioned the competence of the Irish to participate in civic affairs. Suspicion of Catholic connections to the Vatican certainly played a part, but Maryland Know-Nothings placed more emphasis on immigrants as a voting bloc. The allegedly ignorant and pliable Irish, according to Know-Nothings, enabled and supported corrupt politicians. The political focus of conflicts between the Irish and Know-Nothings in Baltimore politics is illustrated by the fact that Maryland Know-Nothings de-emphasized the anti-Catholic element in their party's platform, focusing instead on issues of citizenship and voting.

The worst conflicts in the 1856 elections in Baltimore occurred between partisans in the Irish Ward Eight and their rivals in the Know-Nothing stronghold in Ward Six. When the Know-Nothings attempted to prevent Ward Eight's naturalized citizens from voting, violent clashes with loss of life erupted.[58] Know-Nothing Governor Thomas Hicks responded to these disorders with criticisms of the Irish based on his objections to immigrants' voting patterns, not their religious practices. In his 1858 inaugural address he voiced his hostility toward "this swarm of immigrants" that has been granted "the power and dignity of Citizenship."[59] Other nativists, of course, sometimes argued that immigrants' voting patterns could be linked to religion, as when they alleged Catholics put obedience to the pope ahead of loyalty to the Republic. But Maryland Know-Nothings apparently found that argument so unconvincing that they attempted to repudiate the anti-Catholic plank inserted in the party's national platform.[60] Maryland Know-Nothings finally accepted the national platform, but the response to the party's anti-Catholic rhetoric revealed the distinctive characteristics of the Maryland Know-Nothings. Even one of the most violent Baltimore Know-Nothing gangs, the Plug Uglies, paid little heed to the national party's anti-Catholic plank: the gang counted among its members some young men from respectable Catholic families.[61]

Ultimately, Baltimore Democrats recovered from the setbacks of the Know-Nothing era, but the outbreak of the Civil War brought new trials for the party. Partly because many of their pro-Southern adherents left the state during the war, and partly because federal authorities excluded openly anti-Union

Democrats from politics, the Democratic Party's conservative core fell into obscurity in Maryland from 1861 to 1866, a period in which a coalition of former Whigs and Unionist Democrats took control. Nonetheless, the loyal base of party members, the Unionist Democrats, sustained the party through the crisis. Referring to themselves as Conservative Unionist, the Democrats opposed secession despite their adherence to the Southern view of states' rights and their belief in African American inferiority. With the end of the war, the mainstream of the Democratic Party regained its dominance in state and local politics. By 1868, when Patrick McDonald is known to have lived in Maryland, Democrats controlled the state, and immigrants in Baltimore, with the Irish in the forefront, played a major role in sustaining the Democratic Party's majority status.

In 1874, an appointment to the police force offered a young Irishman a chance at more economic security than he could hope to find in most laboring jobs. But to win an appointment, it was necessary to establish a connection to a Democratic ward leader. Ward politicians in Baltimore, following a practice that was common in nineteenth-century US cities, reserved positions on the police force for young men who had demonstrated party loyalty.[62] In the 1850s, Know-Nothings filled Baltimore's police force with party loyalists and used them for partisan purposes in elections.[63] In response to Know-Nothing abuses, reformers called for a police force that could remain independent of party control, but the reform they offered failed to solve the problem.[64] Reformers succeeded in transferring control of the police force from municipal authorities to the state legislature, but when Democrats gained control of the state government after the war, the practice of appointing police on a partisan basis continued. The introduction of black voters into Reconstruction-era political calculations increased Democrats' incentive to utilize the police to control elections. In 1870, when party members grew concerned about the Fifteenth Amendment's potential to strengthen the Republican Party with African American votes, Democrats in the state legislature openly discussed their need to control Baltimore's police force, noting that the force played an important role in protecting party interests in election-day skirmishes.[65] In 1874, as a young Irishman, Patrick McDonald was well positioned to claim a place on the police force, provided he could get the attention of Democratic ward leaders.

At some time between 1868 and 1874, Patrick McDonald established the necessary tie to Baltimore Democrats. There is evidence that he had associations with influential figures in Democratic ward-level politics. One of the lawyers who defended McDonald in the Brown case, Joseph S. Heuisler, was a party regular in McDonald's home ward. In the 1870s and 1880s, Heuisler held positions in the city government, including as the ward's representative on the city council's first branch, examiner of titles in the law department, and commissioner in the water department.[66] And McDonald also counted among his associates some of the rougher Democratic Party adherents in the ward. Accounts of a fight in a downtown saloon, for example, show that McDonald socialized with his neighbor Tom Freeze, a neighborhood thug who had a long-standing reputation for violence and intimidation in service to city Democrats.[67]

Some of McDonald's supporters asserted that he was by nature a mild person. At his trial, representatives from the police force stated that McDonald's reputation "as a peaceable, forbearing and humane man was first class," and "that he was known as a quiet and gentle officer all the time he was on the force."[68] McDonald's attack on Daniel Brown by itself counters the assertion of his supporters, but there are additional reasons to believe McDonald could handle himself in violent situations. Baltimoreans established the police force for the purpose of controlling rioters and street ruffians. Ward leaders who recommended young men for appointments to the police force necessarily took into account a potential appointee's capacity to deal with tough characters on the streets, and politicians almost certainly considered an appointee's ability and willingness to protect their party's interests in the rough—often very rough—give and take of city politics. Despite the character witnesses' assertions of McDonald's peaceable nature, some of the statements offered in defense of the policeman suggested he had been involved in violent encounters. Although it was reported that McDonald was a "cool man in excitement," for example, it was also reported that he could be "a terror to roughs."[69] Similarly, one of McDonald's former fellow workers on the Northern Central Railway testified that McDonald was remembered as a man of good character, although he had once heard that "an engineer had beaten McDonald with a boot."[70]

As a police officer on the streets of Baltimore, it may well have been justifiable for McDonald to use force defensively sometimes, but the evidence of his involvement in violent encounters is not limited to the period of his service on the police force. In addition to the fight that the Northern Central Railway engineer alluded to during the trial, McDonald may have been engaged in a street fight shortly before he became a policeman. In February 1873, Baltimore police arrested a man identified as Patrick McDonald and charged him with assault with intent to kill. A police magistrate dismissed the case after the injured party,

Edward Deboines, declined to prosecute.[71] Because more than one person named Patrick McDonald lived in Baltimore in 1873, it is not certain that Officer Patrick McDonald committed this assault.

There is certainty, however, about McDonald's involvement in violent confrontations during his career as a policeman and afterward. In addition to McDonald's altercation with Daniel Brown, there are two other well-documented cases in which he had violent interactions on the streets of Baltimore. While patrolling his beat in January 1875, McDonald intervened in a fight between William Bracken and William Konig. He arrested Bracken, who was charged with assaulting and cutting Konig with a knife and with threatening the life of Officer McDonald while McDonald was discharging his duties.[72] Bracken appeared in Baltimore City Criminal Court in February 1875 to answer the charge of threatening McDonald, but the case was dismissed by Judge Robert Gilmor.[73] The clash with Bracken, of course, did not necessarily indicate that McDonald had a propensity to resort to unnecessary force in resolving conflicts. In carrying out their duties, McDonald and his fellow officers inevitably found it necessary sometimes to defend themselves against violent and disorderly people, and in the case involving Bracken, McDonald intervened in a fight in which one of the participants wielded a knife. After he left the police force, however, McDonald participated in a street fight in which a man was killed. In September 1877, McDonald and a man identified as William Brackenridge took part in a fight that began in a saloon and ended with a fatality on the sidewalk in front of Baltimore City Hall. The fight began after McDonald, accompanied by Thomas Freeze, encountered Brackenridge in a saloon. Brackenridge challenged McDonald, and the two men took the fight outside. A policeman and a bystander, Andrew Weidner, tried to stop the fight, but Freeze intervened and punched Weidner, breaking his nose. According to several witnesses, after Weidner fell to the ground, Freeze kicked Weidner in the head. Weidner died of a cerebral hemorrhage, and police detectives arrested Freeze and McDonald shortly after the fight.[74] A police justice dismissed the charges against McDonald, but Freeze was tried for the murder of Weidner. Despite the testimony of several witnesses who said they saw Freeze kick Weidner, the jury acquitted him after the defense produced several witnesses who asserted that an unidentified man who emerged from among the bystanders kicked Weidner.[75] Although the man who fought with McDonald in this instance was identified as Brackenridge rather than Bracken, he probably was the man McDonald arrested in January 1875.[76] When Brackenridge appeared before a police justice, he admitted that he started the fight with McDonald as an act of revenge because McDonald had beaten him when McDonald was a policeman.[77]

McDonald's involvement with Thomas Freeze is revealing about the former police officer's associations with ward party activists and violent characters. Freeze served as a ward worker in Democratic Party primary elections on the day before the fight that ended in Andrew Weidner's death, and after Freeze's arrest, Joseph S. Heuisler, the same attorney and Democratic Party regular who had defended McDonald in the Brown case, came to Freeze's aid. Whether McDonald worked for the party during the primary contests on the day before the fight with Brackenridge is unknown, but Freeze and McDonald lived near each other in the area of Dolphin Street and Foster Alley, and the two men had spent part of the day together visiting a friend who was being held in the city jail.[78]

By associating with Freeze, McDonald placed himself in the company of a man well known in Baltimore's Ward Twelve for his rowdy behavior. Freeze's reputation for violence was well established by 1877, and his career as a party enforcer went on for decades afterward.[79] As late as 1907, Freeze maintained influence in the Democratic Party as a ward captain.[80] In his defense of Freeze in the Weidner murder trial, Joseph Heuisler stated that he had known Freeze for fifteen years, having first met him through a Sunday school, and found him to be a peaceful man. But Heuisler's characterization of Freeze seems almost absurd in light of Freeze's acts of callousness and violence over nearly a quarter of a century. According to reports of his arrest for the murder of Andrew Weidner, Freeze brazenly flaunted his indifference to the tragedy. As police officers led Freeze to his cell, they passed Weidner's body, which had been placed on a bench in the yard of the station house. As reported in one account of Freeze's arrest, when he noticed the crowd of people who were looking at the body, "Freeze, with an air of bravado, loosened the grasp of the policemen . . . and walked deliberately up to the body, remarking, with an air of assumed coolness, 'Let me look at him too.'" Freeze then asked to be permitted to send for some cigars. And the Weidner killing was not the first instance in which Freeze was charged with committing an act of violence. He was arrested in 1876 and charged with attacking the arresting officer, although in that case a Criminal Court judge exonerated Freeze and admonished the arresting officer.[81] Despite Freeze's success in countering the charges against him in 1876 and 1877, when Baltimore's police marshal sent the grand jury a list of the city's habitual "ruffians and disorderly characters" in 1879, Freeze was included on the list.[82] Freeze later acquired a neighborhood saloon and continued to promote the interests of the Democratic Party in Ward Twelve.[83] But in 1896 his liquor license was revoked, and on election day of that year he was accused of spitting in the face of the city's liquor license commissioner. On the same day, he was arrested for intimidating voters by firing a pistol. In reports of the incident, Freeze was characterized as one of a number of "toughs" who had been intimidating African American voters in the ward for many years.[84] At Freeze's trial in February 1897, witnesses testified that Freeze fired a pistol, then walked back and forth past a group of black men who were standing in line to vote.[85]

As his connections to Joseph Heuisler and Tom Freeze demonstrate, the young immigrant who confronted Daniel Brown in the doorway in July 1875 had made adjustments to life in Baltimore and found ways to ease the insecurities that had troubled his family in Ireland. The Know-Nothings in Baltimore may have despised the lowly Irish, but within the Democratic Party, McDonald and other Irish immigrants found friends and protectors who gave them jobs, offered them a place in the social order, and even sometimes provided legal assistance. But the introduction into Baltimore's social and cultural setting did very little to prepare McDonald for the responsibilities of peacefully settling conflicts or resolving misunderstandings. Instead, McDonald's informal education in the ways of his new land introduced him to a subculture in which violence served as a tool for political advancement and status. In his duties as a policeman, McDonald had some useful qualities, such as strength and an ability to respond forcefully to aggressive lawbreakers, and these qualities had the potential to serve the interests of the city. In mid-nineteenth-century Baltimore, however, some community and political leaders encouraged police officers to use aggressive, even violent, tactics in pursuit of the partisan goals of political dominance and social oppression.

In a confrontation with a black man who was prepared to claim his civil rights and defend his dignity, McDonald's experiences with street violence and his associations with the city's Democratic Party increased the likelihood that he would resort to aggression. Drawing on clues that men like Tom Freeze provided about the city's social hierarchy and political order, McDonald might readily conclude that the city's black men and women were his despised enemies. The Democratic Party, the party that opened the Baltimore police force to men like McDonald, consistently denigrated African Americans and advocated curtailing their rights and privileges as citizens. After 1870, when the Fifteenth Amendment enabled black voters to raise the political fortunes of Republicans and reformers, blacks became the principal targets of Democratic violence and intimidation in election-day skirmishes. Ultimately, the political environment that made McDonald's employment on the police force possible fostered a casual attitude toward violence against African Americans.

And the historical and cultural circumstances of the migrations of Great Famine–era Irish men and women further increased the risk of violence in confrontations between African Americans and Irish immigrants. For an Irishman trying to find a place in a new social order, a black man embodied anxieties that followed him and his family to his new home. As immigrants who believed themselves to be exiles from a European society that relegated them to the status of a racially inferior caste, the status of Baltimore's African Americans stood as a warning of the hazards the Irish faced if they failed to draw clear lines between themselves and blacks. And the anxiety grew more acute when US employers relegated Irish men to pick-and-shovel jobs on canals, railroads, and construction sites—work that native-born Americans rejected because they considered such work more suitable for black workers.[86]

Yet the circumstances in which Daniel Brown and Patrick McDonald confronted each other only heightened the risk of violence. A homicide was not an inevitable outcome. Most Baltimore policemen, even those who held racist views, did not routinely club and shoot unarmed citizens in their own homes. Patrick McDonald's personal weaknesses and character deficiencies cannot be ignored. There is evidence that McDonald chose to put himself in risky, potentially violent settings. He was no stranger to street fighting. He was inclined to see fists, clubs, and pistols as the tools he relied on in conflicts, and he was more willing than most men to use those tools aggressively.

CHAPTER 3

Homicide, Coroners, and Criminal Justice

In the immediate aftermath of Daniel Brown's death, the thoroughness of the homicide investigation depended on the responses of a few key agents of the criminal justice system. The district police captain, the coroner, and the state's attorney all had roles to play. The actions of these officials could sidetrack the case and block a full investigation of the incident. But in Daniel Brown's case, these officials chose not to stop the investigation. Unlike several other cases of killings of African Americans by law enforcement officers in post–Civil War Maryland, the investigation proceeded, signaling the possibility of a trial in the Baltimore City Criminal Court. The location of the killing and the social setting of the encounter between Brown and Officer McDonald made a difference in these critical stages on the path toward a trial.

Daniel and Keziah Brown's house at 41 Tyson Street stood in a narrow passage that cut through a city block in the heart of one of Baltimore's wealthiest neighborhoods. As was the case in many cities in the South, segregation by neighborhood had not yet become the predominant pattern of settlement in 1870s Baltimore. Tyson Street reflected Baltimore's typical pattern. In the cramped passageway, workers and domestic servants found quarters that provided convenient access to the homes of wealthy Baltimoreans on nearby broad avenues. The district surrounding Tyson Street, Park Avenue, and Cathedral Street was one in which police administrators viewed their mission as providing security for "a larger number of wealthy and well-to-do homes than are to be found in all the rest of Baltimore."[1]

A little to the north of the Browns' residence, Tyson Street bent eastward from its north-south axis and curved toward and intersected with Park Avenue, forming a triangular plot. The Browns' residence was close enough to the intersection to allow easy access to Park Avenue from the back entrance.[2] At the tip of the triangular plot, the owner of the Browns' home, Allen Martin, operated a flour and feed business. Martin had emigrated from Ireland some time before 1847, and he had prospered. He held a membership in the Baltimore Corn and Flour Exchange for many years, and in 1870 he owned real estate valued at $5,000 and personal property valued at $3,000, significant sums by the standards of the time. He owned not only the Browns' residence, but also adjacent properties, including his own family home and houses at numbers 43 and 44 Tyson Street.[3]

Just steps away from the residences of the Browns and several other households of domestic servants and laborers, wealthy merchants and old elite families occupied substantial stone buildings along Park Avenue and Cathedral Street. Charles J. Bonaparte, a young lawyer and a grandson of the French emperor's brother, made his home on Park Avenue a few blocks to the south, as did Reverdy Johnson, a banker and lawyer who had served in the US Senate and as an ambassador to England.[4] It was not unusual for the neighborhood's bankers, physicians, lawyers, and merchants to keep three or four live-in servants, but the wealthy residents of the area also employed blacks, who lived in the nearby row houses.[5] During the periods in which Keziah took in laundry, proximity to prosperous families made her work easier.

In October 1874, the city's police commissioners promoted Lt. George W. Earhart to the rank of captain and put him in charge of the police district surrounding the Park Avenue neighborhood. The commissioners' choice of Earhart was consistent with their view of the locality as an enclave of old families with wealth and influence. Captain Earhart was a descendant of a "well-known" Virginia family. Despite the fact that he had been a Baltimore resident since his childhood, Earhart served on the Confederate side in the Civil War because "he felt deeply on the question of constitutional States' rights."[6] He had a close relationship with the wealthy and influential Gilmor family, a family whose members included men who played significant roles in the Daniel Brown case. Judge Robert Gilmor of the Baltimore City Criminal Court presided at Officer McDonald's trial, and Judge Gilmor's brother, Harry, served on the Baltimore board of police commissioners. Earhart's close friendship with Harry Gilmor illustrates the police captain's attachment to the values of the old South. In his memoir, *Four Years in the Saddle,* Harry Gilmor romanticized his experiences as a Confederate cavalry officer, recounting his wartime exploits as "exciting episodes" that were "replete, indeed, with opportunities of adventurous life."[7] After Harry Gilmor died, his family, remembering Captain Earhart as a lifelong friend who appreciated the Confederate veteran's values, presented Earhart with the spurs Gilmor wore throughout his service in the Southern army.[8]

By 1875 the Browns were well settled in the neighborhood policed by Captain Earhart and his officers. Early in that year, they took in two lodgers—John Gresham, an African American sailor, and his wife Minnie. In July 1875 Gresham signed on for a voyage to South America, and as he prepared for his departure, he decided to express his appreciation for the Browns' friendship by hosting a party for the Browns and some of their neighbors. On Friday evening, July 30, about a dozen African Americans, several of whom were servants employed in nearby homes, joined the Greshams and the Browns for the party at the Tyson Street residence. The entertainment, arranged by the Greshams, included amusements, one of which a guest described as "Building the London Bridge," a game "consisting of a couple walking up and down the floor and singing verses."[9] The guests shared cakes, candy, watermelon, and ginger beer. They consumed no alcohol.[10]

Despite the tame character of the entertainment and the absence of strong drinks, the joking and singing grew loud enough to bother some neighbors as the party lingered on past 1:00 A.M. The Browns' landlord, Allen Martin, responded by leaving his nearby house in search of a policeman. He found Patrick McDonald, who at the time had less than a full year's experience on the force.[11] Martin, who was on good terms with Officer McDonald, asked the policeman to go to the Browns' house to see what he could do about the noise. Apparently because Martin wanted to maintain good relations with his tenants, he told McDonald not to mention his name as the complainant.[12] Some time between 1:00 A.M. and 2:00 A.M. Officer McDonald arrived at the site of the party.[13] By 2:00 A.M. Daniel Brown lay bleeding and unconscious on the floor of his home after receiving a blow to the right side of his head from McDonald's club and a bullet to the left side of his head from McDonald's pistol.

Captain Earhart took control of the case immediately after Officer McDonald reported the incident. McDonald apparently made contradictory statements about his actions. According to one account, he said he shot Brown in self-defense after Brown pulled him into the house and he had been "surrounded by a crowd of angry negroes." In another statement he said he had chased Brown into the house after a confrontation on the doorstep. Captain Earhart did not rely on McDonald's accounts or on investigators, but instead went to the scene of the shooting himself. When he found that Daniel Brown had died, he relieved McDonald of his duties and turned the matter over to police district coroner Dr. George C. Ogle.[14]

Dr. Ogle played a critical role in the development of the case. For the matter of Daniel Brown to get a fair test in the justice system, the case would have to get past the coroner and his inquest jury. From 1867 to 1910, in case after case in which a Maryland law enforcement officer killed an African American, a coroner's jury established a basis for exonerating the officer. Without probing deeply into the facts of the cases, coroners' juries routinely decided that law enforcement officers killed black men and women in self-defense or as a result of accident. Inquest verdicts did not necessarily block Maryland state's attorneys from bringing criminal charges. But state's attorneys were elected officials with prosecutorial discretion, and the inquest rulings opened welcome paths around cases that might prove unpopular.[15] Following a finding of self-defense or accident by a coroner's jury, it was easy to drop the matter without exposing the actions of patrolmen, sheriffs, or prison guards to the closer scrutiny that would be applied if the cases advanced through formal criminal proceedings. And police commissioners and other public officials as well as prosecutors found it uncomfortable to have their policies reviewed in trial courts. Thus, state's attorneys repeatedly took the easy path made available by coroners' inquests.

Coroners' inquests necessarily begin as quickly as is reasonable after discovery of a suspicious death. The need to preserve evidence and identify witnesses drives the process forward. Although Daniel Brown died in the early hours of a Saturday in midsummer, Dr. Ogle had little difficulty in carrying out his first responsibility—assembling a jury for the inquest. In assembling his jury, Dr. Ogle followed well-established customs. The coroner's office was an ancient English institution that had been adopted by colonial Marylanders, and Maryland's nineteenth-century version of the institution still resembled England's.[16] English coroners typically selected jurors from among the local population of prosperous artisans, shopkeepers, and tradesmen, and Baltimore's coroners followed the English practice.[17] When Dr. Ogle intercepted a few downtown streetcars, he found likely candidates among the businessmen, merchants, and tradesmen making Saturday-morning journeys to their offices and shops.

The men Dr. Ogle selected represented the city's prosperous, white, middle-class citizens. Juror Jacob Reindollar was a stair builder in his mid-fifties. According to the 1870 census reports, he owned real estate with an estimated value of $7,000 and personal property valued at $1,000.[18] Juror Thomas J. Shryock, in his mid-twenties, was a lumber dealer, [19] and juror Charles Spilker, a German-born oil merchant, was prosperous enough to maintain two domestic servants in his household in 1870.[20] Others on the jury included James Barroll, a real estate broker; Henry Spilker, a clerk; Alexander Butcher, a confectioner; and William P. Palmer, a carpenter.[21]

Next, Dr. Ogle needed to assemble witnesses while they remained in the area and their recollections were fresh. With little difficulty, Dr. Ogle secured the presence of seventeen witnesses, many of whom had been guests at John Gresham's going-away party. Among them were Richard Coates, a live-in servant at the home of Dr. William Lee; William Coates, who rented a room at 41 Tyson Street; Lorenzo Golston, who worked for Dr. Robert Atkinson; Mary Moore, a Tyson Street resident identified in city directories as a servant; Mary DeShields, who rented a room at 41 Tyson Street; and Abraham Trusty, who lived nearby on Eager Street. Allen Martin testified, as did the Browns' boarders, John and Minnie Gresham, but neither Officer McDonald nor Keziah Brown appeared before the coroner's jury.[22]

To establish the medical basis of the case, Dr. Ogle called on the testimony of Dr. C. B. Gamble, the physician who had treated Daniel Brown at the scene of the homicide. Dr. Gamble lived near the Browns' residence, and he may have known the Browns or some of the guests at the party. He testified that between one and two in the morning, he responded to a call for medical assistance at the Browns' home, and he found that Daniel Brown had two wounds, a gunshot in the left temple and a contusion to the head. According to Dr. Gamble, Brown lingered in an unconscious state for about three-quarters of an hour before he died.[23]

To provide the jury with an outline of the events leading up to and immediately after Patrick McDonald clubbed and shot Brown, Dr. Ogle called on John Gresham.[24] Because Gresham spoke to Officer McDonald before Daniel Brown went to the door, Gresham was able to offer an account of the facts beginning with Officer McDonald's arrival at the house and ending with the immediate aftermath of the policeman's attack. In his testimony, Gresham established several key elements for the jury's consideration. First, Gresham reported that Officer McDonald repeatedly inquired about a permit for a cakewalk, or pay party. Second, Gresham contended that McDonald entered the house before he struck Brown. Third, Gresham's account indicated that McDonald was not in danger when he resorted to the club and pistol. And finally, Gresham asserted that during and after the attack on Brown, the policeman uttered racially charged threats. Several witnesses supported Gresham's testimony, although some witnesses reported variations on his main themes.

Regarding the policeman's inquiries about the permit, Gresham testified that when he responded to McDonald's rap on the door, McDonald complained about the noise and asked whether the hosts of the party had obtained a permit to hold a cakewalk or pay party. Gresham explained that it was not a cakewalk and no admission fees had been charged. According to Gresham, McDonald responded by issuing a warning that he would take the people in the house to the police station if the noise did not stop. Following the warning, Gresham reported, McDonald again asked about the fees for the party, and Gresham repeated that guests had paid no fees. Gresham testified that McDonald then asked to see the proprietor of the affair, and Gresham explained that he (Gresham) was the proprietor of the entertainment, but Daniel Brown was the proprietor of the house. Gresham stated that Daniel Brown then came to the front door to speak to the policeman. Other witnesses corroborated Gresham's testimony about McDonald's repeated references to the need for a permit. Minnie Gresham reported that she heard her husband assure McDonald it was not a pay party, but McDonald, despite John Gresham's assurances, continued the inquiry about the permit when Daniel Brown went to the door. Mary Parker, a party guest, also said she heard McDonald ask Brown whether he had a permit for the event, although she did not say she heard McDonald first query Gresham about the matter.

Gresham's testimony placed McDonald inside the house at the time he struck Daniel Brown with the club, and again, other witnesses presented testimony that was consistent with Gresham's statements. Gresham said after he stepped away from the doorway, he heard a rush from the front door, and then saw McDonald strike Daniel Brown with the club. Mary DeShields supported Gresham in placing the location of the clubbing of Brown inside the house. She said Brown stood near the middle door dividing the front and back rooms when the policeman struck him. Other witnesses provided testimony that, although not inconsistent with Gresham's statements, was not as clear as to whether the initial attack occurred in the doorway or inside the front room. Abraham Trusty stated that he heard the policeman say, "I'll snatch you from the door" before he hit Brown with his club. According to Trusty, Brown pushed the policeman away before the policeman used the club. Mary Moore, who lived across the street from the Browns' house, said she went to her window and heard the policeman threaten to snatch Brown from the door before she heard "something strike" and she saw Brown jump back into the room. Minnie Gresham also reported hearing McDonald's remark about snatching Brown from the doorway before the clubbing.

In his account of McDonald's use of the club and pistol, Gresham outlined facts that clearly implied the policeman was not in danger when he resorted to lethal force. Gresham asserted that Daniel Brown had been clubbed and had retreated into the center of the front room before McDonald fired the shot. According to Gresham's testimony, after McDonald clubbed Brown, Gresham begged the officer to make no more trouble and assured the officer the party guests would obey his order to be quiet, but the policeman responded by saying he would shoot Brown. Gresham said he did not see McDonald fire the shot, but rather he heard the shot after McDonald followed Brown into the back room. Other witnesses agreed that McDonald resorted to the club and pistol when there was no need for self-defense. Mary DeShields stated that Daniel Brown had nothing in his hands at the time McDonald clubbed him. Golston reported that he was in the back room when McDonald fired the shot. He added that before the policeman fired the shot, Gresham had assured the policeman the guests would abide by the order to reduce the noise. Golston said he did not see the policeman fire the shot, but he saw the flash. Golston also testified that Keziah Brown begged McDonald not to shoot her husband before McDonald fired the shot. Mary Moore said she heard the shot after Daniel Brown jumped back into the room. Richard Coates and William Johnson gave accounts of the shooting that seemed at odds with the statements of the other witnesses as to the location of the shooting, although neither man contended that he saw the policeman fire the shot. Coates said he was upstairs when he heard the shot, but he was sure the shooting took place in the front room. William Johnson said he was in the back room when he heard the shot, which, he believed, came from the front door.

Gresham and others testified that Officer McDonald openly expressed his contempt for African Americans throughout the confrontation. In describing Officer McDonald's demeanor, John Gresham and Mary Parker recounted racially charged exclamations, such as "I'll shoot the black ______" and "I'll shoot the black s__ of a b____." Lorenzo Golston and Mary Parker testified that Keziah Brown begged the policeman not to shoot her husband, but as the policeman fired the shot, he uttered that he "didn't give a d__n." Gresham said after McDonald shot Brown, he threatened to "shoot every ______ that was in the House."[25]

John Gresham offered no explanation as to why or how the confrontation in the doorway between Daniel Brown and Patrick McDonald escalated so quickly from a verbal exchange to a burst of violence. Probably Officer McDonald's condescending manner and presumption of entitlement to deference from a black man played a part, but McDonald may also have unwittingly aggravated a bad situation by persisting in his characterizations of the gathering as a dance or cakewalk. Although none of the witnesses emphasized the significance of McDonald's references to a dance or pay party, Daniel Brown probably found McDonald's questioning, and especially his references to cakewalks, insulting. In combination with Officer McDonald's demeanor and the long history of white intrusions into the private affairs of black Marylanders, the references to a cakewalk negated any inclination Brown might have had to temper his responses to the policeman.

The repeated references to dancing probably offended Daniel Brown for religious reasons. Because the event was a going-away party for a sailor, alcohol consumption and dancing would not have been unusual. But the Browns and their guests apparently abstained from alcohol and dancing on the basis of their Christian faith. Keziah Brown was a member of the Sharp Street Methodist Episcopal Church, and it is very likely that most of the party guests were churchgoing Christians.[26] The evidence from the coroner's inquest, as well as testimony at Officer McDonald's trial, established that there was neither alcohol nor dancing at Gresham's party. And Allen Martin, who knew the Browns and probably many of their guests, made it clear that he was confident there was no alcohol at the Browns' social gathering. In a letter to the *Baltimore American,* Allen explained that he had not expected Officer McDonald to have difficulty with the people at the Brown's home because no one there was intoxicated.[27] Allen apparently did not have information based on personal observations of the social gathering; he explained at the inquest that he did not want the Browns to know that he had complained to the policeman. Presumably, therefore, Allen based his belief about the absence of alcohol on his prior knowledge of the habits of the Browns and their guests.

Abstaining from alcohol was a well-established principle among Methodists, and abstaining from dancing would not have been unusual for churchgoing Christians.[28] In the mid-nineteenth century, Protestant denominations, especially Baptists and Methodists, adhered to a centuries-old view of dancing as sinful. In the nineteenth century, Methodist and Baptist religious leaders opposed dancing for several reasons. Some contended that dancing was an expression of vanity and worldly pleasure; some believed that dances encouraged sexual promiscuity; and some argued that formal dances were flagrant displays of luxury that wasted time and money.[29] A white Methodist expressed the antebellum Protestant view of dancing and its influence on blacks: "I have never known, in a single instance, of a colored man of any moral tone who was fond of the banjo or common dance."[30] Most African American Christian ministers followed these Protestant traditions and militantly opposed dancing. In those days, as historian Carter Woodson explained, churchgoing blacks believed "you could abstain from dancing and be saved, or dance and be damned."[31] Abraham Trusty, in his testimony at the coroner's inquest, stated the guests were not dancing, but rather "playing in rings and singing at a right good gait."[32] The reference to ring games is significant. Observers of African American folk traditions have noted that nineteenth-century African Americans sometimes participated in ring games or ring shouts as a way of enjoying social activities associated with music and rhythmic movements without violating religious proscriptions against dancing. Nineteenth-century African American Christians who participated in ring shouts or ring games sometimes defended their activities against charges of immorality by contending that their rhythmic movements were not dancing because the steps did not require their feet to cross.[33]

In light of the attitudes toward dancing among churchgoing Christians, Daniel Brown may have bristled at characterizations of his guests' ring games as dancing. And Officer McDonald's more specific references to the alleged dancing as a "cakewalk" made it worse. Calling the social gathering a cakewalk not only revealed McDonald's perception of the matter as a problem of controlling black behavior, but the questions about a cakewalk may also have offended Daniel Brown as an insult to his social status. Cakewalks or cakewalking had a long and complicated history, at times finding expression in demeaning portrayals of African Americans in minstrel and blackface shows and at other times serving as a basis for the development of respected cultural achievements. Despite the mocking references to cakewalking in the minstrel and blackface shows of the 1860s and 1870s, by the end of the nineteenth century, even classically trained composers were drawing on cakewalk traditions to develop themes in ragtime, jazz, and classical music.[34] From Daniel Brown's perspective in 1875, however, the term *cakewalk* was not associated with positive cultural achievements, but rather with slave experiences and slave behavior—behavior he probably did not want to be attributed to himself and his respectable churchgoing friends. Although cakewalks developed out of European as well as African musical traditions, the cakewalks familiar to Daniel Brown began as plantation social events planned by slaveholders as entertainment for themselves and diversions for slaves. At harvest time or at holidays, plantation owners commonly brought slaves together to dance, with a prize, often a cake, awarded to the dancers the master and mistress of the plantation found to be the most graceful. Although some former slaves remembered plantation cakewalks as pleasant affairs, others remembered the dances as settings for their masters' condescension and abuses. The dances could be fun and a welcome release from toil for field slaves, but often the slaves also considered the affairs demeaning because they were compelled to perform for the amusement of the slaveholders and their guests.[35] In some cases, masters forced slaves to perform in the cakewalks despite the slaves' objections to dancing on religious grounds.[36] To express their displeasure with the demeaning aspects of the cakewalks, slaves were known to covertly mock the manners of slaveholders by performing absurdly exaggerated imitations of European dances.[37]

As respectable black Christians, many of whom were domestic servants, it is likely that Daniel Brown and his guests remembered the demeaning aspects of plantation cakewalks, and they may have considered themselves socially superior to former field slaves who performed cakewalk steps for the amusement of slaveholders. From the antebellum era to the late nineteenth century, observers of class distinctions within black communities reported that the more prosperous members of black communities looked on dancing and cakewalking as behavior attributable to lower classes in their communities. John Dixon Long, a Methodist abolitionist who observed slavery in Maryland and Delaware, contended that field slaves held on large plantations were less likely to be Christians than were slaves held on small farms, and the field slaves, as the "lowest class of slaves," adopted dancing as a favorite diversion.[38] Observing African American society and culture a half century later, W. E. B. Du Bois asserted that cakewalks and balls were amusements found among the poor and the vicious and criminal classes of Philadelphia.[39]

Daniel Brown, apparently without hesitating, took a stand against the policeman's demands rather than join with John Gresham in a more conciliatory response. Facing down the policeman, Brown was not deferential. Witnesses Lorenzo Golston and Mary Parker said they heard Daniel Brown assert that he paid rent for the house and had a right to do as he wished inside the house. Perhaps Officer McDonald failed to understand why his statements provoked Brown. In any case, the evidence at the inquest established that McDonald arrived at the scene with hostile feelings toward blacks and with little inclination to respond patiently or diplomatically when Daniel Brown failed to show deference to police authority. As several witnesses noted, McDonald not only threatened to snatch Daniel Brown from the doorway, but he also, according to Minnie Gresham and Mary Parker, characterized Daniel Brown's statements as "saucy."[40]

The jurors performed their duties conscientiously. Some of them commented on the absence of Keziah Brown. Captain Earhart offered to send for her, but Coroner Ogle decided to ask for a verdict without hearing Mrs. Brown's testimony. One juror, Thomas J. Shryock, apparently emerged in a leadership role as the jury formulated its verdict. Some jurors suggested that the verdict should include a statement that Officer McDonald was called upon to quiet a disorder at the Browns' home, but Shryock, according to newspaper accounts, argued at "some length" that the reference to a disorder should be excluded. The jury ultimately followed Shryock's lead, excluding the reference to a disorder and rendering a verdict simply stating that Daniel Brown came to his death by a shot fired from a pistol in the hands of Police Officer Patrick McDonald. By avoiding language that implied a basis for exoneration of Officer McDonald, the verdict deviated from the well-established pattern in such cases.

The personal characteristics of the Browns and their guests, in conjunction with the social status of Dr. Ogle, Captain Earhart, and Thomas Shryock and his fellow jurors, probably accounted for the unusual inquest verdict. In the antebellum era as well as in post–Civil War Maryland, the families of men like Ogle and Earhart lived in close contact with black domestic servants. White Southerners, as well as African Americans themselves, recognized class distinctions among blacks. John Dixon Long contended that, in Maryland and Delaware, slaves on small farms lived within slaveholders' families and were treated far more humanely than field slaves. Slaves who worked as domestic servants in wealthy households, according to Long, formed a third class—a class that seldom mixed with the "common slave."[41] Elite white Southerners maintained an oppressive social order based on race, but the employment of domestic servants nonetheless brought African Americans of that class into white households, where they mingled regularly with the families of their white employers. Although harsh discipline, and even violence, remained a possibility if servants rebelled against their subordinate status, the relationships between prosperous white Southerners and their trusted domestic servants were commonly paternalistic; a veneer of civility mattered in domestic settings.

As elite Southerners, Captain Earhart and Dr. Ogle understood the ties of paternalism and trust that bound white employers and black domestic servants. Like Captain Earhart, Dr. Ogle had experiences that prepared him to view social relationships from the perspective of a southern gentleman. Dr. Ogle moved to Baltimore to practice medicine in the early 1870s, and in March 1875 Democratic Governor James Groome appointed Ogle to fill the position of Baltimore's western district coroner. Before the Civil War, however, Ogle had lived the life of a wealthy slaveholder in Prince Georges County, Maryland. In 1860, Dr. Ogle held thirty-eight slaves, and Richard Ogle, apparently Dr. Ogle's brother, held thirty-seven slaves on an adjacent property. Before the war, Dr. Ogle's real estate was valued at $33,300 and his personal property was valued at $30,000. Given the scope of the Ogles' holdings, they probably had several domestic slaves in their homes. By 1870 emancipation had taken a toll on the doctor's personal estate, reducing it to a value of $4,000.[42]

Thomas Shryock and the jurors, although less immersed in the culture of the planter class than Ogle and Earhart, were also prosperous enough to employ African American servants. Shryock did not qualify as a southern planter, but his role in leading the jury reflected the fact that, in some ways, his social status might have engendered a paternalistic attitude toward African American household servants. Shryock assessed the matter of Daniel Brown from the perspective of a man accustomed to the wealth and privileges that came with membership in an influential family. His father, Henry Shryock, who was born into a slaveholding Virginia family, did not accumulate wealth as a planter, but instead as a banker and furniture manufacturer in Baltimore. Despite his origins in a family of Virginia slaveholders, the elder Shryock became one of Baltimore's original Republicans. He was an early supporter of Abraham Lincoln.[43] Thomas Shryock followed his father's political lead and eventually became the first Republican to hold the office of Maryland state treasurer.[44] A quarter of a century after the Daniel Brown inquest, when Thomas Shryock was under consideration for a run for the state's governorship, Baltimore's African American newspaper praised him as a man with "largeness of sympathy for the thrifty and hardworking people of color."[45]

The similarities between Thomas Shryock on the one hand and Captain Earhart and Dr. Ogle on the other should not be overstated. In matters of political ideology, these men did not see eye to eye. Yet Earhart, Ogle, and Shryock shared a patrician social status that led them to view the black men and women at the Browns' home from a perspective that would have been unfamiliar to Officer McDonald. As patrician community leaders, Shryock, Earhart, and Ogle may well have viewed African American domestic workers as inherently inferior, but they were also accustomed to viewing them as servants who were sufficiently trustworthy to come into their homes and interact with their families.

Juror Alexander Butcher spoke to the press following the announcement of the verdict.[46] Like Shryock, Butcher did not share the perspective of Earhart and Ogle; according to Butcher's obituary, his son, a private in the Union Army, died while on picket duty in the waning days of the Civil War. Nonetheless, Butcher understood the social relationships that were familiar to Earhart, Ogle, and Shryock. He too had led a life that made it easy for him to understand the perspective of the wealthy residents of Park Avenue. Butcher was a prosperous small business owner with a reputation for geniality. By 1870, he was comfortably retired with real estate holdings worth $10,000 and personal property valued at $5,000. In the 1860s and 1870s, he kept live-in black servants in his household.[47] In commenting on the proceedings of the coroner's inquest, Butcher said that he, in agreement with the other jurors, thought Officer McDonald was not justified in shooting Brown, and that the appearances of the witnesses indicated that "those present at the entertainment were of the better class, several of them being trusted servants in wealthy families."[48] Butcher also stated that, like many others, he believed that policemen were too apt to use their clubs and pistols "without just provocation."[49]

Although the personal views of Ogle, Earhart, and the jurors played a major role in reaching the unusual verdict, those views would not have mattered if well-established characteristics of the office of the coroner had not given the jurors leeway to deviate from the usual pattern in cases of police violence against blacks. The coroner's juries that disposed of homicide cases in Maryland were the product of centuries of custom and tradition, and those customs and traditions help to explain the results of inquests in cases of homicide by law enforcement officers. The established practices of Maryland's coroners encouraged procedural flexibility, and it was that flexibility that enabled the jurors in Daniel Brown's case to decide the matter in accordance with their personal views about the social setting of the crime.[50]

In Maryland, as elsewhere in English-speaking societies, the historical development of the office of the coroner accounted for the institution's procedural flexibility. In 1637, less than five years after the first permanent English settlers reached Maryland, the colony's General Assembly passed an "Act for the Appointment of Certain Officers," which directed the chief judge of the St. Mary's County Court to appoint an inhabitant of the county to serve as sheriff and coroner. The legislators made it clear that they intended to provide the county with an officer who would serve in accordance with customs rooted in English common law: the act assigned the sheriff and coroner the same duties "as a Sheriff or Coroner of any Shire of England hath or ought to have or is or may be charged with by the law or Custome of England."[51]

Despite the ancient origins of the coroner's jury and its importance in the criminal justice system, the institution never developed clear, formal procedural guidelines.[52] In the early years of the Maryland colony, a scarcity of professionally trained candidates made it difficult to find appointees capable of coordinating these functions and establishing precedents for regularizing procedures.[53] In addition, men with appropriate skills shunned the office because it came with limited compensation. In early Maryland, a coroner was entitled to a fee of forty pounds of tobacco for viewing a body, burying it, and holding an inquest. Apparently, however, seventeenth-century colonists found the fee inadequate, and the General Assembly found it necessary to threaten appointees with a fine of "two thousand weight of Tobacco" if they refused to perform the coroner's duties.[54] The office had little prestige, and coroners had little incentive to adhere to formalized procedures. Coroners' inquests developed as open-ended inquiries, not as forums in which defendants were tested in adversarial proceedings. And echoes of that tradition survived. A nineteenth-century handbook for sheriffs and coroners devoted nearly four hundred pages to the duties of the sheriff, but only twenty-nine to the duties of the coroner.[55]

In nineteenth-century Maryland, where standards apparently fell behind the norm of other states, coroners adhered to even fewer formalities. In summarizing practices throughout the United States, the author of the handbook for sheriffs and coroners listed among the duties of coroners the task of reducing all testimony to writing.[56] In nineteenth-century Baltimore, however, testimony at coroners' inquests was not recorded. Newspaper accounts of inquests included far more detail than coroners included in their final reports. In nearly all cases, the meager coroners' records of these proceedings include just enough information to establish the coroner's entitlement to his fee. Some coroner's used mere scraps of paper to record the essential facts needed to support the claim for payment—date, name, age of the deceased, if known, and a phrase encapsulating the jury's verdict usually sufficed.[57] Such record-keeping practices, or lack of them, discouraged the accumulation of precedents that might have served as a basis for consistency in procedures.

As a result of these historical developments, coroner's juries had sufficient latitude to act as a check on actions of the more formal legal institutions of the society. Students of legal institutions have long noted that the informality of inquests allowed coroners' juries to mitigate legal outcomes that seemed unduly harsh. English juries frequently colluded with the families of suspected suicides and "palliated the law" when a verdict of suicide would result in forfeiture of a neighbor's property to the Crown.[58] Some nineteenth-century observers criticized coroners' juries for deferring too readily to public opinion.[59] In the 1830s, responding to public outcries about the harsh consequences of industrialization, juries occasionally went so far as to devise strategies to impose financial penalties on employers in cases in which careless management of hazards in the workplace caused deaths.[60] Thus, long-standing traditions allowed coroners' juries to assert the will of the community—or at least the will of the members of the community who were privileged to participate in inquests. In doing so, they could express a community's social and political norms by acting "as popular tribunals of mitigation."[61]

What is less often noted, however, is the fact that jurors could also use the forum to express a community's intolerance. Verdicts sometimes reflected the community's negative judgments about the behavior of the deceased or others involved in the events surrounding the death. Commonly Baltimore jurors concluded that persons came to their deaths by "intemperance."[62] Not surprisingly, given the sordid circumstances of some cases, jurors were known to express "Great indignation," as when a Baltimore jury reviewed the details of a death brought on by a man's beating, torturing, and starving his wife.[63] And sometimes juries incorporated disapproving comments about the behavior of the deceased. In an 1872 case, a jury found "That Emma Ella Wilkinson came to her death by blows with a cleaver inflicted by the hands of her husband," but the verdict went on to report that John W. Wilkinson's use of the cleaver was "superinduced by jealousy, caused by the intimacy between his wife . . . and William Griswold. . . ."[64]

In nineteenth-century Baltimore, the coroner's discretion in presenting evidence and the coroner's free hand in choosing jurors came into play most significantly as a vehicle to support callous treatment of the community's most disfavored minority—African Americans. In many cases in which law enforcement officers killed African Americans in nineteenth-century Maryland, the circumstances of the homicide or the social status of the deceased made it easy for coroners' juries to shield law enforcement officers from the legal risks of exposure to potentially damaging formal legal inquiries. More often than not in nineteenth-century Maryland, authorities could summarily dismiss matters in which law enforcement officers killed African Americans by characterizing the victims as disorderly persons or vagrants or as lawbreakers who were already justifiably incarcerated.

Numerous cases in the second half of the nineteenth century reflected the tendency of coroners' jurors to focus on the victim's circumstances, and these cases invariably resulted in verdicts of self-defense or accident. Usually the victim's circumstances made it equally easy for jurors to pay more attention to disapproval of the victims than they paid to the facts of the homicide. As a result, inquest juries, often without a thorough review of the evidence, exonerated officials who used lethal force. In 1882, a prison guard shot and killed Robert Taylor, a penitentiary inmate who was allegedly attacking a prison employee, and the jury concluded the killing was justified as self-defense.[65] In 1887, a jury exonerated a Howard County sheriff on the basis of self-defense after the sheriff shot and killed George Thomas, a man who allegedly fit the description of a suspect in the theft of a horse and buggy.[66] In 1896, a deputy warden in the Maryland penitentiary shot and killed Andrew Jackson after Jackson allegedly attacked him with a knife in one hand and a hammer in the other. The circumstances reported by the deputy warden made it easy for the jury to enter a finding of self-defense.[67] Apparently killings of African Americans by law enforcement officers in Maryland increased in frequency by the turn of the century. From 1898 to 1910, at the height of the Jim Crow era, Maryland police officers or jailers killed John Carter, Herbert Brown, Leroy Pendleton, Lawrence Adkins, and William Carter, and in each case a coroner's jury established a basis for a finding of justifiable homicide, either because the officer acted in self-defense or because the killing occurred by accident.[68] Obviously criminals sometimes threaten the lives of policemen and jailers, and just as obviously, accidents can occur in fast-moving, dangerous encounters. Unfortunately, the cursory disposition of these homicide cases, along with limitations in the available records, make it hard to determine whether the facts in these killings by law enforcement officers adequately supported exonerations based on self-defense or accident.

With a tradition of informality and only meager records to provide precedents for procedural guidelines, the institution was open to a wide range of influences. In most cases in which the circumstances revealed the likelihood of unjustified use of lethal force against African Americans by the police, administrators, coroners, and jurors showed a readiness to respond to white citizens' views. Coroners and their juries sometimes showed a willingness to alter procedures and distort facts in order to reach a verdict of accident or self-defense. Two cases, one before Daniel Brown's death and one after, demonstrate the extent to which a coroner's inquest could be manipulated to shield policemen from criminal charges.

In 1867 a Baltimore policeman, responding to an altercation in an alley outside a "bawdy house," shot and killed Eliza Taylor (also known as Eliza Murray), a black woman, and wounded her husband.[69] The policeman claimed that his gun discharged accidentally, but, as reported in news accounts, witnesses contradicted his claim: the officer had fired two shots; he had shouted racial epithets before he fired the shots; and another policeman on the scene had told the shooter not to fire. After crowds of protesters gathered near the police station, the coroner moved the inquest to the home of one of the jurors. When the jury reassembled, the coroner produced two witnesses, both of whom were former policemen with no direct knowledge of the killing. The former policemen demonstrated to the coroner's jury how a pistol could be accidentally discharged—testimony that, according to the *Baltimore Sun,* "did not appear to have any direct bearing on the case," and according to the *Baltimore American,* "simply amounted to nothing."[70] Nonetheless, the coroner's jury in the Eliza Taylor case exonerated the policeman based on a finding that the victim's death resulted from "a wound inflicted by a pistol ball, accidentally discharged from a navy Revolver in the hands of Policeman Gotleib Frey in the discharge of his duty." The coroner's report of the case, in contrast to newspaper accounts, obscured the incriminating details, and, if the newspaper accounts are accurate, the coroner's report also left out some of the unusual maneuverings in the case by misrepresenting the location of the proceedings. The cursory report stated the inquest was held at the address at which the shooting occurred and made no references to the relocation of the proceedings in response to the protests.[71] Neither the newspaper accounts nor the coroner's report noted that the shooter, Gotlieb Frey, a Confederate Army veteran, was the brother of police captain Jacob Frey.[72] Judge Hugh Lennox Bond of the Baltimore City Criminal Court ordered Frey held to await action by the grand jury, but the coroner's verdict, as was the usual case, provided ample cover to shield Frey from great legal peril, and he was never indicted.[73]

In the second case, a Baltimore policeman approached a group of men standing around a bonfire. One of the men, John Carter, an unemployed twenty-one-year-old African American from Georgia, ran when he saw the policeman approaching. Carter was unarmed and was not accused of any crime. After the policeman called to him to stop, a shot from the policeman's pistol hit Carter in the back. The policeman stated he only intended to frighten the fleeing man, but stumbled at the moment he fired the shot. Before Carter died, Justice Wood, the magistrate assigned to Baltimore's northwestern police station, visited him in the hospital and took his deposition, which allegedly included Carter's statement that he did not think the policeman intended to shoot him. The report of the investigation included no explanation of how Carter, while running with his back to the policeman, might have become aware of the policeman's intentions. A coroner's jury found that the death was the result of an accident.[74] Several witnesses corroborated the policeman's account, but the victim's suspiciously convenient deposition was the most compelling evidence, and the jury "took only a few minutes" to exonerate the officer.[75]

In contrast to the above examples, in the Daniel Brown case the coroner and his jurors disapproved of Officer McDonald's resorting to lethal force. The social context of Daniel Brown's case made all the difference. The coroner and his jurors found the black men and women who witnessed the crime credible, and they listened to them. What the jurors heard led them to the conclusion that Officer McDonald did not act in accordance with what Baltimore's majority residents expected of policemen. Like citizens in other major cities, Baltimore's white citizens wanted policemen to shield them from the dangerous and disorderly conditions they feared were spiraling out of control as a result of changing economic and social conditions in nineteenth-century cities. Black men stood front and center among the allegedly dangerous persons white citizens wanted their policemen to suppress and incarcerate.[76] But for elite Baltimoreans, not all blacks fit the mold. The coroner and the jurors understood that the black men and women present at the Browns' home were not people Baltimore's prosperous white citizens feared. Historians differ in their interpretations of the urban conditions that led nineteenth-century cities to expand and modernize their police forces. Some have focused on the shift from personal relationships to bureaucracies as mechanisms for control of disorderly behavior; some have stressed capitalists' will to control and discipline labor; and some have suggested that police forces needed to "civilize" city dwellers by establishing social service bureaucracies.[77] Despite such differences in emphasis, historians agree that cities shifted from watch and constable arrangements to uniformed police because middle-class and elite residents feared groups perceived as dangerous classes—variously characterized as immigrants, rioters, vagrants, labor radicals, ruffians, or drunkards.[78] The wealthy residents in Daniel Brown's neighborhood, like elites in other growing cities, relied on their police force to shield them from these dangerous classes.[79] But most Park Avenue residents did not consider Daniel Brown and his guests representatives of the dangerous classes; they were not criminals, immigrants, vagrants, labor radicals, ruffians, or drunkards. Keziah and Daniel Brown did not resemble Eliza Taylor and her husband: the Browns did not inhabit an alleged bawdy house in a poor neighborhood. Nor did Daniel Brown resemble John Carter: Brown was not a vagrant from the Deep South and he did not flee at the sight of a policeman. Brown and his friends were perceived by their wealthy neighbors as subordinate partners in personal relationships that echoed slavery-era paternalism. And Coroner Ogle, Captain Earhart, and Thomas Shryock understood the Browns' wealthy Park Avenue neighbors far better than Officer McDonald did.

Although Captain Earhart fulfilled his obligation to support his officers by telling newspaper reporters that McDonald was "one of the most trustworthy men in the district," Earhart nonetheless promptly arrested McDonald.[80] Obligations to his patrolmen or not, Earhart knew unnecessary violence offended the sensibilities of the wealthy residents of Park Avenue. Dr. Ogle and the jurors shared Earhart's understanding of the social context of the case, and, accordingly, they diligently sought to ascertain the facts.

Racism and the subordination of African Americans was fundamental to Baltimore's social order, but the methods of social control favored along Park Avenue differed from the methods used by tough policemen or plantation overseers in places where blacks were isolated from polite society. The wealthy residents of Daniel Brown's neighborhood preferred to forego whips, clubs, and pistols; they favored more genteel methods to subordinate servants they looked upon as racial inferiors.[81] As Frederick Douglass noted, whites in cities, unlike slaveholders on remote plantations, felt some constraints on their most violent impulses because overt brutality might offend their more discreet neighbors.[82] Violence might be tolerated as a method of reasserting social control in the city's rougher districts or in response to recalcitrant field hands on remote plantations. But within the subculture of the elites of Park Avenue and their Tyson Street servants, the resort to violence by an Irish immigrant policeman represented a breakdown in the social order. And the clubbing and shooting of an unarmed man in the middle of the night at a place within sight and hearing of the backdoors of the residents of Park Avenue made it worse.

Captain Earhart, Coroner Ogle, and the coroner's jurors understood the sensibilities of the prosperous, influential residents in Daniel Brown's neighborhood, and the adaptability of the coroner's procedures enabled them to act in accordance with those sensibilities. In doing so, they cleared the way for further legal actions against Officer Patrick McDonald. On August 4, 1875, four days after Brown died, McDonald was committed to the city jail. When the state's attorney brought the charges against McDonald before the grand jury, he presented most of the same witnesses who had appeared before the coroner's inquest. But the prosecuting officer apparently acted with some confidence in his case: once again the state's most compelling witness, Keziah Brown, did not appear. On August 28, 1875, four weeks after Daniel Brown's death, a Baltimore Criminal Court grand jury issued a presentment charging Patrick McDonald with murder. A week later, the state's attorney issued a true bill, formally indicting McDonald. In October McDonald appeared in Baltimore City Criminal Court and filed a plea of not guilty. A trial was set for November 1875.[83]

CHAPTER 4

Black and White Views of Law Enforcement

Public officials—the police captain, the coroner, and the state's attorney—took the necessary steps to advance the Daniel Brown case though the criminal justice system. But public perceptions also mattered in high-profile crimes, especially in cases in which police violence called attention to the city's racial divisions. Black and white Baltimoreans agreed the city had a problem with police misconduct, but blacks saw racism as a major cause of the problem and most white, middle-class citizens did not.

After Captain Earhart relieved Officer McDonald of his duties and an investigation went forward, hints of the white Baltimoreans' ambivalence surfaced. Newspaper accounts that appeared on the Monday following Brown's death did not present Officer McDonald in a bad light. It was noted, for example, in reporting Officer McDonald's actions, that Brown had been "tapped on the head," and that the policeman had a reputation for being a "cool man in excitement." One article quoted Allen Martin as saying he "could speak in the highest terms" of McDonald. As for Daniel Brown, the newspapers focused on his character. The deceased was remembered as "a sober man, but stubborn" and as a man who was "strong in urging his own way."[1] Allen Martin, it was reported, said that he knew Brown to be "a very stubborn, surly sort of man, but he never heard of him getting drunk." It was also noted that Martin described Brown as "a sober and industrious man, but a little strong in the Civil Rights questions."[2] Brown's employer at Woods, Weeks and Company, a sugar refinery, said "he had always known [Brown] as a sober, industrious and attentive man during his two years in the employ of the firm."[3]

When the city turned its attention from the personal characteristics of McDonald and Brown to the issue of police violence, public discourse grew heated. In an editorial on Tuesday, August 3, the *Sun* offered the opinion that, apart from any question of the merits of the particular case, the shooting of Daniel Brown was "calculated to direct public attention to the general question of the right of police officers to use deadly weapons in the discharge of their duties." The *Sun*'s editors stated that the police force was "no place for passionate and excitable men." Noting reports that Officer McDonald may have been investigating the Browns' failure to obtain a permit to hold a cakewalk or a pay party, the *Sun*'s editors asserted that a policeman would not be justified in using deadly force as a response to a citizen refusing to comply with the city's licensing ordinance. In addition, it was noted that "mere impudence" did not justify the use of the policeman's club and, unless an officer believed with probable cause that his life was in danger, there would be no justification for use of the pistol. The *Sun*'s editors noted that the circumstances raised serious questions about the officer's actions: "Still, it may be permitted to observe that, if not criminal, he was undoubtedly hasty."[4] The *American,* a Republican paper, covered the story under headlines referring to the "POLICE MURDER" and printed several citizens' statements under the heading "OPINIONS ABOUT THE OUTRAGE." The *American*'s editors attributed the tragedy to the "almost unlimited license" permitted to the police.[5] The Baltimore *Daily Gazette,* however, criticized the other papers for implying that the "police force are in the habit of shooting negroes for violating ordinances."[6]

In an editorial entitled "Mordwaffen in den Händen öffentlicher Beamter" (Deadly weapons in the hands of public officials), Baltimore's leading German-language newspaper, *Deutsche Correspondent,* decried the prevalence of careless violence by officers acting in the line of duty. The *Correspondent*'s editors compared the killing of Brown to the shooting of a German sailor in August 1873, a shooting the *Correspondent* characterized as thoughtless and unprovoked.[7] In that case, a customs official had arrested a German resident of Baltimore after he had allegedly tried to smuggle a few bottles of gin off a German ship. In the course of transporting the accused smuggler from the harbor to downtown Baltimore, the customs officer noticed some German sailors walking behind him and his prisoner. Feeling threatened by the Germans, the officer turned and fired a shot, hitting one of the Germans in the forehead and killing him instantly. The German sailors, it turned out, had been unarmed, and the evidence did not indicate they intended to interfere with the customs official. The customs official was convicted of manslaughter and sentenced to two years in prison, a sentence that, in the opinion of the *Correspondent*'s editors, was very light for such a crime.[8] At the time of the shooting of the German sailor, the *Correspondent*'s editors had complained that in the English-language press, the attitude toward the matter was "Es War ja nur ein Deutscher!" ("It was only a German!").[9] For those in the city's German-language community, however, the actions of the customs official was "kaltblütiger Mord" (cold-blooded murder);[10] and in view of the fact that they believed Officer McDonald had shown little understanding of his responsibilities and had abused his authority, the *Correspondent*'s editors considered McDonald's action comparable.[11]

In strongly worded editorials, both the *Sun* and the *American* criticized the Baltimore Board of Police Commissioners for inadequate control of patrolmen. In the *Sun* it was stated that "all citizens of whatever color or degree, rich or poor, white and black, have the same personal immunity and protection before the law."[12] Furthermore, in the view of the *Sun*'s editors, police violence such as occurred in the killing of Brown was becoming increasingly common: "Too many cases have happened lately—fewer, perhaps, in Baltimore in proportion than elsewhere—of a brutal and lawless use by the police of the powers with which they are clothed."[13] On its editorial page, the *American* placed the responsibility for patrolmen's abuses on the Baltimore police commissioners. The *American* reminded the commissioners that patrolmen had no right to enter the house of a private citizen without a proper warrant, and that "The singing and dancing of colored people is neither a felony nor a misdemeanor."[14] The cause of Daniel Brown's death, the *American*'s editors asserted, was "the almost unlimited license that has been permitted to [policemen] to use their clubs upon the slightest provocation, and to resort to the revolver when any resistance is made to their unnecessary brutality."[15] It was also stated in the *American*'s editorial that a policeman would never dare to "come pounding on the door of some respectable white citizen, ordering him to keep quiet."[16]

Yet the coverage in the city's major newspapers for the most part expressed denials that police excesses could be attributed to racism. Despite the comparison to what might be expected in the case of "some respectable white citizen," the *American*'s editorial writer went on to challenge African Americans who claimed the McDonald case was one "deeply concerning themselves."[17] According to the *American*'s editors, the source of the problem was poorly trained policemen and unprofessional, corrupt police magistrates who victimized not only black citizens but also "the poorer class of white people."[18] In the *Sun*, which was always less supportive of African American claims than the *American* was, editors voiced disagreement with African Americans who responded to Daniel

Brown's death by organizing protests. They contended such protests mistakenly showed a "disposition to treat the affair as one involving considerations of race or color." [19] In conclusion, the *Sun*'s editors denied the existence of officially tolerated racial oppression in Maryland: "We are not aware of any systematic oppression in this State or city of any class of citizens by another, nor do we believe that there is any disposition or intention on the part of the police authorities or members of the force to oppress, injure or maltreat colored people."[20]

In contrast to white journalists, many African Americans believed that police practices in the city amounted to racial oppression, although factions within the black community differed as to the best way to respond. Within days after Brown's death, black leaders scheduled a protest meeting. At the same time, however, a person the *American* described as a "prominent and intelligent colored citizen" was quoted as saying he opposed plans for the meeting.[21] Although hundreds of African Americans and a few white men attended the meeting, organizers permitted only a few persons to speak.[22] And circumstances surrounding the meeting indicate that black ministers disagreed with plans outlined by black activist businessmen. Protesters initially reserved the Bethel African Methodist Episcopal Church for the gathering, but it was reported that organizers had to move the meeting to the Frederick Douglass Institute after some church members insisted that a place of worship was not a proper location for a protest meeting.[23] The principal organizers included no ministers. John W. Locks chaired the meeting and George Myers served as the secretary. Both Locks and Myers were businessmen who had participated in the acquisition of the Chesapeake Marine Railway and Drydock Company (CMRD) after white workers had forced black skilled workers out of the city's shipyards. A few months before the death of Daniel Brown, Locks had acted as a pioneer in integrating juries in Maryland, at least in federal courts. In response to the federal Civil Rights Act passed in March 1875, the US District Court had sworn in Locks along with two other Baltimore African Americans to serve on a grand jury.[24] Another of the meeting's organizers, Lemuel Griffin, had also participated in the movement to gain control of the CMRD. African American businessman, I. O. B. Williams, a grocer, delivered the meeting's opening statement.[25]

As the first order of business, I. O. B. Williams read Keziah Brown's account of the killing of her husband. According to Mrs. Brown's statement, Officer McDonald had acted with deliberation and a clear intent to kill Daniel Brown. She stated that McDonald had clubbed her husband, then, after her husband had fallen, McDonald had pushed her aside when she begged him not to fire the fatal shot. After reading Mrs. Brown's statement, Williams noted that some African

Americans believed a protest meeting would do their cause harm. He expressed sympathy for those with such fears because, he said, he understood many black citizens "thought it better to silently endure the evils that [African Americans] were forced to bear than to speak, and perhaps bring greater evils."[26]

Williams, in his opening remarks, and George Myers, in his reading of the assembly's resolutions, expressed several grievances that had kept blacks "in a state of most anxious fear."[27] First, Williams noted, the police failed to protect African Americans in cases in which white persons assaulted them. Furthermore, Williams reported, white policemen made frequent arrests of black adults and children by entering their homes without warrants or proper authority. In conjunction with such police harassment, Williams stated, police station magistrates regularly threatened those arrested with imprisonment in order to collect fines and fees for court costs in cases in which charges could not be legally sustained.[28] As reported by George Myers in his capacity as secretary of the meeting, the assembled citizens resolved that Daniel Brown was "shot down like a dog . . . for no other cause but that he was a harmless colored citizen," and further, that this murderous assault was the "culmination of a series of oppressive acts towards our race." Dr. H. T. Brown, another of the nine men given access to the podium, presented additional resolutions. Dr. Brown's resolutions included one in which the organizers counseled "forbearance and an ample use of discretion," and one stating that the assembly courted "impartial sympathy by appealing to the board of police commissioners, magistrates, judges of courts, and all others in authority, and to all good citizens to give us that support and protection to which every citizen is entitled under the laws of the State." The assembly voted to adopt all the resolutions, and Chairman Locks adjourned the meeting after overruling objections from several persons who had been denied opportunities to speak.[29]

Whether they agreed with the tactics of the meeting's organizers or favored a more cautious response, Baltimore's black citizens had reasons for their dissatisfaction with the Baltimore police force and with the practices of police magistrates. Officer McDonald's belligerence by itself showed a need to examine relations between African Americans and white policemen. But the problem obviously went deeper than isolated instances of misbehavior by individual patrolmen. There were good reasons for the protesters' attempts to bring attention to the policemen on the streets and the magistrates in the station houses. Patrolmen regularly harassed blacks, and the guidelines under which patrolmen operated made it easy to disguise racially motivated arrests. Officers could make arrests based on their entirely subjective assessments of people they encountered on the streets. By simply identifying someone as a "suspicious character," an officer could haul someone off to the station house. In 1874, Baltimore police made nearly four hundred arrests of persons they deemed "suspicious."[30] Officers, of course, also arrested white men and women for being suspicious, but for an officer inclined to see dark skin as an indication of criminality, making a habit of selectively arresting suspicious characters could readily serve as a cover for racial harassment. And harassment by patrolmen on the streets could be continued in the station house if magistrates with discretionary leeway chose to deny black citizens fair hearings. In fact, the day-to-day injustices African Americans faced in Baltimore occurred most often not in the criminal courts but rather in street encounters with police and in informal proceedings before station house magistrates. Episodes of abusive behavior and bullying by policemen on their beats could easily escape notice by the general public, and when officers took the more public step of making arrests, station house magistrates disposed of many times more cases than judges in the criminal trial courts tried.[31]

Records from the city's police stations, although sparse, show a basis for the complaint that the police did not protect black citizens from white aggression. Police arrested black citizens far more often for assaults on whites than they arrested whites for assaults on blacks. And for those brought before police magistrates, the outcomes for whites and blacks differed significantly. Nearly all whites charged with assaulting blacks were released on bail or had their charges dismissed. For blacks, the procedure more frequently led to jail time; magistrates released barely half on bail and rarely dismissed them.[32]

In fact, the idea that an African American could effectively bring charges against a white aggressor was relatively new to Marylanders in the 1870s. Until 1867 a Maryland statute barred African Americans from testifying against whites in proceedings before police magistrates or in any of the state's courts.[33] Without testimony from the person charging an assault, the result was almost inevitably a dismissal by the station house magistrate. Even with federal intervention, Maryland's black citizens found it difficult to bring legal actions against white aggressors in the decade following the Civil War. In 1866, using federal civil rights laws as a vehicle to seek justice for an African American, a Freedmen's Bureau agent managed to get a conviction in a case in which a white man "committed an outrage upon a negro." The white defendant challenged the constitutionality of the federal law and argued that the African American witnesses in the case were incompetent. Freedmen's Bureau officials were elated when the Maryland Court of Appeals upheld the conviction, but new obstacles to prosecutions of white aggressors quickly became apparent.

When Freedmen's Bureau officers tried to bring additional criminal prosecutions, constables refused to serve subpoenas and juries habitually disregarded the testimony of black witnesses.[34] As the protesters at the meeting following Daniel Brown's death pointed out, the obstacles to justice observed by Freedmen's Bureau officers in the 1860s had not vanished in the 1870s.

The black men and women who joined the protest following Daniel Brown's death almost certainly remembered the outcome of criminal prosecutions that followed a riot in 1873. As criminal charges resulting from the riot moved through the courts, the case unfolded as a notorious example of the failure of the criminal justice system to protect African Americans from attacks by whites. The obvious bias in the police department's handling of the matter drew criticism not only from the black citizens, but also from one of the city's major newspapers. In an 1873 editorial, the *Baltimore American* charged that policemen failed to protect the African Americans from a stone-throwing mob, and that the Board of Police Commissioners and the state's attorney acted improperly in the case.

The so-called "Essex Street riot" began when white boys threw stones at a Sunday school group from the Asbury AME Church. The church group had spent the day on an excursion in the country, and when the excursioners alighted from train cars at the President Street Depot, they attempted to march back to the church with a band at the head of their procession. As they started through the streets of east Baltimore, some white boys taunted the marchers and threw stones at them. Fighting broke out, and the incident threatened to become a major disturbance; hundreds of men, women, and children marched with the African American group, and white adults joined the fight on the side of the stone throwers.[35] According to the account of the incident in the *American,* the mob chased the African Americans through the streets for several city blocks. The *American*'s reporter described scenes of "women flying with children in their arms, and a howling, infuriated mob following and indiscriminately beating all they overtook," while some of the policemen "seemed to enjoy the scene." Worst of all, according to the reporter, the sergeant who led the police detail on the scene drew his revolver and fired shots in the direction of the fleeing African Americans.[36] The *American*'s editors demanded an investigation and argued that police officials would have responded differently if an African American mob had attacked whites. If the races had been reversed, the *American* hypothesized, there would have been a demand for punishment of every black rioter, the whole police detective force would have been detailed to "ferret out the guilty ruffians," and the station houses would have been filled with African American men arrested on suspicion of involvement in the crime.[37]

The police commissioners investigated the riot. Their primary goals seem to have been to calm the African Americans and to convince all city residents of the police force's ability to maintain order. Although the police commissioners barred the public and the press from the hearings, they made an exception for the pastor of the Asbury AME Church, who not only attended the hearings, but apparently participated in questioning the witnesses. The commissioners called more than fifty witnesses, including several African Americans. Some of the testimony indicated that the *American*'s account erred in details. One of the police officers, not the sergeant in charge of the police contingent, fired the shots. The officer who fired the shots testified and admitted resorting to his pistol, but he claimed he fired in the air in an effort to keep the combatants from advancing toward each other. Several witnesses, including some black men, testified that the police generally tried to keep the groups apart.[38] Nonetheless, there was ample evidence that some policemen, at the very least, showed poor judgment, and at worst, sided with the whites. And the police commissioners agreed the officer who fired shots acted inappropriately, even if his intent was to separate the combatants.

The commissioners published their findings in the form of a letter sent by the commission's secretary to the marshal of the police force. Despite a few concessions to the black community, the letter downplayed the magnitude of the incident and included some evasive, even strange, wording. The source of the trouble, according to the report, was "a few ill-bred urchins," and although the report repeatedly referred to the stone throwers as small boys, some were in fact fifteen years old. White adults had joined in the attacks, but the odd wording obscured the fact: the urchins or small boys, according to the report, were "aided and abetted perhaps by boys of larger growth." The letter concluded by asserting that "It is gratifying to be assured that the police acted dutifully . . . as the conservators of the peace, to the best of their judgment at the moment."[39]

Despite the evasiveness of the final report and the indications that some policemen acted inappropriately, the facts that came to light at least showed that the commissioners and the higher-ranking officers on the force wanted to limit the violence. To some extent, they had succeeded. Only three significant injuries were reported. Given the numbers of people involved and the apparent intensity of anger on both sides, the incident could have resulted in many injuries, loss of life, and widespread property damage. The performance of the police thus provided some benefit to African Americans, who probably would have incurred the most casualties if the violence had not been limited.

At the same time, the policing had served the interests of the entire city; no one would benefit from a full-scale race war.

But for the Baltimore's African Americans, the ultimate outcome of the legal fallout from the riot drove home the message that the highest priority in the criminal justice system was to serve the interests of white, not black, Baltimoreans. The state's attorney obtained indictments for rioting against six men, three black and three white. The balance itself seemed odd, given the overwhelming evidence that whites initiated the violence. But the final disposition of the cases proved to be even more peculiar. In October 1873, as the cases advanced in the criminal justice system, the editors of the steadfastly Republican *American* complained that the state's attorney's handling of the cases showed racial bias. To start with, the state's attorney had obtained two indictments, grouping the three white defendants—James Hagan, Henry Horseman, and Edward Brannan—in one, and the three black defendants—Joseph Butler, Charles Harris, and Mace Pally—in the other. With the defendants so segregated, the white defendants requested removal of their cases from the Baltimore City Criminal Court to the Baltimore County Court in Towsontown. Judge Robert Gilmor of the Baltimore City Court, the judge who would later preside in Officer McDonald's trial, agreed that bias might prevent a fair trial in the city and agreed to the transfer. State's Attorney A. Leo Knott then requested that the trial of the three black defendants also be removed to the Baltimore County Court, and again Judge Gilmor granted the request.[40] The cases were now, in the view of the *American*'s editors, set up neatly for acquittals of the whites and convictions of the blacks. And that is exactly what happened.[41] On January 5, 1874, Joseph Butler, Charles Harris, and Mace Pally were each sentenced to two months in the Baltimore City Jail for rioting, and on the same day, James Hagan, Henry Horseman, and Edward Brannan were acquitted.[42] The incident that began with whites throwing stones at African Americans ended with three black men in jail and no convictions of white aggressors. The verdicts demonstrated what Baltimore's black citizens already knew: the police and the criminal justice system could not be relied upon to protect African Americans from abusive behavior by whites.

And the failure of magistrates and law enforcement officers to protect African Americans from abusive behavior by whites affected blacks in the ordinary course of their daily lives as well as in dramatic events such as the Exeter Street riot. Whites resisted federal civil rights legislation, and white obstruction went unchecked. As a result, measures such as the Civil Rights Act of

1875 had limited effect, discouraging some blacks from trying to desegregate inns and restaurants. Baltimore was not rigidly segregated in the 1870s. Whites found it inconvenient to segregate streetcars. One segregation plan, for example, called for running separate cars, with every third car allocated to blacks. The plan, obviously, would result in less frequent service for whites as well as blacks.[43] Nonetheless, the city maintained strict segregation in some facilities that were very important to the quality of life for African Americans such as schools, hotels, and restaurants. Perhaps because they were aware of the intensity of white resistance to equal access to these facilities, some conservative African Americans denied a need to oppose segregation. In its coverage of the 1875 Civil Rights Act, the *Sun* reported statements from Bishop A. W. Wayman of the AME Church and Mr. Webb, a cashier at the Freedmen's Savings Bank. The *Sun* described Wayman and Webb as men who had "experienced the needs of their race." Both men claimed that the city's blacks were satisfied with segregated accommodations because, as they said, "colored people" have their own churches, graveyards, theaters, and restaurants and "generally take care of themselves and mind their own business."[44]

There is no way of knowing whether these men actually believed that their statements about segregation fairly represented a unified African American community. There is some irony, however, in the assertion in the *Sun* that Wayman and Webb had "experienced the needs of their race." The experiences of those who had different views about segregation and the needs of the black Baltimore residents suggested that police assistance in checking aggressive white behavior could matter a great deal in the day-to-day lives of African Americans in Baltimore. A few days after the *Sun*'s interview with Wayman and Webb, two or three black men tried to make the promise of the new Civil Rights Act a reality, but the results indicated that in the absence of support from law enforcement officials, African Americans would have little chance to desegregate hotels and restaurants. With their rights under federal law in mind, the men tried to have a meal in the restaurant of a Baltimore hotel. Although the proprietor of the hotel at first served the black customers, white diners responded by throwing cups and dishes at the blacks. There is no indication the white assailants were asked to leave. When the black men left and asked a policeman for help, the policeman offered no immediate protection, but instead directed the black men to seek a warrant. In the same article in which the *Baltimore American* reported the incident, it was stated that the passage of the civil rights bill "had created no trouble in this city" and, furthermore, the *American* concluded, "It is not anticipated . . . that the colored people will thrust themselves in places where they would not be wanted."[45] The message to Baltimore's black men and women was clear. Federal laws or not, African Americans could not rely on the Baltimore police to shield them from aggression when they tried to exercise their rights. The people who had political power in Maryland controlled the police, and the police carried out their duties in accordance with the wishes of those in power.

The *American*'s account of the attempt to desegregate the restaurant ended with the statement that, following their unsuccessful attempt to elicit aid from the policeman, the two black men "have not been heard from," implying that the black men lacked a serious commitment to desegregation. The *American*'s reporter apparently found it easy to imagine indifference or lack of resolve where a more empathetic observer might have imagined simmering anger. Day-to-day interactions on the city's streets, however, made it clear that discriminatory law enforcement made many African Americans angry. Inevitably, tensions arose between the all-white police force and black Baltimoreans. And the long-standing frustration of blacks with police intrusions into their social affairs and their homes continued to simmer. On July 12, less than three weeks before Daniel Brown died, a policeman's late-night clash with a group of African American men and women sparked a dangerous outburst of violence that in some ways was a precursor to Officer McDonald's attack on Brown. At about 1:30 A.M., a Baltimore policeman, Officer Moore, on his rounds came across a party of black men and women "talking and making noise." Officer Moore "endeavored to suppress" the noise but, according to the *Sun*'s reporter, Officer Moore's attempt at suppression made the situation worse. As the confrontation escalated, Samuel Johnson, described as a "large and powerful" black man, allegedly swung an ax at Officer Moore. Significantly, however, the facts of the case as reported in the *Sun* showed that Johnson "was followed into his house" before he seized the ax and tried to hit the policeman. Subsequently, several officers arrived at the scene, and in the melee that followed, Johnson was injured by a shot from Officer Moore's pistol. Despite the reported fact that Johnson had attacked the policeman with an ax, the police did not attribute the shooting to self-defense, but instead to an accident—a basis for exoneration of the policeman that fit with the fact that the pistol shot hit Johnson in the back.[46] Fortunately, neither Officer Moore nor Johnson suffered life-threatening injuries, but a few weeks later, Officer Patrick McDonald's encounter with Daniel Brown provided a tragic example of the dangers inherent in tense encounters between African Americans and armed white policemen.

CHAPTER 5

Police and Violence in a Divided City

White Baltimoreans' opinions about police behavior played an important part in responses to the killing of Daniel Brown. Although many white Baltimoreans were reluctant to recognize racism as an element in police violence, they nonetheless acknowledged that police misconduct threatened Baltimore's peace and security and damaged the city's reputation. Many white citizens agreed with blacks' assessment that policemen resorted to the club and pistol too readily, and many white residents shared blacks' anxieties about the perils of interacting with patrolmen. In the two decades preceding Daniel Brown's death, seemingly intractable violence in the city had undermined confidence in the force. By 1875, citizens with allegiances across the political spectrum held the police in low esteem, partly as a result of police complicity in election-day violence, and partly because the habit of resorting to rough tactics in elections sometimes carried over into routine interactions with citizens.

Although Baltimore was not the only nineteenth-century US city that struggled with police interference in elections, conditions in Baltimore exacerbated the problem. Baltimore's experiences during the nation's mid-century crisis differed from the experiences of cities to the north and south. The crisis, of course, ignited conflicts everywhere in the nation. Nonetheless, as measured against conflicts that erupted in cities unambiguously within the Union or the Confederacy, internal conflicts within Baltimore's white population flared up with greater intensity and persisted more stubbornly.

The national crisis obviously traumatized cities in the Deep South, but border cities grappled with a distinctive array of issues. In the border-state politics of Baltimore, neighbors and acquaintances (and sometimes even blood relatives) split into opposing factions during the national debate over slavery, and the divisions intensified as the factions supported opposing sides in a shooting war. The intensity of Baltimore's wartime divisions surfaced, for example, in an incident directly involving Baltimore natives serving in the Union Army. In May 1862, the 1st Maryland Regiment, under the command of Baltimore native Col. John R. Kenly, suffered a decisive defeat at Front Royal, Virginia. The earliest reports from the battlefield indicated that several Marylanders, including Colonel Kenly, had died in the fighting.[1] While friends and family of the fallen soldiers mourned, Confederate sympathizers took to the streets in Baltimore to celebrate. Not surprisingly, fights broke out, and the police struggled to separate the angry factions. Later reports delivered the news that Colonel Kenly had in fact survived the battle, although he had incurred saber cuts and a pistol wound. But at least twenty Maryland soldiers died in the battle and another fifty suffered wounds.[2] Such incidents left many Baltimoreans embittered and the memories lasted long after the war ended.

In contrast, despite inevitable tensions among whites in the cities of the Confederacy, white Southerners, for the most part, directed their hostilities toward African Americans, Northern abolitionists, and Republicans. Although some whites in the Deep South, mostly former Whigs, opposed secession, nearly all of them sided with the Confederacy once the war began.[3] Even many of the pro-Republican so-called scalawags of the Reconstruction era had supported the Confederacy during the hostilities. The ranks of the scalawags included former Confederate officials and slaveholders, many of whom had served in the Confederate Army.[4]

Baltimore's wartime experiences also differed from the experiences of Northern cities. Although Baltimore remained in the Union during the war, its position as the urban center of a slave state set it apart from cities such as Boston, New York, and Philadelphia. Historians of immigration as well as historians of policing contend that wartime conditions in the North attenuated divisions among European Americans. As John Higham notes, the onset of the Civil War had the effect of "absorbing xenophobes and immigrants in a common cause. Now the foreigner had a new prestige; he was a comrade-at-arms."[5] Similarly, Roger Lane, a pioneering historian of policing and urban violence, has noted that despite Philadelphia's reputation for divisiveness, a clear majority of Philadelphians, elites as well as workers, supported the Union, and former rivals, by facing danger together on the battlefields, strengthened their sense of community.[6] Arguably, in light of draft riots and anti-Republican copperhead conspiracies, the alleged unity within Northern cities may be overstated. Nonetheless, as compared to Northern cities, Baltimore's white citizens were more deeply divided and internal conflicts persisted more stubbornly.

In Baltimore, with its deep divisions, as political power shifted from one faction to another, each faction in turn used the police force to dominate the opposition. Police misconduct during emotional and hard-fought political campaigns during the nation's mid-century crisis undermined trust in law enforcement. Control of the police shifted from Democrats to the American Party (the so-called Know-Nothing Party) in the mid-1850s, and then back to Democrats by 1860. But with the outbreak of war, a coalition of Republicans and Unionist Democrats, acting with the assistance of federal authorities, suppressed the Democratic Party's conservative base. In the course of these political shifts, conservative Democrats accumulated grievances as a result of police activities they perceived as abusive.[7] In post–Civil War election cycles, lingering antagonisms prolonged the era of boisterous campaigns and kept alive the temptation to use the police presence in the streets for political advantage. With the withdrawal of federal influence at the end of the war, the Democratic Party regrouped under the leadership of the party's conservative base and overthrew the wartime coalition. After 1866, the Democratic Party in its turn used the police to control elections and repress Republicans and reformers. To ensure the effectiveness of their campaign tactics, party leaders chose tough men for police duty and too often directed them to use rough tactics in elections, and, at least for some policemen, the rough tactics used in elections engendered habits of bullying that were not easily reined in after election day. As a result, in the two decades preceding Daniel Brown's death, many residents of Baltimore had experienced abusive police behavior, and the targets of such bullying included not only African Americans and poor white men and women, but also privileged and prosperous white citizens.

The armed, uniformed police force was a relatively new institution in mid-nineteenth-century Baltimore. In the eighteenth century, the responsibility for protecting the city from crime weighed as heavily on private citizens as it did on town or city officials. Citizens assigned to stand watch at night kept a lookout for fires, but the nature of the assignment also made the watchman the most likely townsman to spot behavior that violated community norms. In his essential responsibilities, the eighteenth-century watchman resembled the medieval villager raising the "hue and cry." When a lone watchman detected a serious crime or emergency, he had little choice but to call on his fellow townsmen.

As Baltimore grew rapidly after the Revolution, the Maryland Assembly took notice of the town's need for a more organized body to "prevent fires, burglaries, and other outrages and disorders." In an Act of 1784, the General Assembly directed Baltimore Town's commissioners to employ paid watchmen and empower them to apprehend "night-walkers, malefactors, rogues, vagabonds, and disorderly persons."[8] In 1798, the Baltimore City Council took another step toward reorganizing police functions. The council created the office of high constable and directed this officer to make the rounds of the city during the day and report on nuisances and violations of ordinances.[9] Along with three deputy constables, the high constable brought a semblance of policing to the city when the night watchmen were off duty.[10] With a paid corps of watchmen for nighttime duty and constables to patrol the city by day, the rudiments of a police force began to emerge. But private policing was a deeply rooted tradition in Baltimore, and at the opening of the nineteenth century, municipal and state control over policing and criminal justice remained minimal. As Adam Malka notes in his study of policing and incarceration in Baltimore, early nineteenth-century citizens "performed seemingly 'public' roles all the time, and this proved especially to be the case when it came to policing."[11]

Early nineteenth-century constables and watchmen faced the task of policing a city that was growing with the energy of a boomtown. From a town of fewer than 14,000 residents in 1790, Baltimore grew into a city with a population of more than 45,000 by 1810, and by 1840, Baltimore was a metropolis with a population of 102,513. The population reached 170,000 by 1850, making Baltimore the third most populous city in the United States, trailing only New York and Philadelphia.[12] And with growth came greater social complexity and economic stratification. Diversity among the city's African Americans presented itself most obviously in terms of freedom and slavery. The presence of an impressively large number of African Americans marked the city as Southern. But slavery never dominated the economy, and by 1850, the city's African American population was 90 percent free and 10 percent enslaved.[13] At the same time, the city's immigrants added diversity within the white population. A substantial number of Germans made the city their home by the first years of the nineteenth century, and new arrivals added to their numbers over the next several decades. French-speaking immigrants blended into the city's ethnic mix during the Haitian Revolution, and the massive emigration from Ireland in the 1840s and 1850s added tens of thousands of new immigrants.[14] The excellent harbor had always given Baltimore commercial advantages, and when railroads improved the harbor's connections to the nation's interior, commerce flourished even more.[15] Commercial growth intensified economic stratification. Wealthy merchants and professionals made their homes in the fine stone houses along the city's wide avenues, but during the workday, they mingled with an economically marginal class of laborers, sailors, laundresses, and dockworkers.[16]

The growth and evolution of the city made many Baltimoreans anxious. Citizens repeatedly complained of daily encounters with the "ruffianism" of wage workers and idle young men, many of whom were immigrants.[17] In the crowded, busy city, episodes of disorderly conduct, public drunkenness, petty crime, and a variety of nuisances troubled middle-class residents.[18] For many, there was a general sense of disorder—the presence of unfamiliar people, the crowding, and the pace of change made the city feel dangerous. It was not uncommon by the 1830s for respectable, middle-class citizens to believe that a simple walk through the city was a risky activity.[19] Troubled by these conditions, prosperous and influential Baltimoreans demanded more protection, and some advocated reforms that would professionalize policing in the city.[20] And state and city officials responded to appeals for more efficient policing. The legislature authorized periodic increases in the watch and day police. An 1826 ordinance provided for three watch districts under the supervision of four captains and eight lieutenants. In 1835 and again in 1845 the watch system was expanded, resulting in four districts.[21]

But additions to security forces also met resistance. An aversion to centralized state power was an enduring element in Maryland's political culture.[22] The Declaration of Rights attached to Maryland's Constitution of 1776 included a warning about the dangers posed by standing armies: in Article 26 of the Declaration, the state's founders declared, "That standing armies are dangerous to liberty, and ought not to be raised or kept without consent of the legislature." When Maryland adopted a new constitution in 1851, Article 26 was preserved word for word.[23] For some citizens, police reforms evoked images of the standing armies their Revolutionary-era forefathers warned them about. With each increase in police presence on the streets, more "captains," "lieutenants," and their patrolmen exercised authority over private citizens' activities. Misconduct and bullying by some watchmen made the case harder for reformers. In response to instances of watchmen bullying citizens, city officials tried to limit watchmen's discretionary authority, but a watchman walking the city at night could not easily be monitored or constrained. It was simply too easy for corrupt or incompetent watchmen in a darkened city to take advantage of their more vulnerable fellow citizens.[24]

Throughout the first half of the nineteenth century, Baltimoreans debated the wisdom of increasing the police force and empowering policemen. As the debate went on, a series of riots periodically added momentum to the advocates of more effective policing. Diversity and economic stratification generated tensions that erupted in outbursts of collective violence, and Baltimore soon earned the nickname "mobtown." In 1812, citizens clashed over differences about the coming war with Britain. In response to taunts in a Federalist newspaper, an angry crowd ransacked the paper's offices. When Federalists retaliated, a battle followed in which a Federalist fired into a crowd, killing one man. The ugly episode almost ended with the arrest of the Federalists, but more violence followed: a crowd broke into the jail to attack the Federalists held there.[25] In 1835 Baltimore's working people protested against unfair banking practices, and the violence of the protesters shocked the city's elite families. After a disastrous bank failure wiped out the savings of thousands of small depositors, investigations exposed shady self-dealing by the bank's managers, who included in their ranks some of Baltimore's leading citizens. Riots broke out and angry mobs looted several of the city's most elegant homes.[26] Rioters targeted, for example, the home of Reverdy Johnson, who accumulated wealth as a bank executive before he served in the US Senate, the Justice Department, and the diplomatic corps.[27] At least nine major riots occurred in the city between 1834 and 1857.[28] When tensions escalated throughout the nation in the Know-Nothing era, the fighting between Democrats and Know-Nothings in Baltimore reached levels that surpassed even New Orleans, a city known for gun violence and high homicide rates.[29] Among cities in the slave states, only Louisville matched Baltimore in its frequency and intensity of Know-Nothing–related disorders.[30]

By the early 1850s, the competing currents of public opinion shifted in favor of increasing security in the streets. In addition to episodic major rioting, almost daily incidents of street violence frustrated prosperous Baltimoreans. Fire companies fought with each other, boys and young men threw bricks and stones, and fights broke out with regularity. Newspaper accounts, at least in the *Baltimore Sun*, reflected an editorial effort to increase public support for the police. Articles in the *Sun* seemed to look for and commend competent policing. In one account, a *Sun* reporter took note of the prevalence of street violence, while taking care to absolve the police of any responsibility for failing to stop it. The article on "yet another" instance of street violence began by relating an episode in which a "gang of rowdies" showered broken bricks and stones on a passing fire company, but the report went on to explain that the high constable and "his posse" were not to blame for failing to intervene because they were on their way to prevent a disturbance in another quarter.[31] In another account, it was observed that the high constable commanded a force in which "a large proportion" of the men were "faithful, industrious and reliable conservators of the peace."[32]

The growing frustration reflected in these reports coincided with a reform movement of international scope. Several mid-nineteenth-century US cities, following a model first adopted in London, transformed ancient constable and watch security forces into bureaucratized (and militarized) metropolitan police forces. In the United States, New York and Boston led the way, followed by several other major cities.[33] Maryland legislators and councilmen observed the reforms carried out in other cities, and they concluded that the plans adopted in London and New York, could serve as useful models for a reorganization of the Baltimore police.[34]

In 1852, Baltimore took the first steps to join the list of US cities that adopted some variation of the London model. An assessment of the city's security forces in 1852 found a total of 318 "guardians of the peace." The day police, including the high constable and his deputy, numbered sixty-eight; the night watch, including captains and lieutenants, totaled 250 men.[35] But the division between the night watch and day police left the security forces poorly coordinated, and the city council was ready to address the perceived inefficiency. A joint committee of the city council examined the police system and issued a report in November 1852. The committee noted that the city's population growth made the system of police and night watch "inadequate." The separation of night and day patrols, they reported, suffered from conflicts of interest and petty jealousies and, even worse, the current arrangement left the city unprotected during transitions between the night watch and the day police. In view of these problems, the committee acknowledged a need to "bow to public opinion," and provide a police force that would forever put to rest "the spirit of rowdyism." The committee concluded by stating that "*the object of the police system is to prevent the occurrence of crime.*"[36] In 1853, the Maryland General Assembly authorized Baltimore's mayor and city council to "strengthen the police by day and night" by consolidating "police officers and men, whether bailiffs, night watch, or however designated." The legislation provided for an increase in the number of patrolmen and authorized equipping officers with uniforms, weapons, and badges.[37] In 1856, the city council passed an ordinance implementing the legislation. The mayor approved the ordinance in January 1857, and by the summer of 1857 a metropolitan police force under a single marshal patrolled Baltimore's streets in new blue uniforms.[38]

Opposition to the plan accounted for much of the delay between the legislature's authorization in 1853 and the mayor's final approval on January 1, 1857. As legislators in Annapolis and councilmen in Baltimore worked out the details, proponents of limiting state-sanctioned authority trimmed some of the measures they considered most offensive. In the General Assembly, an amendment removed a provision that would have made assault on a policeman punishable by a fine double the fine for assaulting a private citizen.[39] A version of an implementing ordnance debated in the city council went considerably too far for even moderate critics of the reorganization. According to a report in the *Baltimore Sun,* the objectionable proposal authorized the chief of police (and presumably the officers under him) "to enter houses and examine premises, after making oath or affirmation that there is good cause to believe that some person is engaged therein in violating the laws of this State, or the ordinances of this city, or is a fugitive from justice." Editors of the *Sun* pointed out the provision's conflict with Article 23 of the Maryland Declaration of Rights, which stated that general warrants "without naming or describing the place, or the person in special, are illegal, and ought not to be granted."[40] The provision may have been aimed at escaped slaves, but white Baltimoreans recognized the provision's potential for abuses against themselves too, and the provision was stricken from the final version of the ordinance.

The General Assembly's enabling act authorized the city to provide arms for the new police force, but the city was not required to equip each patrolman with a weapon to use on regular patrols. Section one of the General Assembly's enabling legislation authorized and *required* (emphasis added) the city to increase and strengthen the police force, but section two authorized and *empowered* (emphasis added) the city to provide weapons for policemen.[41] Baltimore's implementing ordinance was ambiguous as to whether the city would immediately obtain weapons and send each policeman onto the streets armed with a revolver. The ordinance provided that police officers should be equipped "in cases of great emergencies with revolvers and other suitable weapons" and further, that the police marshal should "procure a suitable quantity of such weapons, with which he may arm the police." And finally, the ordinance provided that each person issued a weapon "shall give his receipt for such weapon . . . which shall remain the property of the city."[42]

The ordinance seems to have left to the marshal the judgment as to when to declare an emergency that would justify issuing weapons to policemen.[43] It is unlikely that revolvers were withheld from patrolmen for long. Apparently, watchmen under the old system routinely carried weapons. On January 9, 1857, a few days after Baltimore's mayor signed the reorganization ordinance, a watchman, still patrolling under the old system, fired two shots at a retreating burglary suspect, and there is no indication that the officer's use of the weapon caused a controversy.[44] Despite reservations about weapons in the hands of policemen, many citizens probably recognized that patrolling the streets of Baltimore was dangerous. In 1858, Officer Benjamin Benton died of gunshot wounds incurred while trying to make an arrest. The shooter, Henry Gambrill, was convicted of murder and executed.[45] But Benton's fellow officer, Robert Rigdon, after testifying against Gambrill, was murdered when assassins fired shots into his home.[46] While on patrol during election-day riots in October 1859, Officer William Jourdan died of gunshot wounds.[47] Given the prevalence of weapons on the street, officers probably pressed their superiors for loose control of city-owned revolvers. By the 1860s, all patrolman carried firearms.[48]

Democrats ultimately regretted the interval between the General Assembly's enabling legislation and the city council's implementing ordinance. Despite the Democratic Party's control of the General Assembly and the Baltimore City government, implementing the reorganization plan proved to be a difficult process. Democratic Mayor J. Smith Hollins twice vetoed reorganization bills passed by the Democratic majority on the city council. He refused to give reasons for his vetoes, which made it difficult for the council to arrive at a version that Mayor Hollins would sign.[49] The Democrats failed to complete the reorganization, and the American Party, the so-called Know-Nothings, swept the municipal elections of 1856. With a Know-Nothing mayor, Samuel Hinks, and a majority of their party in the city council, Baltimore's Know-Nothings implemented the reorganization and filled the new police force with their supporters.

Almost as soon as the modernized police force took to the streets, partisan politics undermined the new institution's prestige. The legislature assigned Baltimore's police commissioners the responsibility of ensuring order during elections, but the commissioners lacked the political independence needed to meet the responsibility, and the organized, loyal corps of policemen gave politicians an effective means to promote partisan interests. Nineteenth-century voting procedures were inherently disorderly and vulnerable to corrupt practices. Prior to early twentieth-century reforms, polling places were located in crowded, poorly lit rooms in inns, shops, and even taverns. Voters, without the benefit of secret ballots, often had to make their way past unruly partisan onlookers to cast their ballots in crowded, informal settings.[50] With so many opportunities for intimidation, policemen inevitably assumed responsibilities for crowd control, but policing could be effective only if policemen remained neutral. Often they did not. As Samuel Walker notes in his study of police reforms, in many US cities, newly reorganized police forces readily became creatures of partisan politics.

And, as historians of nativism have observed, with the growing intensity of nativism in the 1850s, Know-Nothing–era politicians commonly used policemen to electioneer, raise campaign funds, and intimidate their opponents.[51]

Baltimore's police force followed the familiar pattern, but with an extra measure of intimidation and violence. As the American Party wrested control of the government from Democrats in the 1850s, political clubs with suggestive names such as Blood Tubs, Butt Enders, Plug Uglies, Rip Raps, Black Snakes, Tigers, and Rough Skins intimidated voters in a series of election riots. Because policemen were hired and fired by elected officials, the patrolmen in the streets had a stake in election outcomes, and in many cases, policemen joined the political clubs.[52] Critics of the American Party contended that by the mid-1850s, Know-Nothing rowdies filled the ranks of the Baltimore force. From the perspective of Democrats and reformers, policemen became nothing more than instruments of violence and intimidation.[53] Throughout the 1850s, election-day violence reached levels that alarmed respectable Marylanders. Combatants resorted to weapons ranging from shoemakers' awls to firearms, and in one instance, combatants fired a cannon in the city streets.[54] As might be expected, these tactics brought rising tolls of serious injuries and fatalities. In battles between Know-Nothings and Irish Democrats in the municipal elections of October 1856, four people died. In the presidential election of November of the same year, street fighters killed ten persons and wounded more than two hundred-fifty.[55]

By the time the newly armed and uniformed policemen began patrolling the city, Baltimore was deeply troubled by election violence. As the city prepared for elections in the autumn of 1857, a controversy arose when Maryland's Democratic governor, Thomas Ligon, proposed state intervention to help keep the peace. Mindful of the violence that led to fatalities in the 1856, the governor offered Baltimore Mayor Thomas Swann a backup force of militiamen. Swann, who had been elected on the American Party ticket, apparently felt confident that the tactics of the city's Know-Nothing gangs could deliver another victory for his party if the militia stayed away. With the help of some prominent citizens, Swann convinced the governor to withhold the militia. Swann's cynical political calculation proved correct, as the Know-Nothing candidates won easily. But opponents of the American Party contended that gangs had attacked anti–Know-Nothing voters and driven many of them from the polls. Democrats and reformers insisted the election had been controlled by fraud and the violence of Know-Nothing gangs.[56] Even citizens who were not allies of the Democrats and reformers had to agree that the new police force had failed to protect voters.

By 1858, violence and intimidation around polling places demoralized Democrats and reformers so thoroughly that Col. A. P. Shutt, the candidate for mayor, announced at noon on election day that he was withdrawing his candidacy. In his written statement to his fellow citizens, Colonel Shutt explained that his supporters' attempts to reach the polls could only raise the danger of "loss of life, and the general disorder of the City." These dangers, according to Shutt, were the result of a "general combination which now prevails between . . . police and the armed bands of lawless men who have, since the opening of the ballot boxes, held possession of the polls to the exclusion of all voters opposed to Mayor Swann."[57]

By the end of 1858, it was clear the new police force was off to a bad start. The first two elections held after the reorganization of the police force left Baltimoreans mistrustful of the new instrument of law and order. Although the editors of the *Baltimore American* suggested that Colonel Shutt exaggerated the level of intimidation in an effort to excuse the inadequacies of his campaign, it was obvious to most citizens that regardless of the shortcomings of Shutt's campaign, the police had failed to curb election-day violence and intimidation. Arguably, the level of partisan animosity and the prevalence of violence-prone party enforcers overwhelmed the police, making it impossible for even a well-intentioned force to keep the peace. Even if citizens chose to view the performance of the police in the most favorable light, however, the fact that the reorganized force had fallen short in its efforts to keep the peace tended to discredit the new institution. In any case, opponents of the Know-Nothings had no inclination to view the performance of the new force generously. City editors asserted that the police had not merely shown themselves to be inadequate, but had actually aided and abetted the street fighters and troublemakers.[58] And there was evidence to support their charges. In his study of Know-Nothing violence in Baltimore elections, Frank Towers contends that 9 percent of the identifiable rioters in elections from 1856 to 1859 were policemen.[59]

Following the embarrassing elections of the mid-1850s, the opponents of the American Party gained momentum by capitalizing on public anxieties about the economic consequences of street disturbances. Fearful that the city's commercial interests could suffer as a result of Baltimore's reputation for violence, opponents of the American Party organized rallies at which they called for a return to law and order. In September 1859, at a gathering before thousands of onlookers, speakers argued that Know-Nothing lawlessness posed a threat to commerce: "Wherever Baltimore is spoken of, the story of its shame is told. Strangers fear to stop in the place, and men of business avoid it." As early as 1857, the Plug Uglies had carried the city's reputation for Know-Nothing violence well beyond the limits of Baltimore. When street fighting erupted in municipal elections in Washington, DC, in June 1857, observers in the capital identified the primary source of trouble as a gang of Plug Uglies who came down from Baltimore.[60] The Baltimore Plug Uglies, according to news reports, seized a small cannon to intimidate their opponents, and when a contingent of United States marines intervened, six people were killed and several suffered serious injuries. In New York, news accounts characterized events in Washington not primarily as disorders involving Know-Nothings based in the capital city, but rather as a "Collision between the Baltimore 'Plug-Uglies' and the U.S. Marines."[61] In 1859 Baltimore reformers, organized as the City Reform Association, focused on the history of unfavorable publicity, alleging that tales of Know-Nothing violence in Baltimore reached as far as London.[62] Organizers of the 1859 rally presented a series of resolutions that called attention to the commercial consequences of the city's disorders, such as "many strangers, business men and others may think it unsafe to maintain existing relations with us, or form new ones."[63]

Although the opponents of Know-Nothings organized under the banner of the City Reform Association and characterized themselves as a nonpartisan movement, their campaign in effect consolidated support behind the Democratic Party.[64] Their movement grew strong enough to offer serious challenges to Know-Nothing dominance in the 1859 elections. With election outcomes increasingly in doubt, the violence continued in the Baltimore city elections of October and in the state elections of November. As disorders persisted in the municipal elections, many respectable citizens directly experienced conditions that further discouraged them about the ability of the police to suppress the city's "ruffians" and "rowdies." And even for those who did not personally encounter episodes of violence and intimidation at the polls, the next day's newspapers presented accounts that further diminished the reputation of the police force.

The *Baltimore Sun*'s account of the October 12, 1859, municipal elections began sardonically with the observation that as there was no shooting, it was the quietest election day in five years. In reporting the details, however, the *Sun*'s account called attention to disturbing facts. It was noted, for example, that several persons were arrested for disorderly conduct, and that the confrontations at polling places included instances such as a group of partisans knocking down an "old citizen" while the police refused to arrest the perpetrators of the violence.[65] The editors of the *Sun* observed that by winning six of the twenty seats on the city council First Branch, the reformers did better than had been anticipated. But the editors also asserted that there had been instances of "shameful dereliction of duty" by police, and the reformers had won their council seats by struggling against "much humiliating exposure to insult, violence, and outrage."[66] The *American* and the *Daily Exchange* included similar accounts of violence, intimidation, and fraud, with ward-by-ward examples of instances in which identifiable perpetrators of violence escaped with little or no consequences. In accounts in both papers, reporters noted cases in which magistrates promptly released persons arrested for violent acts, allowing troublemakers to return to the polls to intimidate more would-be voters.[67]

In assessing the performance of the Baltimore police in the 1850s, it is important to note that many of the officers surrounding the polls apparently tried to maintain order. Even in the *Daily Exchange*, a paper that regularly castigated the Know-Nothings for their tactics, the reports of the October 1859 elections cited instances in which policemen assisted voters. In Ward Two, for example, the *Exchange*'s reporter observed that after "an aged and respected citizen" had been pushed away from the polls, a policeman tried to escort him to the voting window and tried to "see that he got his vote."[68] Accounts of the October 1859 election in both the *American* and the *Daily Exchange* praised Lieutenant Thompson of Ward Three and the officers under his command for their excellent work in difficult circumstances at the polls. And surely many policemen routinely discouraged disruptive behavior that might otherwise have escalated into violence. Understandably, however, incidents of law officers simply doing what they were supposed to do went unreported. Regardless of commendable efforts by some policemen, there was plenty of evidence that with Know-Nothings in control of the mayor's office and the city council, the pattern of behavior by law enforcement officers favored the American Party candidates—and the favoritism went so far as to make the police force complicit in the violence. It is impossible to know with certainty how many of the officers condoned or participated in violence, but even if only a significant minority contributed to the mayhem, citizens had a right to expect more from the force that had been established to shield them from rowdies and ruffians. The perception that the police had failed in that responsibility inevitably undermined trust in the officers on the streets.

Although Know-Nothings prevailed in Baltimore in October 1859, a rapid decline in the fortunes of the American Party followed. Reformers and Democrats attributed Know-Nothing victories in the 1859 city elections to "means against which honest respectable men are almost powerless to contend."[69] Yet the City Reform Association showed that it was not in fact powerless. By exploiting the perception of Know-Nothing rowdyism, reformers checked the momentum of the American Party. When Marylanders went to the polls for the state elections in November 1859, a reaction against the Know-Nothing excesses in the previous month's elections began to take hold. At Reform Party rallies, speaker after speaker cataloged the misdeeds of the violence-prone political clubs that supported the American Party. They asserted that in the last election the political clubs had taken control of the polls and insulted, maltreated, and intimidated anti–Know-Nothing voters. And the same rowdies and ruffians, the reformers contended, had supported the Know-Nothings by depositing fraudulent votes in the ballot boxes. The city, according to one speaker, had "succumbed to the sway of the Plug Uglies, Black Snakes, Swipers and a hundred other clubs."[70] Then, in mid-October, national events added to the momentum of the Baltimore reformers. John Brown's raid at Harpers Ferry enabled reformers and Democrats to link their opponents, especially Congressman Henry Winter Davis, to revolutionary violence and the inflammatory rhetoric of abolitionists.[71] Editors of the *Baltimore Daily Exchange* argued that John Brown was one of the "heroes" of the Republican Party and Brown had been emboldened by proabolitionist statements by Know-Nothing leader Henry Winter Davis and Republican Party sympathizers. Reelection of Davis, it was argued, would be "a direct encouragement" to repeated violent uprisings such as the one at Harpers Ferry.[72] In the weeks leading up to the November 1859 elections, accounts of the reformers' assertions of Know-Nothing misdeeds appeared alongside the *Sun*'s daily page-one accounts of the "Trial of the Harper's Ferry Insurgents."[73]

As the state elections approached, Know-Nothing adherents responded to the growing strength of the reformers by raising the level of intensity at their rallies and openly advocating violence. Know-Nothing agitators flaunted their disdain for polite society by adopting the carpenter's awl as the emblem of their rallies. The carpenter's awl, as a contemporary observer noted, could be easily concealed in a crowd and was as dangerous a weapon as a stiletto.[74] At a huge rally a week before the elections, a procession of Know-Nothing clubs featured a wagon-mounted forge at which men manufactured awls and distributed them to the crowd. Nearly all the displays in the procession used the image of the awl, and the clubs marked their banners with slogans and puns, such as "Come up and Vote; There is room for awl."[75] The "marshal" of the contingent from the Regulators Club paraded through the streets with an awl "about four feet" in length strapped to his back.[76] Henry Winter Davis, the most notable speaker at the event, apparently sensing the vulnerability of his party, advised his audience to avoid "acts of disturbance" that might open the party to criticism. But the editors of the *Daily Exchange* pointed out that Davis delivered his speech while standing under "a huge emblematic awl."[77]

This time the Know-Nothings' tactics failed. The November 1859 statewide elections cost the American Party its majority in the General Assembly. When the General Assembly met in early 1860, Democrats and reformers held a 45–29 advantage over Know-Nothings in the House of Delegates and 12–10 advantage in the Senate.

Although the vote count in November 1859 reversed the momentum that had favored Know-Nothings for several election cycles, election-day violence once again discredited the police. Editors of the *American* contended that voting in Baltimore in November 1859 was conducted "amid scenes of violence and fraud not paralleled in any elections ever held in this or any free country."[78] The hyperbole, no doubt, left some readers skeptical, but anyone present in the city on election day could easily observe enough violence and evidence of fraud to damage the reputations of incumbents as well as the police. For those who had not observed the conflicts in the streets, Baltimore's daily newspapers summarized the misdeeds of officials and police officers. In its account of the election-day disorders, the *American* printed a ward-by-ward survey of events, cataloging instances of voter intimidation and noting that in most wards, the police ignored the perpetrators of the violence or actively assisted them. In Ward One, according to the *American,* the violence drove reformers from the polling places, while the police were observed bantering casually "with the gangs of roughs who were hourly arriving, voting, and departing." In Ward Three, the *American* noted, reformers struggled to keep order and get their votes cast, but the police offered no assistance. In the same ward, when a man named Andrew George tried to help Germans who were being bullied by a "disorderly party," the police did not arrest the bully, but instead hauled Andrew George to the station house. Mr. George's brother, a Reform Party candidate for the legislature, went to the police station to look into the matter, but he was turned away and a policeman struck him "a violent blow to the face." In its account of events in Ward Thirteen, the *American* included a statement from a physician who reported that as many as ten to fifteen men attacked him, and then a policeman arrested him while taking no action against his attackers.[79]

The city's other newspapers reinforced the *American*'s negative portrayals of police conduct. The account of the election in the *Daily Exchange* included similar descriptions of violence and intimidation, along with an assertion that the election was a "farce."[80] An account of "outrages at the polls" filled a column on the front page of the *Sun.* Readers of the *Sun* were informed that a man was stabbed with awls and several persons were "seriously beaten" in Ward One, and that Joseph Vansant, son of Democratic Party leader Joshua Vansant, was "severely beaten" in Ward Five. The *Sun*'s reporter agreed with the other journalists about the complicity of the police: in Ward Nine a German man was "dreadfully beaten" while being held by a policeman, and in Ward Twelve two policemen looked on as attackers knocked a man down and kicked him in the face.[81]

Reports damaging to the prestige of the police continued to command public attention for months after the initial newspaper accounts. In the interim between the November election and the convening of the General Assembly in early 1860, ongoing allegations of corruption and police misconduct raised the level of public anger. Several of the defeated candidates for Baltimore's seats in the House of Delegates contested the elections, and the contests resulted in hearings that kept allegations of police misconduct in the news. More than one hundred witnesses, including residents brought forward from every one of Baltimore's twenty wards, testified as to the violence and intimidation that, according to the defeated candidates, rendered the polling in the city invalid. Witnesses identified gangs of ruffians and partisan election judges as the primary culprits, but they also accused the police of failing to subdue lawlessness. Many witnesses described instances in which policemen looked on and took no action while "ruffians" assaulted and battered citizens around the polling places. In some cases, witnesses claimed policemen were drunk and, in the worst cases, victims of beatings reported that policemen actively participated in the violence.[82] At the conclusion of the hearings, the General Assembly voided the Baltimore election results, leaving the seats won there by the Know-Nothings vacant. The Democratic candidate for controller also contested the election, noting that although the initial vote counts gave him a lead in the counties outside Baltimore, a deficit of more than twelve thousand votes in Baltimore tipped the balance in favor of the Know-Nothing candidate. In the controller's case, the legislature not only voided the ballots from Baltimore, but also, after some wrangling with the governor, awarded the office to the Democratic candidate.[83]

With several of its candidates expelled from the General Assembly and its candidate for the statewide office of controller displaced by the opposition party candidate, the American Party ended the decade in disgrace. Maryland Know-Nothings never recovered from the setbacks of 1859 and early 1860. In October 1860, reformers and Democrats swept the citywide elections by a margin of 17,625 to 9,684, and reform candidate George William Brown defeated his Know-Nothing opponent in the race for mayor.[84]

Once in control of the state, Democrats and their allies promised to reform the police and end the practice of using the police to influence elections. The deluge of damaging publicity about police misconduct provided the reform advocates with public support. In January 1860, the editors of the *Sun* demanded reforms, complaining that without impartial police, "the people of Baltimore will be forever at the mercy of any power which may hold the reins of official authority, corrupt enough to avail itself of an irresponsible ruffianism."[85] Within a few months after the *Sun*'s appeal, reforms became a reality. When state legislators assembled in early 1860, they transferred control of the police from city officials to a Board of Commissioners chosen by the Maryland General Assembly.[86]

Conflicts over the police reforms of 1860 highlighted what most citizens of Baltimore had surely observed in the first few years after the establishment of the militarized police force: those who held political power made it a matter of high priority to gain control of the police. In his reminiscences, Jacob Frey, who would later become Baltimore's police marshal, remembered the intensity of the resistance to the transfer of control of the force. Frey noted that the General Assembly passed the police reform bills in February 1860 only after supporters had overcome "serious and fervent opposition."[87] Frey, a beneficiary of Democratic Party rule, understated the resistance. American Party Congressman Henry Winter Davis, always known for his fiery rhetoric, called the transfer of authority "flagrant usurpation" and charged that the Democrats had "put 'cap and bells' on the bill" by banning the appointment of Republicans."[88] Remarkably, Davis did not exaggerate in his characterization of the blatant partisanship in the reform law. In the section of the new law specifying qualifications for policemen, Democratic legislators included: "*Provided, also,* that no Black Republican or endorser or supporter of the Helper Book shall be appointed to any office under said board."[89] Know-Nothing supporters had good reason to oppose the changes. The reform measures effectively stripped Baltimore's Know-Nothing mayor, Thomas Swann, of his control of the force and ensured that Democrats would appoint their own supporters to the force. Mayor Swann did not accept the new order without a fight. The mayor and the Know-Nothing police commissioners declined to cede control of the force to the new appointees, and the measures went into effect only after the Maryland Court of Appeals sorted out the competing claims and ruled in favor of the reformers on April 17, 1860.[90]

Citizens' responses to the transfer of control over law enforcement reflected the city's discordant politics. The new police force took control of the city on Saturday, May 5, 1860, and the defeated Know-Nothings made sure the significance of the reforms was underscored in a public ceremony. On the following Monday, contingents of the old force, with bands playing martial music ahead of them, proceeded from their station houses to city hall, where they received their final wages and were dismissed. Although no violence marked the transition, the display aroused some supporters of the old order; they disparaged the new order and taunted the newly appointed policemen in their "glittering brass buttons," mocking officers by warning them they might soil their new white gloves.[91] At the same time, other citizens observed the newly appointed policemen in their neat caps, blue coats, and gray pants, and concluded that their appearance warranted commendation as manifestations of proper management and discipline.[92] Far more important than the appearance of the uniformed officers, however, was the fact that the new commissioners had replaced nearly every one of the officers who would now patrol the streets. In a police force of roughly 350 men, a few sergeants and no more than two dozen patrolmen who had served under the Know-Nothing administration remained on duty.[93] The public displays accompanying the transition and the turnover of the force made it clear that those in power controlled the police. Perhaps even more importantly for citizens in a bitterly divided city, events made it clear that patrolmen in the streets would do what those with political power wanted them to do.

By 1860, after a series of crises and controversies, the new Baltimore police force had evolved into the institution that, it was anticipated, would provide security through the period of the impending crisis of national disunity. From 1853 to 1860, the city's security functions had been consolidated; the number of policemen on the force had grown from 64 to 349; and the state legislature had gained control over a city force that was organized under a hierarchy of a marshal, captains, lieutenants and sergeants.[94] At least one nineteenth-century Baltimorean believed the reforms of 1860 left the city poised for a period of efficient government that would bring an end to the "terrible nightmare" of police involvement in "ruffian rule." According to Baltimore's nineteenth-century chronicler, J. Thomas Scharf, the city's new mayor, George William Brown, brought character, ability, and courage to the office, and the new police marshal, Col. George P. Kane, "was perhaps the best man in the city for the task confided to him."

Scharf undoubtedly overestimated the effectiveness of the 1860 reforms. Despite the reforms, the problem of the young institution's susceptibility to political mischief persisted. The reforms merely shifted control of the police force from partisans at the city level to partisans at the state level. The policemen on the streets remained responsive to political leaders and, in an era of bitter ideological divisions and intense racial antagonisms, a corps of armed men offered an almost irresistible means of coercion for any faction with a firm hold on political power. In any case, as Scharf acknowledged, Baltimore's potential for good government under the reforms of 1860 was never to be tested because "that terrible catastrophe that shook the country to its foundations" profoundly disrupted the city's civic affairs in the decade that followed.[95] And with the outbreak of war, the politics of the 1860s introduced a level of internecine conflicts within Baltimore's white population that gave the problem of political interference with the police force a distinctive edge in the postwar era.

The divisive forces unleashed in the national crisis of the 1860s shattered the peace of Baltimore within a week after Confederates first fired on Fort Sumter. When federal authorities tried to move Union soldiers through Baltimore in April 1861, antifederal demonstrators clashed with the Northerners. Mayor George William Brown, reflecting on the crisis from the perspective of the 1880s, remembered the actions of the citizens of his city as an "attack by a mob" that was "a sudden uprising of popular fury."[96] The terse message communicated to President Lincoln at the time of the crisis summed up Brown's response: "A collision between the citizens and the northern troops has taken place in Baltimore, and the excitement is fearful." Mayor Brown and Gov. Thomas Hicks, claiming that they feared the sight of additional Northern soldiers would further inflame Baltimore's pro-Confederate faction, appealed to President Lincoln to send no troops, and they assured Lincoln that officials in Maryland would "endeavor to prevent all bloodshed."[97] But the efforts of Brown and Hicks to prevent bloodshed failed. As a result of the violence in the streets of Baltimore on April 19, 1861, four soldiers died and thirty-six were wounded. Among the citizens of Baltimore, there were twelve deaths and so many injuries that, according to Mayor Brown, city officials never settled on a final tally.[98]

Despite the riots of April 1861 and the undeniable fact that many Marylanders harbored intense states' rights and proslavery sentiments, several factors weighed against secession. Both Governor Hicks and Mayor Brown believed secession would necessarily bring catastrophe to their state, and both men, at least in their public statements, expressed their hopes that Maryland would not secede.[99] In a message to the Maryland General Assembly a few days after the clash with the Northern troops, Governor Hicks argued somewhat cautiously that the best course for the safety of Maryland was to maintain a neutral position. As a result of the state's geographical position, he stated, to do otherwise would make Maryland the "theater of a long and bloody civil war."[100] The state's pro-Confederate faction reacted with great intensity and gained the most attention in the first days of the conflict, but many Marylanders, and especially Baltimoreans, had patriotic sentiments that favored preservation of the Union. In fact, although Southern Democrat John C. Breckinridge carried Maryland in the presidential election of 1860, Breckinridge's three Unionist opponents, John Bell, Stephen A. Douglas, and Abraham Lincoln, polled a combined 54.2 percent of the state's votes.[101] And commercial ties to regions outside the South reinforced Unionist sentiment. The destruction of railroad lines by Marylanders trying to block movements of federal troops, for example, raised anxieties among businessmen whose prosperity hinged on maintaining commerce with the North and West.[102]

Yet the riots in Baltimore, coupled with the fact that thousands of Marylanders chose to fight on the Confederate side, raised Unionists' fears of treasonous activities and, ultimately, elicited a strong response from President Lincoln and his cabinet. Maryland was a slave state and one that, if it seceded, could cut off Washington from the North. When the extent and intensity of antifederal sentiment became clear in April 1861, Lincoln and his advisers acted decisively to secure Maryland's place in the Union. Lincoln ordered a suspension of habeas corpus writs in Maryland, thereby enabling military commanders to arrest civilians without specifying charges. The assertion of federal authority was backed by a strong military presence in Baltimore.

For the city's police force, the presence of Union soldiers brought a new round of crises. With issues of defense and security as the obvious concerns, Union troops took measures to ensure that the city's police force did not constitute an armed contingent that might resist federal authority. In June 1861, an overwhelming force under the direction of Union General Nathaniel Banks arrested police Marshal George P. Kane at his home on St. Paul Street. Arrest of the marshal dealt a demoralizing blow to the police force, and federal troops added to the humiliation of the local police in making the arrest. The soldiers proceeding toward Marshal Kane's home in the middle of the night took into custody every policeman they encountered along the way.[103] The soldiers released the patrolmen once they had secured Kane's arrest, but the episode ended the era initiated by the police reforms of 1860. Barely a year after the reformers' new state-controlled policemen took to the streets, federal authorities assumed complete control of policing in Baltimore. Immediately after the arrest of Marshal Kane, General Banks appointed Col. John Kenly to take command of the police force as provost marshal.[104] When the police commissioners challenged Colonel Kenly's authority, Kenly replaced the city's policemen with a force of four hundred men who were recruited to serve under federal authority.[105]

By 1861, Baltimoreans had suffered through enough episodes of police bullying to leave many citizens apprehensive about heavy-handed law enforcement.

With the introduction of wartime security measures, the new police force, backed by the power of federal troops, increased apprehensions about the patrolmen on the streets. The vulnerability of the national capital forced Lincoln's hand, but, whether justifiable or not, law enforcement measures during the war inevitably stirred up resentment, especially among conservative Democrats with pro-Southern sympathies. Union soldiers with help from Baltimore's federalized police force arrested scores of suspected Confederate sympathizers. Soldiers first arrested Baltimore industrialist Ross Winans, an outspoken secessionist, and then in a case that drew national attention, soldiers arrested and confined a member of the Maryland militia, John Merryman, based on allegations he was storing arms and communicating with Confederate officers. As the reach of federal security measures expanded, authorities arrested prominent and popular citizens, including Mayor Brown, several members of the state legislature, former governor Thomas Pratt, US Congressman Henry May, and Frank Key Howard, an editor of the *Baltimore Daily Exchange,* who was a grandson of Francis Scott Key.

Frank Key Howard's experiences were representative of the political passions aroused among Baltimore's Southern sympathizers during the war. On reaching Fort McHenry at 2 A.M., Howard found that he shared his place of confinement with a collection of men he considered his friends—men who, in Howard's opinion, "were all gentlemen of high social position, and of unimpeachable character."[106] In his protest against these measures, Howard characterized his experiences as comparable to confinement in the Bastille. Not surprisingly, given the sense of grievance expressed by men like Howard, the resentments engendered by such measures lingered long after the national emergency ended.

Although Baltimoreans with grievances about such arrests directed most of their anger at soldiers and the Lincoln administration, wartime security measures also added to Marylanders' mistrust of policemen. Soldiers regularly worked with Baltimore police. Several prominent citizens noted that city police officers aided federal troops in bringing in or arresting suspected Confederate sympathizers. When federal authorities arrested the mayor of Baltimore, the soldiers took positions in front of and behind the mayor's home, while policemen, according to the mayor, "rapped violently on the front door." And it was policemen, not soldiers, who transported the mayor to Fort McHenry.[107] In his account of his arrest, Frank Key Howard reported that he was escorted to Fort McHenry by "Two men wearing the badges of the police force which the Government had organized."[108] And in February 1865 a joint force of soldiers and policemen captured Harry Gilmor in Hardy County, West Virginia, and delivered him to a Baltimore police station before he was transferred to Fort McHenry. In his account of his capture, Gilmor complained that his captors treated him "rudely" and he "had to endure their vulgar taunts all the way to Baltimore."[109]

With the end of the war, the pent-up resentments of men like Mayor Brown, Frank Howard, and Harry Gilmor played a major role in the transition from wartime to peacetime politics in Baltimore. The Unionist coalition that guided the city through the war years could not be maintained in peacetime. In the years leading up to the war, Democrats, with their defeat of the Know-Nothings, had established majorities at both the state and city levels. With the onset of the war, however, a Unionist coalition displaced the Democrats. The wartime Unionist coalition brought together politically diverse factions that were joined primarily by their opposition to secession. Republicans and some independents—leaders who favored federal authority and citizenship rights for African Americans—participated in the wartime coalition with little or no reservations. But the coalition also included a faction of the Democratic Party, which despite opposition to secession, favored a Southern perspective on social and political issues such as African American equality and states' rights. The end of the war brought a resurgence of Maryland Democrats, as the factions of their party once again coalesced into a stable majority.

But the return to Democratic dominance in Maryland took place only after intense political campaigns in which the problem of police interference in elections resurfaced. During the sudden shift in power in the 1865, 1866, and the Reconstruction-era elections of the following decade, Baltimore once again endured episodes of election-day violence, and once again events added to Baltimoreans' mistrust of the city's policemen. Unionists retained control of Maryland in the autumn of 1865 by conducting elections with voter registration lists compiled under wartime conditions. But conservative Democrats wrested control from the Unionists in 1866. The sequence of elections leading up to the victories by conservative Democrats implicated the police force in abuses that were felt by Democrats and Republicans alike. As a result of these shifting political fortunes in the decade preceding Daniel Brown's death, Baltimoreans across the political spectrum felt the sting of abusive policing, not only on election days, but also in everyday interactions on the city streets.

In Baltimore's October 1866 municipal election campaign, conflicts erupted in a dispute over the use of the wartime voter registration lists. As a result of the absence of many Confederate sympathizers and the imposition of loyalty oaths, registration lists in effect in 1865 included a limited number of conservative Democrats. A law passed in March 1865 required registration officials to compile new lists and return them in time for the state and federal elections of November 1866, but Baltimore's municipal elections were scheduled for October 1866. Republicans argued that none of the voters added to the registration lists under the March 1865 law should be effective for the Baltimore municipal elections. Democrats argued that including only voters on the old registration lists effectively disfranchised more than half of Maryland's voters. Maryland Attorney General Alexander Randall, a Republican, issued an opinion supporting the use of the 1865 lists, but Democrats, in an effort to undermine the legitimacy of Randall's opinion, produced alternate opinions drafted by prominent lawyers, including Reverdy Johnson. Relying on these opinions, Democrats argued that Randall's views did not settle the question. Although he had been elected as a Unionist, Gov. Thomas Swann decided his political ambitions would be best served by an alliance with Democrats, and the registration controversy presented an opportunity to demonstrate his shifting loyalty.[110] He refused to publish the Maryland attorney general's opinion, and election judges in Baltimore did not learn of the legal opinion supporting the wartime registration lists until the day before the election. Even then, the election judges debated the question before they decided to accept the 1865 lists.[111]

With the wartime registration lists in use, Republicans won the October 1866 municipal contests, but the election triggered a resurgence of angry Democrats. Emboldened by the challenges to the legitimacy of the 1865 registration lists, disfranchised Southern sympathizers tried to vote in the October 1866 election, sparking conflicts throughout the city. In its account of the election, the *Sun* described it as "a tame affair." But the *Sun*'s account then went on to summarize some of the day's events: one of the city's "most respected merchants" was sent to the central police station for having "excited a riot"; a man who tried to vote was arrested on charges he had participated in the antifederal riots of April 19, 1861; a row occurred near the Belair market in which "pistols were freely used"; a man who tried to vote in Ward Eight was wounded by a pistol shot; men were arrested in south Baltimore for fighting in the street; a procession of thirty-five or forty conservatives was met by people of the opposite side, and a sword and pistol were used in the brawl that followed; and, finally, a heavy afternoon rain "had the effect of pretty generally clearing the polls of bystanders."[112]

But the real crisis came after the election. Enraged Democrats petitioned the governor to bring charges of misconduct against Police Commissioners Nicholas Wood and Samuel Hindes. According to Governor Swann, forty-three hundred citizens of Baltimore signed the petition calling for the removal of the commissioners.[113] A few years earlier, Hindes, like Swann, had aligned with the

Know-Nothings. In 1860, running as the Know-Nothing nominee for mayor, Hindes lost decisively to George William Brown.[114] But with the ascendancy of the Democrats, old Know-Nothing ties between Swann and Hindes did not stop Swann from moving aggressively against Hindes and Wood. Although Maryland law provided for removal of the commissioners by vote of the General Assembly, Governor Swann, arguing that authority devolved to him with the legislature in recess, seized the opportunity to try the commissioners.[115] The trial began in Annapolis on October 26 and ended on October 31, 1866. On November 1, 1866, Governor Swann announced his decision to remove the commissioners, basing his decision on findings that the commissioners had committed several acts of official misconduct. According to the governor's report, the commissioners had permitted the police force to become "a violent partisan organization" that treated all as disloyal who did not adopt the political views of the commissioners; they had appointed election judges and special police exclusively from their own party; and they had delegated to the police marshal and his officers the power to appoint special police for election days without themselves inquiring into the character and qualifications of the special police.[116]

The trial, with several days of testimony alleging partisanship and misconduct, embarrassed the police commissioners, and testimony and affidavits describing abuses by patrolmen stirred up anxieties about the personal security of ordinary citizens. Several witnesses reported incidents in which policemen bullied and intimidated innocent people, condoned criminal activity by gangs, invaded homes, and committed acts of violence. A common complaint was that police had blocked qualified voters from the polls by arresting them and holding them at station houses without hearings until the polls closed.[117]

Most of the complaints came from conservative, pro-Southern partisans. One citizen said he had been marching with conservatives when policemen threw bricks at the procession, and one officer, who was "very drunk," held a pistol to the head of one of the conservatives. He added that these abuses took place in the presence of a police captain, who took no action against the inebriated officer.[118] Another witness stated that a "party of roughs," accompanied by policemen, went to the home of Thomas Bobart, a conservative ward leader, and, in the presence of Bobart's pregnant wife, threatened to kill Bobart with a knife.[119] One witness asserted that he was arrested because he tried to help several German voters who were being denied ballots.[120] John Orem, a policeman and an open supporter of President Johnson, reported that Radical Republican policemen had cursed and threatened him, and as a result of his opinions, he had been disciplined by the police commissioners.[121]

Editors of the Republican *Baltimore American* complained of "flimsy and in many cases false testimony," and there are reasons to doubt the credibility of some witnesses.[122] Thomas Bobart, one of the more colorful figures who provided evidence, for example, faced criminal charges in several instances both before and after the 1866 elections.[123] But some of the allegations of police misconduct came from respected citizens. A. Leo Knott, who nine years later would serve as the state's attorney in Officer McDonald's trial, reported that he was seized and threatened with violence by club-wielding policemen who recognized him as a Democratic Party leader. Knott asserted that he was brought to a station house, but the station house magistrate could not find sufficient reasons to hold him. Nonetheless, according to Knott, policemen in the station house harassed him with shouts of "traitor" and "rebel."[124] Whether from colorful rogues like Bobart or from respected middle-class citizens like Knott, the proliferation of claims that officers bullied voters, tolerated criminal activity, and committed acts of violence had to undermine public confidence in the police force, especially since many Baltimoreans already believed they had been victims of oppressive wartime security measures.

To make matters worse for the public image of the police, the controversy did not end with the decision to remove the commissioners. Governor Swann appointed two replacement commissioners, William T. Valiant and James Young. But Hindes and Wood refused to cede control of the police force, throwing the city into a crisis that lasted nearly two weeks.[125] Unable to occupy the commissioners' offices, Valiant and Young rented office space, issued a written demand to Wood and Hindes to relinquish their offices, and ordered the police force to disregard directives emanating from the "late Board of Police."[126] In collaboration with the sheriff, Valiant and Young assembled a posse of one hundred men, ostensibly to ensure order as crowds gathered, but supporters of Wood and Hindes charged that Valiant, Young, and the posse intended to take possession of the commissioners' offices by force. Lawyers acting for Wood and Hindes brought their claims before Baltimore Criminal Court Judge Hugh Lennox Bond, a well-known Republican. Bond ruled that the posse, as an "array of force," constituted an unlawful assembly, and he ordered Valiant and Young to post security in the amount of $20,000 to keep the peace. When Valiant and Young declined to post security, Judge Bond committed them to jail.[127] For several days the citizens of Baltimore witnessed the spectacle of Governor Swann's police commissioners locked up in the city jail—a spectacle Baltimoreans might have thought was unusual had not the city's police commissioners been imprisoned under federal authority five years earlier. The dispute was finally settled when jail keepers, responding to a writ of habeas corpus, delivered Valiant and Young to the Maryland Court of Appeals, where Judge James Bartol ruled that Valiant and Young were entitled to the offices. On November 15, 1866, Valiant and Young, the preferred candidates of the Democrats, finally took control of the Baltimore police force.[128] Thus, immediately after serious allegations of misconduct had been voiced against many of the city's policemen, the citizens of Baltimore witnessed a two-week-long struggle in which the state's judicial and executive authorities disputed the conduct and legitimacy of the police commissioners.

In finally yielding to the claims of Valiant and Young, Police Commissioners Hindes and Wood recognized that Maryland's wartime coalition of Unionists had suffered a devastating defeat. Although Baltimore election judges had used the 1865 registration lists in the municipal elections of October 1866, Governor Swann had ordered election officials to prepare new lists for the state balloting in November 1866. Just in time for the state elections, Governor Swann's appointees delivered the new lists—lists that, according to Republicans, included "the most notorious out-spoken and malignant revilers of the Government during the entire period of the rebellion."[129] On November 6, 1866, Democrats swept the elections, winning control of both houses of the Maryland General Assembly, as well as the state comptroller's office and seats in the US Congress.[130]

The era of Unionist dominance came to a close with the elections of November 1866. Democrats remained firmly in control of Maryland for nearly a decade, but memories of their setbacks in the 1850s and 1860s persisted. They believed they had been abused by the police when Know-Nothings, Unionists, Republicans, and Union soldiers had controlled the city, and party leaders found it easy to tap into the old resentments. In 1870 the impending ratification of the Fifteenth Amendment renewed Democrats' anxieties. At a gathering of Maryland Democrats in January 1870, party leaders distributed a circular alerting members of the General Assembly to the importance of electing police commissioners who were "democrats and white men" in view of the impending ratification of the "infamous XVth amendment." The drafters of the circular took care to highlight the anxieties about police that motivated their constituents. They insinuated that some men currently on the police force might be the same Republican Radicals who, they contended, had terrorized Democrats a few years earlier: Democratic Party propagandists warned that "Many of these men went into the houses of their political opponents during the war, searched and robbed them, as well as insulted their wives and children."[131]

These lingering animosities within Baltimore's white community provided the context as legal proceedings went forward in Officer McDonald's case. By 1875, many middle-class and elite white Baltimoreans doubted abusive police practices could be easily remedied. And when the circumstances of Daniel Brown's death came to public attention, the image of a club-wielding, pistol-brandishing policeman invading a private home and attacking an unarmed citizen frightened and angered many white residents of Baltimore. The policeman's attack aroused respectable white citizens not only because the killing of Brown was repugnant in itself, but also because they knew the police could be, and actually had been, turned against white citizens. Even as late as the mid-1870s, Democrats had not forgotten wartime police actions against them, and for the Republicans and reformers who opposed the Democrats, police bullying was an ongoing issue.

Although the Fifteenth Amendment added African American voters to the Republicans' constituency, the addition proved insufficient to give Republicans a majority, and Democratic control remained secure for a few election cycles.[132] Even in this lull, however, episodes of recklessness with lethal weapons by law enforcement officers troubled Baltimore residents. The *Sun*'s reports of the incident in which the customs officer had shot and killed a German sailor in 1873 included a disturbing account of the sudden and unprovoked use of deadly force by the official.[133] More anxieties about aggressive law enforcement surfaced in the month preceding the killing of Daniel Brown. In June 1875 Baltimore newspapers reported the accidental killing of a young girl by a Delaware policeman who fired wildly at a fleeing suspect.[134] Both the *Sun* and the *American* took the opportunity to address their community's concerns about police violence. The account in the *American* attributed the tragedy to carelessness and the "free use of the pistol."[135] In the *Sun* it was asserted that the use of the pistol was irresponsible because the fleeing suspect was accused of nothing more than a breach of peace. Furthermore, the *Sun*'s editors added, "the free use of weapons has become too common with all classes in this country, not excluding those entrusted with the execution of the law." And finally, the *Sun*'s editors, in June 1875, urged Delaware officials to set an example that would teach policemen to be "careful how they use pistols in a way which renders them destructive, instead of constructive of human life."[136] Less than two months later, the killing of Daniel Brown would give Baltimore authorities a chance to set such an example for their own city.

CHAPTER 6

The Police on Trial

The Baltimore City Criminal Court scheduled the trial of Patrick McDonald for November 1875. As it turned out, police violence and the problem of police interference in elections was very much in the public eye as the trial date approached. Elections in the autumn of 1875 were especially disorderly, and mistrust of the police force was more intense than ever. As Officer McDonald's trial proceeded, the entire police force was, in effect, on trial.

In the autumn of 1875, the Democratic Party's grip on power began to loosen, resulting in intensely fought election campaigns at both the city and state levels. After an acrimonious session at the Democrats' state convention, a faction broke from party regulars and joined a reform movement of independents and Republicans. Party regulars, who identified themselves as conservative Democrats, mocked the breakaway faction as "potato bugs," but with a strong field of candidates and fusion with the Republicans, the reformers presented a serious, if ultimately unsuccessful, challenge to the majority party. And as had happened in periods of heightened political activity in the preceding two decades, the campaigns of October and November 1875 brought unwanted attention to the police. The accounts of police misconduct in these election campaigns set the stage for the murder trial of Officer McDonald, which was scheduled to begin in mid-November.

Although discontent with regular Democrats had been growing in the early 1870s, the sudden surge in the fortunes of the reform movement came as a surprise to most observers. Republicans and reformers grumbled about the strength of Democrat ward bosses as early as 1871 after Joshua Vansant won the mayoralty race. Vansant, they argued, represented the growing influence of "machine" politics.[1] To most observers in early 1875, however, antimachine sentiment did not pose a viable threat to Democratic dominance. Even as the city's major parties prepared for the upcoming political season, advocates for reform believed they had little chance to unseat regular Democrats in the upcoming municipal and state elections. In June, when the Democratic city convention nominated Ferdinand C. Latrobe as its candidate for mayor, editors of the Republican-leaning *Baltimore American* lamented that Latrobe would not have much opposition. An *American* editorial conceded that the Democrats' nominee was "in all probability" the next mayor.[2]

When state Democrats convened on July 22, 1875, however, a bitter struggle over the nomination of a candidate for governor brought an abrupt shift in the political landscape at both the state and city levels. Led by Arthur P. Gorman and I. Freeman Rasin, party regulars forced through the nomination of John Lee Carroll for governor after an acrimonious struggle with supporters of William T. Hamilton. Many Democrats resented the tactics of Gorman and Rasin, and dissidents recognized that the simmering resentment gave rise to an opportunity for opponents of the party regulars. The defeated supporters of Hamilton, identifying themselves as independent Democrats, immediately began organizing an opposition movement. In secret meetings from late July to the middle of August, they established alliances among disaffected Democrats, independent reformers, and Republicans.[3] Late in August the new coalition made its plans public. Calling themselves the Citizens' Reform Party, they invited opponents of the regular Democrats to a mass meeting. When the new party convened on August 30, 1875, the assembly nominated Henry M. Warfield to oppose Ferdinand Latrobe in the mayoralty election.[4] Shortly afterward, the new party nominated J. Morrison Harris for governor, Severn Teakle Wallis for attorney general, and Edward Wilkins for comptroller.

The *Baltimore American*'s June prediction that regular Democrats would "not have much opposition" turned out to be shortsighted. The Citizens Reform Party went into the fall campaigns with a team of strong candidates. Before he joined the reform movement, J. Morrison Harris had vacillated in his party affiliations, aligning at times with Know-Nothings and at times with Democrats. Despite his indifference to party affiliations—or perhaps because of it—he was a proven campaigner, having won three terms in the United States Congress in the 1850s as a candidate of the American Party.[5] His experience in the US Congress gave him stature and name recognition. As Baltimore's representative, he had participated in discussions with President Lincoln during the crisis of April 1861.[6] Severn Teakle Wallis was one of the most able and respected lawyers in the city. Like Harris, Wallis had earned a reputation as an independent leader. He was known as a brilliant and effective campaigner with a gift for satirizing his opponents.[7] Edward Wilkins helped the Citizens Reform Party solidify its standing among Republicans, who recognized him as one of their regulars.[8] And mayoral candidate Henry Warfield was a well-known and well-liked figure who had earned respect in the Baltimore business community, but he had experience in politics as well as in business, having been elected to the state legislature in 1861 as a candidate on the States' Rights ticket.[9] With credible candidates leading the party's ticket, the reformers gathered support among Baltimore's business leaders and lawyers in the weeks leading up to the elections.[10]

The Citizens' Reform candidates rallied opponents of the conservative Democrats by relentlessly voicing accusations of corruption in the "ring" controlled by Gorman and Rasin. The reformers did not win, but they made the races close and, according to the Maryland House of Delegates Committee on Elections, brought "an unusual degree of political excitement" to the campaigns.[11] In the excitement, violent confrontations erupted in the streets and at polling places—first during the municipal elections in October and then with even greater intensity during state elections in November. Recognizing their vulnerability, Democrats could not resist the temptation to use the police force to influence the elections. Once again, election day violence threw a spotlight on the conduct of policemen at polling places.

In the contest for mayor, Democrat Ferdinand C. Latrobe beat Reform candidate Henry M. Warfield by 28,238 votes to 25,571.[12] In its initial coverage, the *Sun* downplayed election day disorders, contending that, in view of the extraordinary voter turnout and the "passions and prejudices enlisted in the election," the day was "peaceful and orderly." But the *Sun*'s editors may have based their initial assessment on municipal pride and a desire to convince readers that Baltimore's civic affairs had improved since the era of Unionist and federal control. The editorial explicitly contrasted, on the one hand, election day in October 1875, and on the other, the period prior to the Maryland Constitution of 1867—an era in which, they contended, Baltimore's citizens were "disfranchised and proscribed and not entrusted with the right of managing their own affairs."[13] The facts, as presented by the *Sun*'s own reporters, however, contradicted the *Sun*'s editorial. Accounts of the day's events indicated that there were as many as eighty-three arrests.[14] And the arrests involved incidents in which combatants attacked each other with knives and guns.[15] On the day after the election angry partisans continued to confront each other, and there were reports of assaults with guns and clubs.[16] A few days later, in the wake of continuing disorders in

November's state elections, the *Sun*'s editors conceded that their initial comments might have understated the problem of "ruffianly disorder."[17]

Just as Democrats had done in 1866, representatives of the Citizens Reform Party now took a turn in challenging the election results based on allegations that they had been the victims of voting irregularities and police misconduct.[18] Reform Party leaders failed to have the 1875 elections vacated, but once again testimony about mistreatment of citizens called attention to police conduct that disturbed many Baltimore residents. With the Fifteenth Amendment now in effect, more often than not Democratic partisans directed their violence at African Americans, and when some blacks fought back, racial tensions increased.[19] But white voters identified as Reform Party supporters also suffered abuses. W. H. Hoyt, an insurance agent, testified that he saw repeated acts of bullying and intimidation directed at white as well as African American voters. He observed that some policemen wanted to do their duty, but they dared not. In Mr. Hoyt's view, because the police took no action to stop the violence, they were "a disgrace to a civilized community."[20] In some cases, witnesses identified well-known Democratic partisans who assaulted voters. Several observers identified John Carter, a deputy warden at the city jail, as a "ruffian" who intimidated people throughout the day. In one instance, police failed to arrest Carter after he chased a man and fired a pistol at him.[21] In another instance, a witness said that, after Carter intimidated him, he left the polling place without voting. He testified that he feared the police would arrest him, rather than Carter, if he tried again to deposit his ballot.[22] Despite a special committee's recommendation to nullify the election, the Baltimore City Council voted to uphold the results.[23]

The 1875 state elections followed the municipal elections by just six days. Once again, in an intense campaign, the behavior of unruly partisans drew the police into conflicts in which the conduct of patrolmen on the streets undermined community respect for policemen and tarnished the reputations of the police commissioners. Reports in the *Sun* tried to downplay the violence, but once again the detailed accounts Baltimoreans read in their daily newspapers made the police look ineffective at best and thuggish in the worst instances. Although no one was killed, partisans committed assaults with firearms, and there were many incidents that "could not fail to inspire regret."[24] Republican publications emphasized the mayhem and condemned the police for their complicity in illegal acts. Articles in the *American* described "Election Outrages." In one instance, according to the *American*'s account, a mob led by a policeman shot at a black man, then chased him to his home. The mob then broke in and ransacked the house, while the black man and his family escaped out the back door.[25] The *American* also recounted the difficulties white Reform Party members encountered on election day. One voter, for example, while trying to vote, was surrounded by a "party of rowdies who recognized him as a prominent Reformer." He called out to a nearby policeman for help, but the policeman ignored him. Persevering, the reformer finally located a police sergeant, who placed him in the voting line.[26]

Reports of the violence reached other cities and added further damage to Baltimore's already tarnished reputation among observers outside Maryland. National news accounts about the failure of the police to maintain order alarmed Baltimore businessmen, who feared commerce would suffer as a result of the growing perception of the city as a "mobtown" where business transactions could not be carried on in safety. An account in the *New York Times* described Baltimore's election day as a "reign of terror from dawn till sunset" in a city that was in the "hands of roughs, supported and sustained by the police."[27] In reporting Baltimore's election returns, the *Washington Evening Star* claimed that "the most outrageous frauds and violence" accounted for the Democrats' success.[28] And in Chicago, accounts of the Baltimore elections characterized the conflicts as "Plug-Uglyism."[29]

Reform candidates contested the results of the state elections and charged that "at least ninety-seven individuals, all Reformers or colored men" were "assaulted, beaten, kicked or maltreated," and "shot and knocked down," while policemen "gave either a laughing approval or an active assistance to these outrages."[30] Despite the allegations of police misconduct, the Democratic majority in the House of Delegates validated the election results and resolved that the "police force of Baltimore city did their duty thoroughly and fully."[31] Although the legislature rejected the Reform Party's challenges, when the police and the police commissioners were tried in the court of public opinion, independents and reformers found the allegations of fraud and violence credible. J. Thomas Scharf, a chronicler generally sympathetic to the Democrats, noted that "Great frauds were alleged."[32] For decades a general belief persisted that Democrats in Baltimore stole the election, and many citizens remembered the 1875 elections as a disgraceful episode in the city's history.[33]

As a result of the chaotic election campaigns of October and November 1875, public mistrust of the Baltimore police peaked just as Officer McDonald's trial began. On November 15, 1875, with jury selection in progress, editors of the *American* described the Baltimore police as "blue coated ruffians" and as men who did "villainous work."[34] On November 19, 1875, the day Keziah Brown testified, recounting the horrifying details of McDonald's clubbing and shooting of her husband, the *American* printed a letter from an angry citizen who complained that the police "have so degraded the uniform that they are below contempt. Timid men fear to pass them in lonely places." The writer concluded, "Until we are relieved of the present police force we can neither hope for justice or safety."[35] The complaints about "villainous work" and men who "degraded the uniform" were not references to McDonald's killing of Daniel Brown, but rather to police misconduct during the elections. When both the *Sun* and the *American* printed detailed accounts of Keziah Brown's testimony, however, the citizens of Baltimore could not avoid noticing a connection between, on the one hand, general reports of "villainous" acts by policemen and, on the other, Officer McDonald's brutality in the Daniel Brown matter. The *American,* of course, represented the Republican view in the wake of the Democratic victories, and the angry letter writer probably represented the extreme of public opinion. Nonetheless, under the leadership of partisan commissioners, members of the police force had committed enough misdeeds to make the citizens of Baltimore—black and white, Republican and Democrat—mistrust and even fear policemen.

With public opinion still aroused in the wake of the disorderly elections, McDonald and his attorneys prepared for the November trial with reasons to be concerned about the general public's unfavorable views of the police force. But they also had reasons to believe an acquittal was possible. In the matter of Daniel Brown, the state's attorney presented Baltimoreans with an unusual case. Despite the proliferation of complaints about police behavior, state's attorneys seldom held individual officers accountable for using force, and the murder charge was unprecedented. McDonald's lawyers apparently hoped they might convince a jury the policeman was merely trying to preserve law and order. Defense attorney J. Douglass Hambleton argued that "rarely in the history of the Criminal Court" had an officer of the law faced such charges, a fact that, the lawyer suggested, "was strong presumptive evidence of innocence."[36]

Even more than the unprecedented nature of the charges, the homicide victim's race gave the white policeman and his defense counsel reasons to believe they might win. The recent elections had aggravated racial conflicts. Conservative Democrats countered complaints of police misconduct with inflammatory accounts of African American violence during the November elections. The Democratic-leaning *Baltimore Gazette* alleged that unruly behavior by African Americans on election day amounted to "the most outrageous insult which has been offered to a civilized community." The *Gazette*'s correspondents alleged that hundreds of black men armed with pistols, guns, and razors took control of some streets and fired into crowds surrounding polling places.[37] In a city divided by such racial tensions, McDonald and his attorneys could find hope in the fact that McDonald had been processed through a law enforcement and criminal justice system in which black citizens appeared as witnesses, but were excluded from positions of authority.

There is no evidence that any Baltimore authorities, whether Democrat, Republican, or independent, gave serious consideration to hiring black police officers or to appointing blacks as coroners or officials in the criminal justice system during the post–Civil War era. All of Officer McDonald's fellow patrolmen were white, as were the sergeants and captains on the Baltimore police force in 1875. The police commissioners would have vigorously resisted any attempts to integrate the force. Conservative Democrats controlled the General Assembly that had selected all three commissioners, and the Conservatives made no secret of their opposition to African American equality. William H. B. Fusselbaugh began his first term on the Board of Police Commissioners in 1867 as the choice of the resurgent Democrats in the legislature. Fusselbaugh's allies in the Democratic Party elevated him to the board's presidency in 1871. According to the police department's chronicler, Fusselbaugh was a lifelong Democrat, having first held office in 1852, when he was appointed to the state's Board of Tax Control and Review.[38] Commissioners John Milroy and Harry Gilmor had gained their offices with the approval of the Democratic majority in the General Assembly in February 1874.[39] Milroy, like Fusselbaugh, had a long history of supporting conservative Democratic causes.[40] Harry Gilmor, through his Confederate military service, had demonstrated his sympathies for the white-supremacist view of the place of blacks in the city's social order.

In any case, even Republican whites would not have advocated hiring black policemen in Baltimore in 1875. In the decade following the war, African Americans in the South served on police forces only in cities where strong Radical Republican administrations gained control as a result of Reconstruction.[41] In Raleigh, for example, three African American men joined the police force in July 1868.[42] But such appointments were rare anywhere in the South, and in Baltimore, a city that remained in the Union, Reconstruction was not a factor. The federal forces that controlled the city during the national crisis withdrew when the war ended, and conservative Democrats regained control of the state and city governments shortly afterward. Even during the war, when Republican influence crested, Unionists did not consider adding black men to the force. Because Unionists and federal authorities shaped their policies in accordance with the goal of discouraging support for the Confederacy, they had no incentive to propose changes in the racial makeup of the police force that might stir up Southern sympathizers. In fact, the Baltimore police force did not add an African American officer until more than seventy years after emancipation. Policewoman Violet Hill Whyte became the first African American on the force when she took a post at the city's northwestern station in 1937. The first four male black officers joined the force a year later.[43]

In the legal proceedings subsequent to the coroner's inquest, State's Attorney A. Leo Knott, a lawyer with a long association with Baltimore's Democratic Party, guided the matter of Daniel Brown through the criminal justice system.[44] During the war, Knott supported a faction aligned with the Southern view of states' rights, but he opposed secession. He played a major role in reviving the Democratic Party in the 1860s.[45] In postwar politics, reformers viewed Knott as a moderate who kept his distance from the so-called Democratic ring. When US Senator Arthur Gorman designated party loyalists for patronage appointments in 1885, reformers characterized most of Gorman's appointments as unwholesome examples of the spoils system, but they made an exception for Knott, finding him an acceptable candidate for an appointment as an assistant postmaster general.[46]

When Knott brought the Daniel Brown case before the grand jury and prepared the case for trial in the Baltimore City Criminal Court, it was almost a certainty that white jurors would decide McDonald's fate. Maryland law gave blacks only the slimmest of chances to be selected for jury service. An 1870 statute, applicable to grand juries and trial juries, required county clerks to provide courts with lists of "white male taxable inhabitants or residents" from which jurors could be selected.[47] The Federal Civil Rights Act of 1875 cast doubt on Maryland's racial qualification for jury selection, but, ultimately, the federal law had little effect in state courts.[48] In a few isolated cases, black men served on juries in Maryland state courts after the 1875 Act. One African American served on a jury in a state court in Garrett County in September 1875, and another apparently sat on a jury in Anne Arundel County in 1880.[49] But the idea of desegregating juries was not taken seriously in the Baltimore courts as of November 1875. The *Sun* treated the matter lightly in its reports of the Garrett County African American juror; it was noted in the *Sun* that the juror was the only African American voter in the district, and that he was a registered Democrat, a fact, the *Sun* jested, "argues much for his social judgment and political good sense."[50] And the US Supreme Court rendered the Civil Rights Act of 1875 ineffective as to the desegregation of juries within a few years after the Garrett County juror had his day. In an 1880 case, *Strauder v. West Virginia,* the Court invalidated a state statute requiring all-white juries, but almost immediately thereafter, in *Virginia v. Rives,* the Court ruled that local officials could exercise discretion in ways that resulted in whites-only juries, provided the local officials did not act under a statute that explicitly excluded African Americans from consideration.[51] As constitutional historian William M. Wiecek has noted, after *Rives* "It took little imagination for whites to devise techniques of black exclusion that were implicit and based on a universal understanding of how things work in a segregated society."[52] In Baltimore, procedures gave judges and clerks more than enough discretionary authority to devise such techniques of black exclusion.[53] In any case, even a whisper of a suggestion that a black man might serve on a jury in the matter of Daniel Brown would have created a major controversy and would have been widely reported in the accounts of the trial.

The judge and trial attorneys in the matter of Daniel Brown were all white men. A statute enacted in 1831 reserved the right to practice law in Maryland's courts to "free white male" citizens of Maryland. Despite the provision's apparent inconsistency with the Fourteenth Amendment to the US Constitution, the exclusion of African Americans from the practice of law in the state remained in effect throughout the 1870s.[54] In 1877, Charles S. Taylor and James H. Wolff, two African American lawyers, attempted to gain admission to practice in Maryland's state courts, but the Maryland Court of Appeals ruled against their applications. A black attorney living in Elkton, Maryland, Charles S. Wilson, finally succeeded in having the whites-only provision overturned on the basis of its unconstitutionality in 1885.[55] But Maryland's legal establishment turned to new methods to limit the presence of African American lawyers in the state's courts. Beginning shortly after Wilson's admission to the bar, the University of Maryland excluded blacks from legal training, and the state's law school remained closed to blacks until well into the twentieth century.[56]

The presiding judge in the Baltimore City Criminal Court, Robert Gilmor, was the oldest of eleven children born to a prominent Baltimore County family.[57] The Gilmor family, which was among the wealthiest families in Maryland, maintained strong ties to the Confederacy during the war. Police Commissioner Harry Gilmor was not the only one of Judge Gilmor's siblings who served in the Confederate Army; the judge's brothers, Meredith Gilmor and Richard T. Gilmor, also took up arms in service to the South.[58] Judge Gilmor did not serve in the war, but he supported the state's conservative Democrats and won his place on the bench as part of a slate of candidates who defeated Baltimore's coalition of Unionists and Republicans when the war ended.[59] According to his obituary, Judge Gilmor had influence beyond Baltimore; it was reported that Gilmor was on "intimate terms" with President Johnson and had frequently conferred with Johnson on questions of public interest.[60]

Two lawyers, one Democrat and one Republican, represented the state. State's Attorney A. Leo Knott had guided the case through the grand jury, and he continued on the case as the chief prosecutor. Knott, although undoubtedly a loyal Democrat, brought in Republican Henry Stockbridge to assist him in the trial. Stockbridge stood alone among the lawyers in the trial as a man who had taken stands in favor of African American rights. He had gained prominence early in his career as an unconditional Unionist and antislavery lawyer. Although he opposed the Know-Nothings in the 1850s and ran against their candidate, Henry Winter Davis, in 1859, he later joined with Davis in support of Radical Republican policies.[61] As a delegate to the Maryland constitutional convention of 1864, he argued vigorously against a proposal to grant Orphan's Courts the authority to place all African American minors in apprenticeships. Stockbridge called the attempt to perpetuate the slave labor system a "monstrous proposition" and castigated its supporters, stating, "I have no sympathy, no respect, even, for that feeling, or that fear, whatever it is, that is so eternally afraid of negro equality."[62] Stockbridge continued his support of African Americans after emancipation in Maryland. When former slaveholders seized black children in sham apprenticeships, Stockbridge joined a team of lawyers who helped the Freedmen's Bureau rescue some of the children.[63] In later years, Stockbridge provided legal service to Baltimore's black businessmen.[64]

All three of Officer McDonald's defense attorneys maintained close ties to the Democratic Party. John Prentiss Poe served as chief defense counsel. An "arch-conservative," Poe complained bitterly of the federal presence in Baltimore during the war, referring to federal security measures as "tyrannical usurpation which has trampled our rights."[65] In his long career, Poe took some notable stands in opposition to African American rights. As the dean of the University of Maryland Law School, he led the movement to defeat attempts to integrate the school in the late 1880s.[66] When Maryland Democrats attempted to disfranchise blacks in 1905, Poe drafted the proposed state constitutional amendment that was intended to block African Americans from registering. The measure that finally went before Maryland voters was so closely identified with John Poe that it bore his name. Maryland voters rejected the "Poe Amendment" in November 1905.[67]

Poe's assistants in the trial, J. Douglass Hambleton and Joseph S. Heuisler, were both active in Baltimore's ward politics. Hambleton was the youngest son of prominent Baltimore business executive, Thomas E. Hambleton.[68] In his early twenties, the younger Hambleton opened a law office in Baltimore, but he left Maryland for several years in the mid-1860s to practice in San Francisco. When he returned to Maryland, he established himself as a loyal Democrat, addressing meetings around the state "on political topics from the Democratic standpoint." In his speeches he opposed African American voting rights and argued against what he termed the "unconstitutionality and tyranny of the proposed fifteenth amendment."[69] Later, he served the Democratic Party as president of Baltimore's Ward Nineteen association and as counsel to Democratic candidates who faced challenges following the 1875 elections.[70] The third member of the defense team, Joseph S. Heuisler, was an experienced criminal defense lawyer, as well as an active politician.[71] Less than a month before the trial, he had fallen short in his contest for reelection to his seat on the Baltimore City Council, losing by a narrow margin to Reform Party candidate Henry Loney.[72] His opponents in that election characterized him as a candidate of the Democratic ring.[73] Heuisler's status as a party favorite became clear in the aftermath of his defeat. When Heuisler applied for the position of examiner of titles in the Baltimore city attorney's office, prominent Democrats and businessmen supported his application. Heuisler's cocounsel in the McDonald trial, Hambleton, submitted a supporting statement in which he emphasized Heuisler's party loyalty rather than his professional qualifications. In his letter to Mayor Latrobe, Hambleton based his support on Heuisler's "great exertion" in his services to the party.[74]

Officer McDonald's ability to assemble a defense team of three prominent lawyers suggests that the city's Democratic organization came to his aid. It is unlikely that McDonald, a suspended patrolman with a work history as a laborer, could have paid three prominent attorneys without help. John Poe's account book covers the period of the trial, but it includes no records of payment for the McDonald trial.[75] Poe and Heuisler both appeared in other cases in defense of policemen or other persons with ties to Democratic ward politicians. When Baltimore Patrolman John McKenna faced charges of attempting to rape a thirteen-year-old African American girl in 1876, Poe took the case and got the officer off with only one month in prison and a fifty-dollar fine.[76] Heuisler represented a Democratic city councilman in his successful defense against a challenge to his election victory in November 1875.[77] And in 1878 Heuisler defended Democratic Party ward enforcer Tom Freeze, a friend of Officer McDonald, in a murder trial.[78] Like McDonald, both Officer McKenna and Tom Freeze appear to have been men who might have found the cost of hiring an experienced trial lawyer with a statewide reputation daunting.

Jury selection began in mid-November 1875, but after the first session Judge Gilmor and the attorneys had exhausted the first pool of potential jurors while seating only five. Some of those excused may have been trying to avoid the inconvenience and stress of a weeklong murder trial, but many probably had prejudged the case; several articles about the so-called "cake-walk homicide" had appeared in the press.[79] In addition to those who had formed opinions about the defendant, a "considerable number" disqualified themselves based on conscientious objections to the death penalty.[80] Out of the first group of fifty potential jurors, twenty-seven admitted they had already made up their minds about McDonald, ten said they could not as a matter of conscience vote for a verdict calling for the death penalty, and seven failed to meet residency or age requirements. After the state's attorney used arbitrary challenges to eliminate four others, the clerk brought in one hundred more.[81] Judge Gilmor and the attorneys continued to struggle with the selection of jurors on the second day. Once again, as many as three-quarters of those questioned had formed opinions about the matter, but before the end of the second day, the judge and the attorneys completed the jury selection process.[82] To the extent the jurors can be identified, they appear to have been representative of the city's white middle-class citizens. J. Hanson Thomas Jr. was a bookkeeper; Duncan Robb, an agent for a piano company; Albert Shook, a real estate agent; and John M. Getz, a carpenter.[83] The *Sun*'s reporter observed that the jurors had "the appearance of citizens who have some stake in the community, and of good sense, their ages generally ranging between thirty and forty years."[84]

With the jury finally in place and the courtroom crowded with observers, attention shifted to the presentations of evidence by the attorneys. Over the course of the first two days of testimony, each side revealed major points of emphasis in their strategies.[85] State's Attorney Knott stressed the fact that the killing occurred inside Brown's home, and that McDonald shot Brown "in the presence of and almost in the arms of his wife." Brown fell and died, Knott told the jury, "on his own hearthstone." Resorting to a familiar adage, Knott reminded the jurors that Brown's home, although humble, was nonetheless his castle, and it was "made so by one of the most glorious maxims of the law of English liberty."[86] By drawing the jury's attention to the location of the killing, Knott obviously played to the jurors' sympathies, but he also kept the focus on critical issues of fact and law in the trial. The jurors would base their decision on their beliefs about how the conflict moved from the doorstep to the interior of the house and on their conclusions about the significance of the policeman's entry into the house without a warrant.

The location of the conflict and the movements of Daniel Brown and Patrick McDonald mattered to both the prosecution and the defense. The prosecution argued that the policeman rushed into the house without proper authority and this egregious disregard of the residents' rights demonstrated McDonald's state of mind and criminal intent. Defense attorneys contended the location of the conflict had an entirely different—although no less important—bearing on the case. According to the defense attorneys, the location of the conflict supported a theory of self-defense because, they argued, Daniel Brown, possibly with help from others in the house, pulled McDonald into the house and threatened him. Another aspect of the defense strategy became apparent with the questioning of the state's second witness, Minnie Gresham. Beginning with the cross-examination of Mrs. Gresham, McDonald's attorneys sought to establish another element of a self-defense claim by eliciting statements about objects in the house that Daniel Brown might have tried to use as weapons.

The prosecution planned to begin witness testimony with a series of eyewitnesses and medical experts, but McDonald's attorneys attempted to blunt the anticipated weight of the state's eyewitnesses before the first witness took the stand. Officer McDonald could not testify because Maryland law barred defendants charged with indictable offenses from giving evidence for or against themselves.[87] The law was intended to deter juries from drawing negative inferences when criminal defendants declined to testify. In the matter of Daniel Brown, however, the only witness who might have been in a position to counter the prosecution's eyewitness's accounts was McDonald himself.[88] Defense attorney Hambleton asked Judge Gilmor to have witnesses removed from the courtroom while they were not testifying.[89] Judge Gilmor granted the motion, but the sequestration of witnesses proved counterproductive for the defense. Minor, understandable variations in wording and details surfaced in the eyewitnesses' testimony, but the state's witnesses for the most part did not, as defense counsel hoped, falter or contradict each other. And the fact that each witness testified without having heard the others only enhanced their credibility. After observing several of the witnesses, the *Sun*'s correspondent reported, "It is remarked how clearly the colored witnesses testify, and how hard it is to shake or confuse them."[90]

Much as they had at the coroner's inquest, the state's witnesses described a violent intrusion by an angry policeman and the intentional killing of an unarmed man. John Gresham testified first. The *Baltimore American*'s reporter described him as "a stout honest looking man and very dark colored."[91] Gresham stated that he was not sure what time of night it was when the policeman came to the door. He said his wife answered the policeman's knock, but when she saw it was a policeman, she called to him, and he went to speak to the officer. The policeman asked if the event was a cakewalk, pay party, or ball, and Gresham responded that it was not, but rather it was a "sociable entertainment." The policeman then said, according to Gresham, that he had heard a great deal of noise and if he heard any more such noise, he would take all the party guests to the station house. McDonald, Gresham reported, asked again about the admission charge for the party. Gresham said he then responded, "All right, sir, we have your orders and will obey them," and he started away from the door, but McDonald asked to speak to the proprietor of the house.[92] Before he went off to retrieve Daniel Brown, Gresham, according to his account, again responded politely to the policeman's orders, saying, "We have your orders, Sir, and calculate to abide by them."[93]

Gresham's testimony presented the jury with a version of the facts that suggested Gresham's acquiescence in Officer McDonald's order to stop the noise might have, and probably should have, ended the matter before the encounter turned violent. Gresham offered no explanation for McDonald's persistence beyond the initial exchange about the pay party and the noise, and he did not describe McDonald's demeanor during the conversation at the door. Gresham simply reported that Officer McDonald was not satisfied with the promise to abide by the order to stop the noise. Apparently, Gresham was not, in the moments after his first encounter with Officer McDonald, anxious about the policeman's presence; he testified that he left the front door, returned to the back room, retrieved a soda he had been drinking before the interruption, and was about to "make a jocose remark about a toast to a Mr. Boston." At that moment, however, according to Gresham's account, the tone of Daniel Brown's interaction with the policeman changed suddenly. Gresham stated that he heard "a rushing and a noise at the front door" and saw the policeman strike Daniel Brown with his club.[94]

Gresham went on to describe the moments before McDonald used his pistol, and his account, if accepted, established a basis for a murder conviction. A conviction of first-degree murder required proof of "willful, deliberate and premeditated killing."[95] Gresham indicated that McDonald fired the fatal shot after some deliberation, and his testimony suggested facts inconsistent with a defense based on accident. According to Gresham, after McDonald struck the first blow, an interval passed in which Gresham spoke to the policeman and repeated his promise to abide by the policeman's orders. Gresham testified that he tried to intervene by appealing to the policeman, saying, "Mister, please don't make a disturbance here."[96] But McDonald responded by cocking his pistol and hesitating "a quarter of a minute," then saying, "I'll shoot the black s__ of a b____."[97] Gresham's testimony also countered McDonald's claim of self-defense. According to Gresham, Daniel Brown retreated after he had been struck, but McDonald went after the injured man and shot him. Gresham conceded that he did not actually see McDonald fire the shot, but Gresham stated that, after shooting Brown, McDonald cocked his pistol again and threatened to shoot others in the room.[98]

In concluding his testimony, Gresham reported that Mrs. Brown asked him to go for a doctor.[99] Dr. Gamble came to the house in a "few minutes," but could do nothing to save Daniel Brown. Gresham also stated that the refreshments at the entertainment included "cakes, candy, watermelon, and ginger beer, but no intoxicating liquors." Gresham did not know the number of guests at the entertainment, but he believed "almost all" had been summoned as witnesses. The guests, according to Gresham, played "ring plays," but there was no dancing.[100]

In cross-examining Gresham, defense counsel John Poe tried to establish a basis for a claim of self-defense based on the contention that Brown and/or other party guests pulled Officer McDonald into the house and posed a threat to his life once he was inside. Poe asked whether the policeman was outside the door during the exchange with Gresham and whether the door remained opened at all times until the shooting. Gresham, however, stated that during his initial conversation with McDonald, he and the policeman were both on the front steps and the door remained open at all times until the shooting.[101]

John Gresham's wife, Minnie, next took the witness stand. On direct examination, Minnie Gresham for the most part reinforced her husband's testimony. She said the policeman asked John Gresham about a cakewalk or pay party, and Gresham responded that it was a sociable entertainment and assured McDonald the guests would comply with the order to reduce the noise. Minnie Gresham also backed up her husband's statement that the policeman was not satisfied with the assurances of John Gresham and asked to speak to the proprietor of the house. Minnie Gresham stated that she did not see the policeman strike Daniel Brown with the club or shoot Brown, but she heard Keziah Brown call out that the policeman was going to shoot Daniel Brown. In one detail, Minnie Gresham's testimony differed slightly from her husband's; Daniel Brown, after he was struck with the club, according to Minnie Gresham, "ran into the back room to the cupboard."[102] Minnie Gresham's reference to Daniel Brown's movement toward the cupboard gave defense counsel an opening to add details that might support the self-defense claim. Defense attorney Hambleton asked about the contents of the cupboard, and the witness stated that Keziah Brown had been ironing that day and the flatiron she had used was in the closet. On further questioning, Mrs. Gresham responded that there was a coal stove in the room and the raker used to stoke the fire was hung near the stove. She also testified that Daniel Brown owned a razor. In agreement with John Gresham's testimony, Mrs. Gresham testified that the party guests sang and played games, but they did not dance and they had no intoxicating drinks.[103]

After the testimony of John and Minnie Gresham laid out the state's version of the events leading up to and including the shooting, the prosecution presented medical experts. Dr. Gamble, who had treated Daniel Brown in the moments after the shooting, testified first. Coroner Ogle, who had participated in the postmortem examination, and Dr. Charles F. Bevans, a professor of anatomy, supplemented Dr. Gamble's testimony.[104] Dr. Gamble based his testimony on his observations when he tended to Daniel Brown on the night of the shooting as well as on what he found in the postmortem examination. He described two wounds. There was, according to Dr. Gamble, a one-and-one-half-inch-long ragged opening on the scalp on the left side. Dr. Gamble added that in his opinion, the wound was "done with a stick of some kind." The second wound, according to Dr. Gamble, was a small round wound from a gunshot, which, as shown by the postmortem examination, entered the left temporal bone and passed through Daniel Brown's brain.[105]

The defense attorneys objected to some of the medical testimony and tried to raise doubts about it on cross-examination. Dr. Ogle and Dr. Bevans supported Dr. Gamble's statements as to the presence of two wounds, and the defense did not counter their clinical descriptions of the wounds.[106] But the attorneys clashed when the prosecution's medical witnesses offered judgments about the relative positions of Daniel Brown and the shooter at the moment the shot was fired. Dr. Gamble stated that the pistol ball struck Daniel Brown's temple and then the ball ranged forward and downward. Therefore, in Dr. Gamble's opinion, the shot came from above and behind Brown. Defense attorney Hambleton objected, arguing that an opinion about the trajectory of the ball could only come from an expert with the proper qualifications, but the court allowed the jury to hear the testimony. On cross-examination, Dr. Gamble conceded that it was not impossible for the shot to have come from a different angle. Coroner Ogle followed Dr. Gamble on the witness stand and testified as to the findings on the postmortem examination. In agreement with Dr. Gamble, Ogle stated that the shot that killed Daniel Brown came from above, but he differed from Dr. Gamble in that he said the shot came from the side rather than from behind Brown.[107] The second day of the trial ended with Dr. Ogle's testimony.

On the third day, spectators again crowded the courtroom. With the possibility of a first-degree murder conviction advancing with each day's proceedings, the tension in the courtroom was apparent. One reporter noted that Officer McDonald's face showed a "deep, unbroken gravity."[108] The day's testimony opened with Dr. Bevans, who supplemented the medical testimony of Dr. Gamble and Coroner Ogle. In conjunction with Dr. Bevans's testimony about the bullet wound, the prosecution exhibited a skull, and it was noted that the exhibit elicited an emotional response from Officer McDonald as his "eyebrows contracted and a painful expression came over his face."[109] Using the skull to clarify his description of the wound, Dr. Bevans stated that the shooter must have been behind Daniel Brown and Brown must have been bending over or with his head turned to the side. When the prosecutor asked him about the severity of the club wound, Dr. Bevans replied, "some men might have been stunned by it and some men might have been infuriated."[110]

The prosecution next brought forward Joseph Boston, a witness who had not testified at the coroner's inquest or before the grand jury.[111] As a trial witness, however, Boston provided a dramatic account of the killing and significantly bolstered the prosecution's case. Boston's testimony, if believed by the jury, negated Officer McDonald's claim of self-defense. Boston stated that he witnessed the moment the confrontation between McDonald and Brown turned violent, and it was McDonald, not Brown, who was the aggressor. According to the account in the *Baltimore American*, Boston said McDonald "had hold of the lapel of Brown's coat." According to the account in the *Baltimore Sun*, Boston said the policeman took Daniel Brown by the breast, rushed him back into the room, and clubbed him.[112] Boston added that he was within five feet of the confrontation when Officer McDonald resorted to his club and he could see that Brown "did not even resist him."[113] On further questioning about the moments before McDonald struck Brown, Boston said he heard the policeman threaten, "If you say much more, I'll snatch you out of the door," to which Brown replied, "No, you won't." The policeman then, according to Boston, snatched at Brown and chased him, running close behind, until Brown pushed him away and the policeman reacted by clubbing him. Boston stated that Brown then staggered into the back room. After Brown retreated into the back room, the policeman drew his revolver, and John Gresham, according to Boston, appealed to McDonald not to shoot Brown. Boston said he did not hear the policeman respond to Gresham's attempt to intervene, but he saw the policeman run into the back room, and he heard Keziah Brown say, "Oh, don't shoot him, it's my husband." Officer McDonald's actions, at that point, as described by Boston, showed malice and a cold-blooded intent to kill: McDonald, Boston testified, answered Keziah Brown's plea by saying, "Yes, I will shoot him, the black s__ of a b____." Boston added that he heard the report of the pistol and saw the flash after McDonald's response to Keziah Brown.[114]

On cross-examination of Boston, defense attorney Heuisler elicited testimony showing that the officer went to the Browns' home in response to neighbors' complaints about noise and singing. State's Attorney Knott objected, arguing that whether there was singing was irrelevant to the question of the policeman's right to enter the house. Judge Gilmor overruled Knott's objection, explaining that evidence of McDonald's response to complaints of noise involved more than the policeman's right to enter the house. Evidence of the noise and singing, according to Judge Gilmor, was relevant to the issue of whether the policeman acted out of malice or out of an honest misunderstanding of the extent of his authority to enter a home.[115]

Although he ruled in favor of the defense, Judge Gilmor's explanation of his ruling added to the defense team's troubles. With the attention of the jury drawn to the fact that Officer McDonald entered the house without a warrant, Judge Gilmor took the opportunity to educate the jury about the law applicable to warrantless searches. If there is no crime being committed or threatened, Judge Gilmor explained, even when guests are noisy and disorderly, a policeman "may not force his way into a house of a citizen and invoke the badge of his office for so doing." There are exceptions that allow for warrantless entries into private homes, Gilmor noted. These exceptions, he said, apply in cases of great emergency—cases of "imminent danger to life, or the immediate probability of one of the high felonies," But, he added, "these are exceptions: the rule is otherwise." In the absence of an exception for great emergency, the judge explained, "the complaint must first be made, and competent authority in the form of a legal warrant obtained, by whose sanction alone he [the policeman] is enabled to proceed."[116] Judge Gilmor's explanation of the law, in light of the testimony presented up to that point in the trial, gave the jury a basis to conclude Officer McDonald entered the Browns' home without proper authority. The jury had heard testimony from several witnesses describing the event at the Browns' home as a tame affair—clearly not one within the exceptions defined by Judge Gilmor. If the jury accepted the testimony, the rule stated by the judge applied: Officer McDonald needed a warrant to enter the house.

Abraham Trusty next took the witness stand. Trusty identified himself as a live-in servant in the home of W. P. Harvey, a provisions merchant.[117] Trusty's testimony added important details about the moment the confrontation between Officer McDonald and Daniel Brown erupted into violence.[118] According to Trusty, after an extended conversation with Daniel Brown, the policeman said, "I will snatch you out of the door," and Brown replied, "No, you won't." McDonald then ran at Brown, who retreated "half way into the front room" before McDonald "ran up close to him." When the policeman caught Daniel Brown, Trusty said, Brown pushed the policeman away, but the policeman immediately pulled out his club and struck Brown. Trusty added that Brown staggered to the back room and fell against the cupboard door after being struck with the club. In agreement with the earlier witnesses, Trusty gave an account that showed deliberation by McDonald; Trusty said the policeman disregarded Gresham's attempt to prevent further violence. And Trusty reiterated the details most damaging to McDonald's defense. He reported that Keziah Brown asked McDonald not to shoot her husband, and that McDonald ignored her pleas and prefaced the gunshot with the angry remark, "Yes, I will shoot him, the black son of a b____."[119]

Richard Coates, who reported that he was a live-in servant of Dr. Lee, of Eutaw Street, testified that it was common for policeman to inquire about permits "when there is a party or anything like that." He added, however, that the guests at the Browns' home were not dancing.[120] Mary D. Shields, Mary Moore, and William Johnson also testified before the day's testimony ended. According to the *Sun*'s reporter, these witnesses, "all colored," provided testimony similar to the testimony of the preceding witnesses.[121]

When the third day's testimony ended, the prosecution had established a strong case. The most important witnesses—Gresham, Boston, and Trusty—had given mutually reinforcing accounts of McDonald's actions, actions that presented the jury with a vision of an angry, violent policeman attacking an unarmed man in his own home. And the details added to the strength of the prosecution's case. The testimony showed not only anger and violence, but also intervals in which McDonald revealed his willfulness and deliberation by disregarding appeals for restraint and by announcing his intent to shoot. Furthermore, defense attorneys may well have hurt their case by calling attention to the noise at the gathering in an attempt to convey an image of a wild, disorderly party. When questions about the singing and noise came before the jury, witness after witness drove home the fact that the noise was not indicative of a wild, disorderly party, but rather a social entertainment in which there was no consumption of alcohol and no dancing, and the main activity was an innocent game of building London Bridge.

The fourth day of the trial "attracted quite a crowd." A reporter from the *Baltimore Sun* observed that Officer McDonald "Wore his usual look of firmness, with a slight dash of something like haggardness in his expression." Not all observers, however, made the same subjective judgment about McDonald's demeanor. In the *Baltimore Gazette* it was reported that the policeman showed a "cool, calm and almost unconcerned look" throughout the trial.[122]

Mary Parker, who lived on North Charles Street with a "Mrs. McCoy," began the day's testimony, offering further details about the exchange in the doorway between Officer McDonald and Daniel Brown.[123] The witness reported that she heard Daniel Brown say, "I rent the house and pay the rent for it, and I think I ought to have the right to use it to suit myself." In response to Brown's assertion of his rights, according to Parker, the policeman answered, "If you give me any more of your sauce I'll snatch you out of the door."[124] The policeman then, Parker said, grabbed Daniel Brown by the collar as he jumped back into the room, following which the policeman struck Brown "as hard as he could strike."[125] At this point, Parker's testimony gave the defense an opportunity to elicit details that might support a self-defense claim. Parker said Brown, after being struck, "sidled into the back room into a little closet." At least one juror apparently recalled the earlier reference to the possibility that the closet contained a flatiron. The jury requested clarification, asking whether Brown retreated into the closet or to a point near the closet. Parker responded, "He went onto the closet."[126] Regarding the shooting, Parker agreed in substance with the earlier witnesses. She said Keziah Brown begged the policeman not to shoot her husband, but the policeman responded, "I'll shoot the black son of a b____." After the shooting, according to Parker, the policeman said, "Let him die."[127]

With the case for the prosecution about to close, Knott brought forward the state's most compelling witness, Keziah Brown. Other witnesses, by noting Keziah Brown's proximity to the shooting and her pleas to the policeman, had portrayed Officer McDonald's actions as callous and cruel. Keziah Brown herself, however, had made no public statements about the killing before she testified at the trial, and the jury and courtroom spectators undoubtedly gave her their full attention. Mrs. Brown had been in a position to witness the entire confrontation between her husband and McDonald. She reported that the outburst of violence followed an exchange in which Daniel Brown asserted his rights as a man who paid rent for his home, and the policeman replied by threatening to "snatch" Brown. Mr. Brown, according to Keziah Brown, defied the policeman by responding, "Snatch!" Mrs. Brown then described the violence that followed in detail. The policeman, she said, was on the steps and her husband was in the doorway; her husband "backed into the house."[128] She said after her husband backed into the house, the policeman struck him on the left side of the head and he "staggered back nearly into the cupboard or closet."[129] As she described the violence, Keziah Brown dramatically underscored her direct involvement in the confrontation: according to Mrs. Brown, when McDonald said, "I'll shoot the black son of a b____," she faced the policeman and pleaded, "don't shoot him, he's my husband," but McDonald retorted, "Damn your husband." In recounting the moment McDonald fired the fatal shot, Keziah Brown said she was between her husband and the policeman, but "he took me by my right shoulder and wheeled me from before him and he shot my husband over my shoulder."[130] Keziah Brown ended her testimony on direct examination by reporting that she said to the policeman, "You have killed him," to which the policeman replied, "Let him die."[131]

On cross-examination, defense attorney Hambleton tried to blunt the impact of Keziah Brown's account of the violence, but his questions elicited responses that seemed to harm more than help the defendant's case. Keziah Brown's responses underscored her credibility and presented the jury with a repetition of some of the most horrifying details of the killing. When questioned about whether she had conversed with other witnesses about the evidence brought forward at the coroner's inquest, she answered that she had not talked about the case with anyone until she spoke to the state's representative on the preceding Saturday; she had relied, she said, on her own memory in testifying. When Hambleton tried to bring out details about Daniel Brown's approach to the cupboard door, Keziah Brown explained that her husband's head was down and she tried to support him, "but he fell from her arms into the cabinet door." She added that when she faced the policeman before he fired the shot, she was within an arm's length of him before he wheeled her around and shot over her shoulder.[132]

On the same day Keziah Brown delivered her account of the killing to the jury, the prosecution brought its case to a conclusion, and McDonald's defense team began its case. To open its case, the defense attempted to counter the prosecution's portrayal of McDonald as hot-tempered and aggressive. Attorney John Poe began with a statement characterizing Officer McDonald as a thirty-six-year-old family man. This family man, he said, had formerly worked for the Northern Central Railway as an engineer or fireman, and had been on the police force for about a year. Policemen, Poe reminded the jury, were expected to exhibit qualities of coolness and courage, and their duties "called for the exposure of their lives." The defense then brought forward several character witnesses, including Police Marshal John T. Gray, Deputy Marshal Jacob Frey, and Captain Earhart. Marshal Gray testified that Officer McDonald "was a quiet and gentle officer all the time he was on the force." Frey testified that McDonald's reputation as a "peaceable, forbearing, humane man was first class."[133]

But a successful defense would obviously require more than generalizations about McDonald's character. Lead defense attorney Poe promised the jury more. Poe assured the jury that the evidence would show that McDonald "was assaulted on the pavement and got into the house in the struggle, when the door was locked on him" before he used his pistol.[134] In an effort to present the jury with an alternative account of the policeman's encounter with Brown, the defense attempted to enter into evidence the report McDonald filed at the northwestern district police station after he shot Daniel Brown. The state objected to the report, asking Judge Gilmor to exclude not only the content of McDonald's report, but also the reference to the fact that McDonald made such a report. Defense counsel contended that the fact that the report existed should be admitted into evidence to support the contention that McDonald "was not conscious of having committed any wrong act." As to the content of the report, defense attorney Hambleton argued that "an officer's lips should not be closed utterly when called to perform a duty, hazardous, perhaps, at the hour of midnight, with no citizen present, except the friends of the disorderly violators of the law." Judge Gilmor allowed admission of the evidence as to the fact that McDonald filed the report, but, in view of the clear statutory prohibition of testimony by the indicted defendant, he denied admission of the content of the report. He noted that he had excluded such evidence based on the well-established principle many times.[135]

A second item of evidence offered by the defense ignited a heated exchange between attorneys and ultimately focused attention on the roots of citizens' anxieties about aggressive policing. As justification for Officer McDonald's entry into the Browns' home, defense counsel attempted to place in evidence a document identified as Police Order No. 13. Under this order, Baltimore's police commissioners authorized patrolmen in cases in which they observed breaches of public peace to make arrests without obtaining warrants and, when necessary, to break open doors in doing so. The prosecution objected, arguing that officers had only the powers of peace officers under common law and such powers could only be increased by statute. In opposition to admission of the order into evidence, State's Attorney Knott argued, "if this order of the police board can shield a police officer from the consequences of his violence, and he can stalk through the streets red with the blood of his brothers, but free from all responsibility, then it is time the community knew it."[136] Then, reminding the court of Baltimoreans' lingering grievances over federal emergency police measures during the Civil War, Knott went on to state, "Somewhat of this sort of power was familiar to the people of this country a few years ago, when a plea of necessity was set up to justify the most startling and pernicious departures from the principles of the constitution."[137] In ruling on the question, Judge Gilmor noted that the order had probative value for the purpose of grading Officer McDonald's offense as first or second degree in the event he was found guilty of murder.[138] But Judge Gilmor went on to observe that his earlier opinion about the limits on a police officer's authority to act without a warrant also needed to be taken into consideration. Despite the importance of the order in grading the offense, Gilmor concluded, admission of the order into evidence "might lead the jury to give it too preponderating an influence."[139] Accordingly, the judge denied defense counsel's request to admit the order, thereby ensuring the jury would not undervalue the importance of restrictions on an officer's authority to enter a home without a warrant.

Defense counsel's most successful presentation to the jury—and one that may have saved Officer McDonald from a death sentence—came when they called to the witness stand Thomas Gill, an unemployed railroad worker. Gill testified that he was sleeping on a pile of lumber near Daniel Brown's house on the night of Brown's death, but the noise from the Browns' house awakened him. He said he saw the policeman in front of the Browns' house, and he observed that one black man came down the steps and two others came out onto the steps. One black man, according to Gill, defied the policeman and called him an "Irish s__ of a b____." Following the insult, Gill testified, the policeman came back toward the black men, then one of the men struck the policeman and the two men on the steps shoved the policeman inside. Gill said he then walked past the Browns' house and as he went by, he heard someone say, "Unlock that door."[140] In response, State's Attorney Knott produced two witnesses who testified that Brown's front door could not be seen from the location Gill described as his vantage point.[141]

The case went to the jury at 4:30 P.M. on Tuesday, November 23, and at 11:00 A.M. on Wednesday, November 24, the jury returned a verdict of not guilty of murder, but guilty of manslaughter. According to the account of the jury's announcement in the *Sun*, it was evident that Officer McDonald was satisfied with the verdict, as he "looked earnestly at the jury and bowed his head twice in thanks." Apparently at least one juror spoke to members of the press afterward: the *Sun* reported that the jury first voted eight in favor of guilty of first-degree murder and four in favor of manslaughter, but the proponents of the manslaughter verdict could not be moved. After an attempt to reach a compromise verdict of second-degree murder failed, the majority acquiesced to the manslaughter verdict.[142]

CONCLUSION

Elusive Justice

Even with the manslaughter verdict, Patrick McDonald's conviction stands as a notable anomaly. Although the worst years of the Jim Crow era were yet to come, the trial of Officer McDonald occurred in a period in which a majority of Baltimore's white citizens stood firmly against equal rights for African Americans. In 1867 the state adopted a new constitution that withheld the franchise from black citizens.[1] In the post–Civil War era, Baltimore established a segregated school system and limited African American participation in government at every turn.[2] And by 1874, despite the benefits Republicans might have derived from courting black voters, some Baltimore Republicans launched vicious attacks against African Americans and advocated "laying the nigger on the shelf" and creating a party "exclusively of white men."[3] Although federal civil rights legislation gave African Americans hope, and the Fifteenth Amendment gave them the right to vote, by 1875 a majority of white Marylanders had rallied behind states' rights and white supremacist politics. Black workers fought for their jobs, and black citizens struggled to win equal rights, but advocates of white supremacy were gaining momentum. Evenhanded justice was unlikely in a case of white-on-black police violence in Maryland in 1875.[4]

Despite the unfavorable climate for real justice for African Americans, several factors motivated authorities to pursue an investigation into the underlying facts of the matter of Daniel Brown and advance the case through the criminal justice system. The most obvious factor was the shocking nature of the policeman's actions; by any standard, McDonald's attack on an unarmed man was an egregious criminal act. But other factors mattered even more. Above all, social and political differences among Baltimore's residents came into play at each stage of the criminal justice system. Patrick McDonald wound up in the Baltimore City Jail because social divisions were important in Baltimore's white population as well as in the city's black population. Ideas about race mattered; lines were drawn on the basis of beliefs about racial differences. But neither the black population nor the white population of Baltimore was an undifferentiated mass. Some black men and women had been born into slavery and some into freedom, limited as that freedom was. Among the former slaves, some had sweated in the fields and others had served slaveholders in manor houses. In the city, some blacks worked as common laborers and servants, while other performed skilled tasks as caulkers and carpenters, and some launched businesses of their own. Whites chose opposing sides in a Civil War and for years afterward found it difficult to forgive each other for their choices. Wealthy white merchants and professionals lived in fine stone houses on the city's wide avenues, while white common laborers found accommodations wherever they could, including in the cramped alleys and backstreets. When they thought of their origins, some white men and women looked back to England; others remembered Ireland or Germany.

Beginning on the night Patrick McDonald clubbed and shot Daniel Brown, these differences came into play as the events were examined. From the first moments of the tragedy, the city's social and cultural complexity made a difference. The confrontation between the Irish policeman and the black laborer in Daniel Brown's doorway was in itself a collision between men with histories that made their interaction dangerous. The case advanced through the first stages of the criminal justice system, in part, because many of the African Americans who witnessed the attack worked in wealthy white citizens' homes and were accepted by their employers as trustworthy servants. Paradoxically, the persistence of some elements of a slavery-era culture encouraged the inquest jurors to give credence to the testimony of the African American witnesses to the crime. Many of the white jurors and authorities who participated in the inquest undoubtedly viewed the African American witnesses as inferiors—but they also saw them as subordinates who accepted their place within the city's racial hierarchy, and, accordingly, could be trusted. Had the killing occurred elsewhere in the city—in the places where poor black and white workers lived in clusters isolated from prosperous white citizens—the inquiry into the matter might easily have been sidetracked by a quick inquest verdict of accident or self-defense.

Avoiding an abrupt disposition of the matter at the coroner's inquest, however, was only the first step toward holding Officer McDonald accountable. Even with the inquest verdict, the state's attorney could have dropped the matter, the grand jury could have failed to indict McDonald, or the trial jury could have acquitted him. But the proceedings went forward and the jury voted for a conviction. The reason criminal proceedings advanced all the way to a jury trial and conviction can be explained by the community's anxieties about the police force, and, most importantly, about the way that police force had been used for partisan ends by bitterly divided factions of white citizens. As a result of the deep-rooted mistrust of state-sanctioned authority that characterized Baltimore's political culture, the plans to reorganize and modernize that police force had moved along haltingly. Conflicting opinions about the wisdom of empowering and arming policemen made citizens wary of the metropolitan police force from the start. And the timing of Officer McDonald's trial—a period in which images of police misconduct in the 1875 elections remained fresh in Baltimore residents' minds—underscored divisions among white citizens and amplified anxieties about police violence. At the same time, white middle-class citizens expected, even wanted, the police force to act as an instrument of oppression, primarily because population growth and economic development brought the city an uncomfortable level of diversity. This was a city living with memories of rioters who invaded the homes of some of its elite families. Prosperous Baltimoreans wanted the police force to control vagrants, street ruffians, ghettoized blacks, immigrants, and others perceived as socially isolated from the city's "respectable" citizens. But McDonald, in effect, in the eyes of the city's respectable citizens, brought the weapons of oppression to bear against the wrong victim.

It is important to note that Officer McDonald was not convicted because the city's white citizens as a general matter objected to the oppression of African Americans. Although many Baltimoreans distrusted and even feared the police, there was no consensus among whites that African Americans suffered disproportionately from police violence. At two points in Officer McDonald's trial, Judge Gilmor issued rulings that revealed his priorities (and presumably the priorities of other prosperous citizens), and in each instance his rulings underscored the fact that Officer McDonald's attack on Daniel Brown was seen, not as racist violence, but rather as aggressive policing that disturbed the peace and security of all citizens' homes. When the question of warrantless searches and arrests came up in the trial, Judge Gilmor took care to remind the jury of common-law protections against police intrusions into private homes. The judge returned to that point of emphasis when defense attorneys offered evidence in the form of a police order that suggested policemen were free of traditional common-law constraints when they observed breaches of peace. As explained by Judge Gilmor, the relevance of the police order as evidence of the defendant's state of mind was not sufficient to outweigh the risk of inducing the jury to undervalue constraints on police intrusions into private homes.

The compromise verdict of manslaughter and a peculiar twist in the posttrial legal proceedings revealed the ambivalence of white Baltimoreans when confronted with white-on-black police violence. Although Judge Gilmor sentenced McDonald to five years in the Baltimore City Jail, McDonald served less than a year, even counting the days he was held awaiting trial. The statutory punishment prescribed for manslaughter called for up to ten years in the penitentiary or, in the discretion of the sentencing court, imprisonment for not more than two years in the city jail.[5] Because Judge Gilmor designated the city jail rather than the penitentiary as the place of McDonald's proposed five-year incarceration, the Maryland Court of Appeals, the state's highest appellate body, ruled in June 1876 that the sentence was without legal authority. Furthermore, in its decision, the Court of Appeals stated its only recourse was to reverse the Criminal Court's judgment of guilt because it had no authority to impose a proper sentence or to remand the case to the trial court for resentencing. As a result, McDonald could not be resentenced unless he was tried and convicted again.[6] Following the Court of Appeals' ruling, the state's attorney sought a new indictment, but defense attorneys successfully argued that a retrial would unlawfully subject the policeman to double jeopardy. On July 15, 1876, less than a year after Daniel Brown's death, McDonald went free with complete immunity from further prosecution.[7]

In the end, Officer McDonald's actual punishment was nowhere near proportional to the severity of his crime. Some jurors simply were not willing to find a white policeman guilty of murder in a case in which the victim was black, and Judge Gilmor, despite several years of experience in the Baltimore City Criminal Court, committed a sentencing error. In an editorial, the *Baltimore American* complained that, in sentencing McDonald, Judge Gilmor intended to make the policeman's incarceration easy by placing him in the city jail, where fellow officers could look after him, and, in doing so, Gilmor "lost sight of the law."[8] The criticism is well founded: during his years of experience in the Baltimore City Criminal Court, Gilmor had issued sentences in several manslaughter cases. He should have known better.[9]

The *American* limited its criticism to Criminal Court Judge Gilmor, offering no comment on the decision of the Court of Appeals. But it is doubtful whether the law required the appellate body to issue the decision that led to McDonald's freedom. Although the law applicable to the appellate court's options was not completely clear, the Court of Appeals might have remanded the case for the limited purpose of correcting the sentencing. Such a remand would not have required a new trial and would not have raised the issue of double jeopardy. McDonald would then have served his entire five-year sentence. In an odd interpretation of the applicable law, however, Associate Justice Oliver Miller of the Court of Appeals asserted that he had no authority to remand the case for resentencing.[10] Justice Miller's assertion was not based on a thorough examination of the applicable law. In fact, a statute dating from 1800 authorized the Court of Appeals to reverse a "judgment, or part of a judgment, at law" and to replace it with "such judgment as ought to have been given."[11] Justice Miller circumvented the Act of 1800 by relying on an 1859 decision, *Watkins v. State,* in which the Court of Appeals ruled that a reversal of judgment in a criminal case required negation of all former proceedings, including the trial.[12]

In considering whether the Act of 1800 applied in McDonald's case, Justice Miller stated that the question had been "fully argued" in *Watkins,* and that the Court in *Watkins* had decided that the Act did not apply in criminal cases.[13] But Justice Miller's statements misrepresented the decision in the *Watkins* case. The question had not been "fully argued" in the *Watkins* case; the report of the *Watkins* case indicates that the question of the applicability of the Act of 1800 had not been argued at all. In the *Watkins* case, the lawyers had made no references to the Act of 1800. The *Watkins* Court based its decision on general principles of common law, with no discussion of the Act of 1800.

To understand what Justice Miller should have reviewed in reaching the decision in McDonald's appeal, it is helpful to remember that the Court of Appeals had to answer two separate questions. First, Justice Miller had to decide whether the trial court erred in sentencing McDonald. The second question arose only after Justice Miller found error in the sentence: because Justice Miller found an error in the trial court's sentence, he had to decide what remedy might be available. The two-step process in Justice Miller's decision seems obvious enough. The error was clear; Justice Miller needed to decide what to do about it. The two-step process became important, however, when the Court reviewed the legal authorities applicable to remedies in such cases.

To thoroughly address the applicable legal authorities, Justice Miller should have considered and discussed an 1865 case, *Isaacs v. State.* In that case, the Court of Appeals also reviewed a question of error in sentencing a criminal defendant. The *Isaacs* case warranted consideration by Justice Miller because in *Isaacs* Maryland Attorney General Alexander Randall, in his arguments before the Court of Appeals, stated that the Act of 1800 applied in criminal cases.

Attorney General Randall made his position on the issue clear: "The Court of Appeals, if they do not approve of this sentence of the Court below, have the power to modify the same, and give judgment as ought to be given by that Court, and may do the same in this case."[14] The two-step process required in such cases became important, however, because in *Isaacs* the Court of Appeals found no error in the trial court's sentence. No remedy was called for and the second question—whether the Act of 1800 was applicable—did not need to be answered by the Court. Consequently, *Isaacs* did not establish a precedent for Justice Miller to follow in McDonald's case. But *Isaacs* and Attorney General Randall's reasoning were, nonetheless, important. A thorough analysis of McDonald's appeal called for a discussion of *Isaacs* and of Attorney General Randall's position. If Justice Miller had first analyzed *Isaacs* and Attorney General Randall's position, he could have presented a reasoned opinion as to why the Act of 1800 did or did not apply. But Judge Miller did not cite the *Isaacs* case; he did not address the attorney general's opinion; and he offered no reasoning to explain why the Act of 1800 did not apply in criminal appeals.

In a matter as serious as a homicide, it is fair to hold Justice Miller to a higher standard of jurisprudence than he demonstrated in Officer McDonald's appeal. The *Isaacs* case and Attorney General Randall's statement made it clear that the applicability of the Act of 1800 was a question warranting consideration in an appeal concerning a sentencing error. If Justice Miller had not erroneously stated that the question of the applicability of the Act of 1800 had been "fully argued" in the *Watkins* case, and if he had acknowledged the attorney general's position in the *Isaacs* case and offered some legal reasoning to counter the attorney general's argument, Justice Miller's decision might have been merely questionable, perhaps even defensible as a reasonable interpretation of ambiguous legal standards. But as it stands, Justice Miller's decision is inadequate in its citation of legal authorities and deficient in its legal reasoning.

Ultimately, the ambivalence of the white community shielded Officer McDonald from what might have been a considerably more severe punishment. As admitted by the one juror who spoke to the press, the manslaughter verdict represented a compromise that negated the judgment of eight jurors who concluded that the evidence supported a murder conviction. As to the posttrial proceedings, the historical record is insufficient to show with any certainty that the judges intentionally bent the law to shorten McDonald's incarceration, but their rulings indicate that they did not believe the crime was one warranting the harshest penalties the law allowed. By sentencing McDonald to the city jail rather than the state penitentiary, Judge Gilmor intended to allow McDonald to benefit from the proximity of his fellow officers. The legal precedents guiding Judge Miller in his appellate decision may have been sufficiently ambiguous to justify the termination of McDonald's incarceration, but the judge read the applicable cases carelessly and he wrote a decision that failed to address important aspects of the case.

With the early release of Officer McDonald, real justice must have seemed elusive to Baltimore's black residents in 1875. From the perspective of the twenty-first century, however, the conviction of the policeman is nonetheless noteworthy. Officer McDonald killed Daniel Brown in a vicious attack that warranted vigorous prosecution, and the egregious nature of the crime accounts in part for the fact that McDonald was tried and convicted. But, in the wake of the Civil War, many whites—law enforcement officers and civilians alike—escaped punishment for crimes committed against African Americans. What made the difference in Baltimore in 1875 was the city's social and political diversity—diversity made especially complex by Baltimore's border status. As a result of shifting political fortunes in this deeply divided city, some authorities allowed—and sometimes even encouraged—policemen to bully and intimidate influential citizens. When policemen bullied and intimidated white middle-class citizens, the constraints that might have inhibited prosecutions of miscreant officers loosened, and prosecutors, judges, and jurors more readily turned to the courts to rein in offending officers.

Yet some aspects of the Daniel Brown case reflected new trends rather than lingering slavery-era values or animosities carried over from Civil War–era conflicts. Daniel Brown understood the potential for social changes that came with emancipation, civil rights laws, and voting rights; he was, as his landlord described him, "a little strong in the Civil Rights questions." Although his spouse and many of his guests were domestic servants, Brown was a laborer. When he faced Officer McDonald in the doorway, Brown did not take on the role of the subordinate in a lingering slavery-era culture; he asserted his rights as a citizen and as the proprietor of his own home. And the policeman Brown faced in the doorway was not a representative of the old South. Officer McDonald, an Irish immigrant, found his place in Baltimore as a wageworker in the industrializing city, first as a laborer, then as a patrolman. Neither man was grounded in the culture of slavery-era paternalism.

In some ways, the Daniel Brown case seems familiar to a twenty-first-century observer. When black citizens protested in response to Brown's death, they raised complaints and concerns remarkably similar to those voiced by African Americans protesting the killings of black men and women in twenty-first-century cities: police tactics calculated to intimidate black citizens, arbitrary arrests, harassment of African American teenagers, use of excessive force. Then, as now, protesters were frustrated by the fact that racial differences control perceptions; when blacks in 1875 insisted that police abuses were manifestations of racism, white journalists, even those outraged by the killing, answered that racism was not a factor. And black citizens' complaints that Daniel Brown "was shot down like a dog . . . for no other cause than he was a harmless colored citizen" make it easy to imagine that the protesters of 1875 would understand twenty-first-century protesters' declarations that black lives matter.

Notes

Introduction

1. Baltimore City Court of Common Pleas, Marriage Index, Male, 1851–1885. MSA CM205-3; Baltimore City Health Department Death Record 1875–1972, 1:129, death certificate no. 4503, MSA CM1132-2. In the 1870 US Census record Daniel is recorded as "James," but the 1870 census entry shows the Browns as residing next door to Matilda Philips, which is in agreement with the 1870 and 1871 city directory entries showing Daniel and Keziah Brown at 114 Sarah Ann Street and Mrs. Matilda Phillips at 112 Sarah Ann Street. US Census, 1870, Population Schedules, Maryland, Baltimore Ward 13, 200; *Woods's Directory,* 1870, 468 and 683; *Woods's Directory,* 1871, 473, 678–79.

2. The city's major newspapers, the *Baltimore Sun* and the *Baltimore American and Commercial Advertiser* (hereinafter *Baltimore American*) carried detailed accounts of the events surrounding Brown's death and its aftermath in issues from August 2 to August 7, 1875, and the details of the trial of Officer Patrick McDonald from November 16 to November 24, 1875.

3. Adler, "Shoot to Kill," 236.

4. "Many Obstacles to Prosecuting Police," *Baltimore Sun,* July 14, 2015, p. A.13; "Thousands Dead, Few Prosecuted," *Washington Post,* Apr. 12, 2015, p. A.1; Kevin Rector, "Charges Dropped, Freddie Gray Case Concludes with Zero Convictions against Officers," *Baltimore Sun,* July 27, 2016.

5. Adler, "Shoot to Kill," 254.

6. Hahn and Jeffries, *Urban America and Its Police,* 74. Investigating authorities classified only one of the 319 deaths unjustifiable.

7. Bernasconi, "When Police Violence Is More Than Violent Policing," 145.

8. Generalized statistical analyses of the history of criminal justice often exclude records of the first stages of proceedings in favor of trial records because trials are more thoroughly documented than are arrests and coroner's inquests. A pioneer in the study of policing and urban violence, Roger Lane, for example, in his study of violence in Philadelphia, acknowledges the limitations of nineteenth-century sources. He notes that, as a result of the characteristics of the nineteenth-century justice system, very few homicides were labeled as murder at the coroner's inquest stage. Despite his acknowledgment of

the importance of the coroner's role in processing homicide cases, Lane concedes that the limitations in the available sources led him to rely on trial records as the "most direct and significant evidence about justice, black and white." Lane, *Roots of Violence in Black Philadelphia,* 89.

9. Malka, *Men of Mobtown.*

10. Studies of northern cities include Lane, *Policing the City: Boston;* Richardson, *The New York Police;* Monkkonen, *The Dangerous Class;* Miller, *Cops and Bobbies;* Schneider, *Detroit and the Problem of Order;* Harring, *Policing a Class Society;* Lane, *Roots of Violence in Black Philadelphia;* Steinberg, *The Transformation of Criminal Justice in Philadelphia;* Mitrani, *The Rise of the Chicago Police Department.*

11. Examples of studies of southern cities include Hindus, *Prison and Plantation;* Rousey, *Policing the Southern City—New Orleans.*

12. Monkkonen, *Police in Urban America.*

13. Ruffner, *Maryland's Blue and Gray,* 7.

14. Scott and M'Cullough, *Maryland Code, 1860,* Art. 66, §§ 1–94; accessible at *Arch. Md. Online,* 145:450–68.

15. Miller, *Emigrants and Exiles,* ch. 7.

1. *The Black Man in the Doorway*

1. *Journal of the House of Delegates, 1865,* Document EE, Report of the Select Committee, 18, accessible at *Arch. Md. Online,* 753:1930. The Eastern Shore included eight counties in the antebellum period: Cecil, Kent, Queen Anne's, Talbot, Caroline, Dorchester, Somerset, and Worcester. Wicomico County was later carved out of northern portions of Somerset and Worcester counties. Fisher, *Gazetteer of the State of Maryland,* 5.

2. *Journal of the House of Delegates, 1865,* Document EE, Report of the Select Committee, 10, accessible at *Arch. Md. Online,* 753:1922.

3. Douglass, *Life and Times of Frederick Douglass,* 67–69. In one instance, Douglass reported that the mistress of a teenage slave girl murdered the girl and "mangled her face and broke her breastbone" because the girl fell asleep while babysitting the child of the mistress; the coroner determined that the death was attributable to the beating administered by the mistress and a warrant was issued, but never served.

4. Douglass, *Life and Times of Frederick Douglass,* 27.

5. Whitman, *Challenging Slavery in the Chesapeake,* 19–22.

6. Berlin, *Slaves without Masters,* 26–27; Fields, *Slavery and Freedom,* 4–5; Wright, *Free Negro in Maryland,* 39–42. Over the course of the nineteenth century, Ohio Valley growers outpaced Maryland tobacco planters; in the report of an 1865 survey of Maryland's resources, tobacco barely warranted a mention as an agricultural product of the Eastern Shore counties. *Journal of the House of Delegates, 1865,* Document EE, Report of the Select Committee, 19–22, accessible at *Arch. Md. Online,* 753:1921–34. By 1870 Kentucky's tobacco production was eight times that of Maryland, and even Ohio's output was greater than Maryland's. *Compendium of the Ninth Census, 1870,* table LXXXIX, p. 700.

7. Wright, *Free Negro in Maryland,* 44–49; Berlin, *Slaves without Masters,* 20–25. In "Slavery in the Age of Revolution," 304–7, William Calderhead contends that in the Revolutionary era, ideological considerations had more effect on the decline of slavery in Maryland than economics had.

8. Fields, *Slavery and Freedom,* table 1.7, p. 13.

9. United States Census Office, *Compendium of the Seventh Census, 1854,* 248; *Population of the United States in 1860,* State of Maryland table no. 1, pp. 211–13; Fields, *Slavery and Freedom,* table 4.1, p. 70.

10. Dodson Journal, Apr. 5, 1855.

11. Dodson Journal, Feb. 22, 1855.

12. Brackett, *Negro in Maryland,* 66. Turner's uprising gave new life to anxieties that had troubled Marylanders for decades. During insurrections in Santo Domingo from 1791 to 1804, many of the whites who managed to escape found new homes in the southern United States, and they brought with them tales of atrocities that perpetuated white Southerners' apprehensions about the dangers around them. Memories of Santo Domingo lingered until the 1830s. Then Nat Turner's insurrection in 1831 brought a heightened sense of immediacy to southern fears. Jordan, *White over Black,* 380; Potter, *Impending Crisis of the South,* 39–43.

13. Scott and M'Cullough, *Maryland: Code, 1860,* Art. 66, §§ 1–94, accessible at *Arch. Md. Online,* 145:450–68.

14. Scott and M'Cullough, *Maryland: Code, 1860,* Art. 37, § 1. In a recent study of African Americans' claims to birthright citizenship, Martha S. Jones explains how some blacks, through determination and creativity, found ways around such legal limitations. Jones, *Birthright Citizens,* 26–27.

15. Brown, *Road to Jim Crow,* 9–10.

16. "The Course of Maryland," 468.

17. Provisions in the code regulated the movements and activities of "free negroes" and mandated enforcement through harsh penalties and intrusive surveillance. Sections applicable to the "Immigration of Free Negroes" prohibited African Americans from relocating to Maryland from other states and limited Maryland blacks in their interstate travels. The level of anxiety about African American immigrations into Maryland is reflected in the severity of penalties for violations, which included fines up to $500 and sale into slavery. Scott and M'Cullough, *Maryland Code, 1860,* Art. 66, §§ 44–51, accessible at *Arch. Md. Online,* 145:458–60. Other sections of the code authorized private citizens and local officials to intrude into the affairs of ostensibly free black men and women. Sections regulating "Vagrant Free Negroes" directed constables or sheriffs to round up "any free negro, male or female," residing in the county "without visible means of support" and bring any such man or woman before an Orphan's Court judge, who then had the authority to sell the vagrant into slavery for one year. At the end of the year in slavery, the vagrant was required to hire out to "some respectable white person" for another year's service. Scott and M'Cullough, *Maryland Code, 1860,* Art. 66, §§ 52–57, accessible at *Arch. Md. Online,* 145:460–61. Other provisions prohibited blacks from opting out of contracts of employment, barred blacks from navigating on Maryland's waterways without an adult white male aboard the vessel, and limited blacks' rights to own dogs or guns. Scott and M'Cullough, *Maryland Code, 1860,* Art. 66, §§ 67–73 and 76–87, accessible at *Arch. Md. Online,* 145:463–64 and 465–67.

18. Scott and M'Cullough, *Maryland Code, 1860,* Art. 66, §§ 74–75, accessible at *Arch. Md. Online,* 145:464–65.

19. "Who Pays the Costs?" *Cecil (Md) Whig,* Sept. 23, 1854, p. 2.

20. Scott and M'Cullough, *Maryland Code, 1860,* Art. 66, §§ 58–60, accessible at *Arch. Md. Online,* 145:461.

21. Scott and M'Cullough, *Maryland Code, 1860,* Art. 66, §§ 61–65, accessible at *Arch. Md. Online,* 145:461–62.

22. Scott and M'Cullough, *Maryland Code, 1860,* Art. 66, § 66, accessible at *Arch. Md. Online,* 145:462.

23. Baltimore City Court of Common Pleas, Marriage Index, Male, 1851–1885. C205-3 (MSA).

24. In *Woods's Directory,* 1871, 677, Brown is still listed as living on Sarah Ann Street. Keziah Brown testified in November 1875 that she and Daniel had lived in the Tyson Street house for four years. "Court Proceedings," *Baltimore Daily Gazette,* Nov. 19, 1875, p. 4.

25. Halpin, *Brotherhood of Liberty,* 12.

26. Halpin, *Brotherhood of Liberty,* 7.

27. Phillips, *Freedom's Port,* 75.

28. Della, "Problems of Negro Labor," 27–28. Della made these calculations based on listings in *Matchett's Directory, 1849–50* and *Woods's Directory,* 1860.

29. Phillips, *Freedom's Port,* 204.

30. Della, "Problems of Negro Labor," 15.

31. Brugger, *Maryland,* 255.

32. Phillips, *Freedom's Port,* 195–96.

33. Towers, "Job Busting at Baltimore Shipyards," 234.

34. "Trouble Among the Brickmakers," *Baltimore Sun,* May 18, 1858, p. 1; "The Trouble among the White and Black Caulkers," *Baltimore American,* July 8, 1858, p. 1.

35. Towers, "Job Busting at Baltimore's Shipyards," 229–32. Towers argues convincingly that conflicts among caulkers centered on competition between blacks and native-born white workers, with the white workers gaining advantage through their influence in city government, especially the police force. White employers often, according to Towers, favored black skilled labor, but whites, especially those with Know-Nothing affiliations, used their connections to city government to overcome resistance from white employers and black workers.

36. Della, "Problems of Negro Labor," 28; Rockman, *Scraping By,* 42.

37. Phillips, *Freedom's Port,* 102–4; Della, "Problems of Negro Labor," 20; Wade, *Slavery in the Cities,* 61.

38. By 1860, the ratio of free blacks to slaves in Baltimore was 25,680 to 2,218. Ira Berlin, *Slaves without Masters,* 62; Groves and Muller, "Evolution of Black Residential Areas," 177; Garonzik, "Racial and Ethnic Make-up of Baltimore Neighborhoods," 392.

39. Groves and Muller, in "The Evolution of Black Residential Areas," 177–78, contend that Baltimore's racial residential distribution did not resemble the pattern found in the Deep South, but rather was characterized by segregated clusters of African Americans scattered throughout the city. But in many areas of antebellum Baltimore, the clusters of African Americans were in alleys directly behind the residences of prosperous white families who employed black alley residents. Baltimore's pattern differed from the familiar pattern of the Deep South, but Baltimore's pattern of residences was nonetheless similar to the pattern typical of the Deep South, at least as it demonstrates the proximity of black workers to white employers.

40. United States Census, 1880, Maryland, Baltimore, Ward One, EDs 11, 12, 14, 15, and Ward Eight, ED 259 (East Side); Ward Eleven, ED 97, Ward Twelve, ED107, and Ward Twenty, EDs 205, 206 (West Side).

41. As early as 1870, for example, many hod carriers lived in mostly African American blocks northwest of the city center. United States Census, 1870, Maryland, Baltimore Ward Thirteen, pp. 243–45. Many laborers and laundresses lived in the area of Camden Station, just to the west of the harbor. United States Census, 1880, Maryland, Baltimore,

Ward Fifteen. By the 1890s this area, which came to be known as Pigtown, would be identified by social reformers as a notorious area of squalor. An article in the *Baltimore News,* of September 20, 1892, included the following description of Pigtown: "Open drains, great lots filled with high weeds, ashes and garbage accumulated in the alleyways, cellars filled with filthy black water, houses that are total strangers to the touch of whitewash or scrubbing brush, human bodies that have been strangers to soap and water, villainous negroes who loiter and sleep around street corners and never work; vile and vicious women, with nothing but a smock to cover their black nakedness, lounging in the doorways or squatting upon the steps, hurling foul epithets at every passerby; foul streets, foul people, in foul tenements filled with foul air; that's Pigtown." The *News* article is quoted in Power, "Apartheid Baltimore Style," 290.

42. United States Census, 1880, Maryland, Baltimore, Ward One, EDs 12, 14, and 15. The numbering of Baltimore's street addresses changed after the 1880 census. In the 1880 census, the Baltimore Street residences referred to here are numbered from 400 to 499. In subsequent census reports, the same residences are numbered 2101 to 2299. One African American live-in counted here was a two-year-old child of a female live-in servant.

43. United States Census, 1880, Maryland, Baltimore, Ward One, EDs 11 and 12.

44. United States Census, 1880, Maryland, Baltimore, Ward One, EDs, 11, 12, 14, and 15.

45. Douglass, *Life and Times of Frederick Douglass,* 181.

46. Towers, "Job Busting at Baltimore Shipyards," 25.

47. Whitman, "Manumission and Apprenticeship," 64–65.

48. "Trouble Among the White and Black Caulkers," *Baltimore American,* July 8, 1858, p. 1.

49. Towers, "Job Busting at Baltimore Shipyards," 225–28.

50. Fuke, *Imperfect Equality,* 113.

51. Fuke, *Imperfect Equality,* 132.

52. Thomas, "A Nineteenth Century Black Operated Shipyard," 1–12.

53. Halpin, *Brotherhood of Liberty,* 24.

54. Fuke, *Imperfect Equality,* 134–36.

55. "The Fifteenth Amendment," *Baltimore American,* May 20, 1870, pp. 1 and 4; "The Fifteenth Amendment," *Baltimore Sun,* May 20, 1870, p. 1.

56. Foner, *Reconstruction,* 353.

57. Md. Const. of 1867, art. I, § 1.

58. *Laws . . . Made and Passed, 1867,* ch. 71, accessible at *Arch. Md. Online,* 133:4312; Wallis, *Writings of Severn Teakle Wallis,* 1:143–44.

59. "The Taney Statue Inauguration," *Baltimore Sun,* Dec. 11, 1872, p. 1.

60. Hyman and Wiecek, *Equal Justice under the Law,* 177; Harris, *Two Against Lincoln,* 20–21 and 99.

61. Johnson, *Further Consideration of the Dangerous Condition,* 20.

62. Harris, *Two Against Lincoln,* 109–10.

63. William E. Sinn to John T. Ford, Mar. 4, 1875.

64. "The Civil Rights Law," *Baltimore Sun,* Mar. 4, 1875, p. 1.

65. Brackett, *Negro in Maryland,* 204.

66. *Baltimore City Code: Ordinances of the Mayor and City Council,* Ordinance No. 37, approved June 5, 1858.

67. Scharf, *History of Baltimore,* 196–98; *Laws Made and Passed, 1853,* ch. 46, passed Mar. 16, 1853, p. 43, accessible at *Arch. Md. Online,* 403:43.

68. "Suit against the City," *Baltimore Sun,* Sept. 4, 1858, p. 4; "Verdict against the City," *Baltimore American,* Sept. 6, 1858, p. 1.

69. "Police Intelligence," *Baltimore Daily Exchange,* May 12, 1859, p. 1; "Descent on a Dance House," *Baltimore Sun,* May 12, 1859, p. 1. In the *Daily Exchange,* it was reported that all thirty-three African Americans were sent to jail; according to the account in the *Sun,* the police magistrate released seventeen of the arrested persons on bail.

70. "Local Matters," *Baltimore Sun,* Oct. 3, 1860, 1 (quotation): "City Affairs: Disorderly House," *Baltimore American,* Oct. 3, 1860, p. 1.

71. "Disorder at a Ball," *Baltimore Sun,* May 11, 1859, p. 1.

72. "Five Shots at a Policeman by a Negro," *Baltimore Daily Gazette,* Aug. 6, 1875, p. 1.

73. "A Policeman Shot at by a Colored Man," *Baltimore Sun,* Oct. 26, 1870, p. 4.

74. *Baltimore City Code, 1879,* Art. 33, Licenses, § 13.

75. Wright, *Free Negro in Maryland,* 124–25. Although the Maryland General Assembly enacted legislation intended to lessen some of the hardships caused by enforcement of the black code in the City of Baltimore, these measures nonetheless reflected the presumption of white entitlement to control the private affairs of "free colored persons." In order to facilitate meetings of African American charitable associations, for example, an 1846 statute permitted meetings of charitable associations formed by "colored persons" of "good moral character," but the statute nonetheless required the mayor of Baltimore to appoint a police officer to attend the meetings of such associations. Act in Relation to the Free People of Color in the City of Baltimore, ch. 284, passed Mar. 9, 1846. *Baltimore City Code: Ordinances of the Mayor and City Council , 1858,* p. 559. According to its preamble, the act was passed because an earlier act of the Maryland General Assembly banning assemblies of free blacks caused "much hardship upon honest, industrious, and peaceable colored people."

76. "Colored People's Mass Meeting," *Baltimore Sun,* Aug. 6, 1875, p. 1.

77. "A Homicide in Northwest Baltimore," *Baltimore Sun,* Aug. 2, 1875, p. 1; "A Police Murder," *Baltimore American,* Aug. 2, 1875, p. 4.

78. Euchner, "The Politics of Urban Expansion," 270; Kemp, *Housing Conditions in Baltimore,* 58 and 66–67.

79. Jones, *Labor of Love, Labor of Sorrow,* 125–26.

80. Keziah Brown is listed as a laundress in *Woods's Directories* for the years 1871, 1872, and 1873, but her name disappears in 1874 and 1875. Sadly, the widowed Keziah Brown's listing as a laundress reappears in *Woods's Directory,* 1876, p. 710.

81. *Woods's Directory,* 1870, p. 710; United States Census, 1870, Maryland, Baltimore Ward Thirteen, p. 200. In the census report, the lodger is reported as Minor Hennesen, a blacksmith; in the city directory, he is reported as Minor Henderson, a hod carrier.

82. "A Police Murder," *Baltimore American,* Aug. 2, 1875, p. 4; "Court Proceedings," *Baltimore Gazette,* Nov. 16, 1875, p. 4.

83. Maryland Bureau of Industrial Statistics and Information, *Bureau of Industrial Statistics and Information, 1884–1885,* p. 40.

84. Niccol, *Essay on Sugar,* 26–35; "A Fearful Accident," *Baltimore Sun,* Aug. 27, 1855, p. 1.

85. Casual laborers in Baltimore earned about $1.25 per day and worked irregularly; Brown earned $2.50 per day as a hod carrier and about $1.65 per day as a laborer in the sugar refinery. Young, *Cost of Labor in the United States . . . 1869,* 48. *Woods's Directories* for the years 1871, 1872, 1873, 1874, and 1875.

86. United States Census, 1870, Maryland, Baltimore Ward Thirteen, p. 200.

87. "A Homicide in Northwest Baltimore," *Baltimore Sun,* Aug. 2, 1875, p. 1.

88. Genovese, *Roll, Jordan, Roll,* 561–66.

89. Douglass, *Life and Times of Frederick Douglass,* 136.

90. Mary Bradbury to Lewis Jackson, Oct. 16, 1855, series 1, box 1, Mary Elizabeth Bradbury Papers.

91. Bureau of Refugees, Freedmen and Abandoned Lands, *First Semi-annual Report,* 8.

92. Douglass, *Life and Times of Frederick Douglass,* 111.

93. Davis, *Narrative of the Life,* 17–35.

94. Fuke, *Imperfect Equality,* 88–89; Browne, "The Expenses Are Borne by the Parents," 407–10.

2. *The Irish Policeman on the Doorstep*

1. According to one newspaper account, McDonald was "almost thirty years of age" in August 1875. "A Police Murder," *Baltimore American,* Aug. 2, 1875, p. 4. An 1880 census entry lists a Patrick McDonald, age thirty-seven, and born in Ireland. This is probably the correct Patrick McDonald, although not all the details match the news reports. The entry lists his children as ages twelve, nine, seven, four, and two, all of whom were born in Maryland. United States Census, 1880, Maryland, Baltimore City, Ward Twelve, Enumeration District 109, p. 3, sheet 92C. This census entry is consistent with newspaper accounts of his arrest, in which it was reported that he was a native of Ireland, and had three children and a wife who was "in very delicate health." "A Homicide in Northwest Baltimore," *Baltimore Sun,* Aug. 2, 1875, p. 1.

2. Reilly, "Modern Ireland: An Introductory Survey," 90; Miller, *Emigrants and Exiles,* 291.

3. Kenny, *New Directions in Irish-American History,* 14; Miller, *Emigrants and Exiles,* 346; Doyle, "The Remaking of Irish America, 1845–1880," 215.

4. Tóibín, "The Irish Famine," 28.

5. Gray, *Famine, Land and Politics,* vii; Lee, "Introduction: Interpreting Irish America," 21 (quotation).

6. Tóibín, "The Irish Famine," 22–23; Pim, *Conditions and Prospects,* 71–72.

7. Society of Friends, *Transactions of the Central Relief Committee,* 192.

8. Society of Friends, *Transactions of the Central Relief Committee,* 153–55.

9. Dufferin and Boyle, *Narrative of a Journey,* 6

10. O'Rourke, *History of the Great Irish Famine,* 272–73.

11. O'Donovan, *Brief Account of the Author's Interview,* 5. The themes of oppression and exile appeared repeatedly in Irish songs and poems. O'Donovan introduced his work with a typical beginning with "Irishmen are ev'ry where; Oppression made them roam." See also Miller, *Emigrants and Exiles,* 312.

12. Miller, *Emigrants and Exiles,* 283; Gray, *Famine, Land and Politics,* 96–102.

13. Trevelyan, *The Irish Crisis,* 8–9.

14. O'Rourke, *History of the Great Irish Famine,* 197 (quotation); Pim, *Condition and Prospects,* 76.

15. Tóibín, "The Irish Famine," 16.

16. Pim, *Conditions and Prospects,* 69–73; Society of Friends, *Transactions of the Central Relief Committee,* 181.

17. Dufferin and Boyle, *Narrative of a Journey,* 9–10.

18. Miller, *Emigrants and Exiles,* 318; Noel Ignatiev, *How the Irish Became White,* 117; Melton, "Michael J. Redding," 323.

19. "The Cake-Walk Homicide," *Baltimore Sun,* Nov. 19, 1875, p. 4; *Woods's Directory,* 1870, p. 381.

20. United States Census, 1880, Maryland, Baltimore City, Ward Twelve, ED 109.
21. Miller, *Emigrants and Exiles*, 290–91; O'Rourke, *History of the Great Irish Famine*, 418.
22. Brugger, *Maryland*, 4 and 55–56.
23. "Baltimore: Ancient and Modern," *Baltimore Sun*, Jan. 10, 1880, p. 5.
24. Brugger, *Maryland*, 56.
25. Spalding, *Premier See*, 5.
26. Miller, *Emigrants and Exiles*, 144.
27. Spalding, *Premier See*, 57.
28. Spalding, *Premier See*, 21.
29. Spalding, *Premier See*, 31–32.
30. Spalding, *Premier See*, 139.
31. Scharf, *History of Baltimore*, 668.
32. Rohr, "Charities and Charitable Institutions," 659.
33. "Irish Social and Benevolent Society," *Baltimore Sun*, Sept. 20, 1852, p. 2.
34. Society of Friends, *Transactions of the Central Relief Committee*, 232–33.
35. Society of Friends, *Transactions of the Central Relief Committee*, 341.
36. Scharf, *History of Baltimore*, 601; Spalding, *Premier See*, 139.
37. "Irish Social and Benevolent Society," *Baltimore Sun*, Sept. 20, 1852, p. 2.
38. Baker, *Ambivalent Americans*, 18; Spalding, *Premier See*, 133.
39. Baltimore Citizens, *Proceedings of the Great Meeting*, p. 4.
40. "Great Excitement," *Baltimore Sun*, Aug. 19, 1839, p. 2; "The Convent Case," *Baltimore Sun*, Aug. 23, 1839, p. 2.
41. Greenberg, "Mayhem in Mobtown," 166; Steiner, *Life of Henry Winter Davis*, 101; Schmeckebier, *History of the Know Nothing Party*, 52–53.
42. Malka, *Men of Mobtown*, 62–63.
43. Baker, *The Politics of Continuity*, xiv.
44. Towers, "Violence as a Tool," 15–16; Baker, *Ambivalent Americans*, 28–29.
45. Schmeckebier, *History of the Know Nothing Party*, 68.
46. Brugger, *Maryland*, 260; Schmeckebier, *History of Know Nothing Party*, 101–2.
47. Scharf, *History of Baltimore*, 787; "Mass Meeting of the American Party at Monument Square," *Baltimore Daily Exchange*, Oct. 28, 1859, p. 1.
48. Steiner, *Henry Winter Davis*, 101.
49. "City Affairs," *Baltimore American*, Oct. 28, 1859, p. 1.
50. Baker, *Politics of Continuity*, xiv.
51. "Serious Negro Riot," *Baltimore American*, Sept. 10, 1856, p. 1; "Violent Demonstration," *Baltimore Sun*, Sept. 10, 1856, p. 1.
52. United States Census, 1860, Maryland, Baltimore City, Ward Eight. Irish immigrant women, at least as compared to other European immigrant women, preferred domestic work, such as housecleaning or laundering, over other occupations. Diner, *Erin's Daughters*, 74.
53. United States Census, 1860, Maryland, Baltimore City, Ward Eight, p. 264.
54. United States Census, 1860, Maryland, Baltimore City, Ward Eight, p. 266.
55. United States Census, 1860, Maryland, Baltimore City, Ward Eight, pp. 263–64.
56. United States Census, 1860, Maryland, Baltimore City, Ward Two.
57. United States Census, 1880, Maryland, Baltimore City, Ward One, ED 11.
58. Brugger, *Maryland*, 263; Frey, *Reminiscences of Baltimore*, 96.
59. *Journal of the House of Delegates, 1858*, Document E, The Inaugural Address of Gov. Thomas H. Hicks, p. 4, accessible at *Arch. Md. Online*, 665:1456.

60. "Political Intelligence," *Baltimore American,* July 13, 1855, p. 1. The Maryland delegates, however, ultimately accepted the national platform. "Proceedings of the American State Convention," *Baltimore American,* July 19, 1855, p. 1.

61. Melton, "The Case of the Catholic Know-Nothings," 352.

62. Anbinder, "We Will Dirk Every Mother's Son," 107.

63. Towers, "Violence as a Tool," 16.

64. "The First Fruits," *Baltimore Sun,* Jan. 10, 1860, p. 2

65. "Letter from Annapolis," *Baltimore Sun,* Jan. 21, 1870, p. 4.

66. *Register of Corporation Officers, 1874,* p. 4; *Register of Corporation Officers, 1876,* p. 4; *Register of Corporation Officers, 1887,* p. 14.

67. "Homicide in Front of City Hall," *Baltimore Sun,* Sept. 15, 1877, p. 4; "The Freeze-Weidner Murder Trial," *Baltimore Sun,* Jan. 11, 1878, p. 4; "Acquittal of Freeze," *Baltimore Gazette,* Jan. 12, 1878; "Lawlessness in Baltimore," *Baltimore Sun,* May 12, 1879, p. 1; "Trial of Tom Freeze," *Baltimore Sun,* Feb. 16, 1897, p. 6.

68. "The Cake-Walk Homicide," *Baltimore Sun,* Nov. 20, 1875, p. 5.

69. "A Homicide in Northwest Baltimore," *Baltimore Sun,* Aug. 2, 1875, p. 1.

70. "The Cake-Walk Homicide," *Baltimore Sun,* Nov. 19, 1875, p. 4.

71. "Police Items," *Baltimore Sun,* Feb. 21, 1873, p. 1; *Woods's Directory,* 1873, pp. 392 and 382. The police magistrate's name is spelled Maddox in the *Sun,* but the Ward Three magistrate's name is spelled Maddux in the City Directory.

72. Baltimore City Jail Assault and Battery Docket, Jan. 2, 1875. MSA C2058-5.

73. "Proceedings of the Courts," *Baltimore Sun,* Feb. 15, 1875, p. 4. Judge Gilmor later presided in McDonald's trial for the killing of Daniel Brown.

74. "Homicide in Front of City Hall," *Baltimore Sun,* Sept. 15, 1877, p. 4.

75. "The Weidner Homicide," *Baltimore American,* Jan. 12, 1878, p. 4; "Acquittal of Freeze," *Baltimore Gazette,* Jan. 12, 1878, p. 4.

76. Baltimore newspapers as well as Baltimore courts commonly reported various spellings of subjects' names. Although Thomas Freeze was a well-known character on the streets of Baltimore, his name was sometimes spelled Frieze. See "The Weidner Homicide," *Baltimore American,* Jan. 11, 1878, p. 4, and "The Police Board," *Baltimore Sun,* June 2, 1897, p. 2. Variations in spellings in court records include, for example, spellings of the name of an important witness in the Daniel Brown case as Gressen in grand jury records, while the same man was identified as Gresson in Baltimore City Criminal Court trial dockets. *State v. Patrick McDonald,* no. 486, May Term 1875, folio 61, Baltimore City Criminal Court Grand Jury Docket, MSA, T494-22; *State of Maryland v. Patrick McDonald,* Oct. Term 1875, folio 29, Baltimore City Criminal Court Trial Docket, MSA C1849-63.

77. "The City Hall Homicide," *Baltimore Sun,* Sept. 15, 1877, p. 4, and Sept. 17, 1877, p. 4.

78. United States Census, 1880, Maryland, Baltimore City, Ward Twelve, ED 109, p. 3, sheet 92C and p. 33, sheet 107A; *Woods's Directory,* 1875, p. 385; *Woods's Directory,* 1877, p. 246; "The City Hall Homicide," *Baltimore Sun,* Sept. 17, 1877, p. 4.

79. Freeze's brushes with the law as a result of violent encounters spanned more than twenty years, beginning at least as early as 1874, when he appeared in court for assaulting a policeman. "Proceedings of the Courts," *Baltimore Sun,* Feb. 28, 1874, p. 5.

80. "To Lead Mayor's Fight," *Baltimore Sun,* Jan. 7, 1903, p. 12; "Mayor Mahool in Office," *Baltimore Sun,* May 22, 1907, p. 14.

81. "Homicide in Front of City Hall," *Baltimore Sun,* Sept. 18, 1877, p. 4; "Proceedings of the Court," *Baltimore Sun,* Jan. 24, 1877, p. 4.

82. "Lawlessness in Baltimore," *Baltimore Sun,* May 12, 1879, p. 1.

83. "Tom Freeze," *Baltimore Sun,* Nov. 6, 1895, p. 8; "Arrests by Police," *Baltimore American,* Nov. 4, 1896, 11.

84. "A 'Frost' for Freeze," *Baltimore Sun,* Nov. 4, 1896, p. 8.

85. "Trial of Tom Freeze," *Baltimore Sun,* Feb. 16, 1897, p. 6.

86. Miller, *Emigrants and Exiles,* 318; Roediger, *Wages of Whiteness,* 134.

3. *Homicide, Coroners, and Criminal Justice*

1. Folsom, *Our Police,* 379.

2. "A Police Murder," *Baltimore American,* Aug. 2, 1875, p. 4.

3. "Funerals Yesterday," *Baltimore Sun,* Nov. 24, 1880, p. 4. Allen Martin, grocer, is listed with an address on Tyson Street in *Matchett's Directory, 1847–1848,* p. 213; United States Census, 1870, Maryland, Baltimore Ward Eleven, p. 45; *Woods's Directory,* 1875, p. 372. Newspaper accounts of Daniel Brown's death report Allen Martin's residence as 190 Park Avenue.

4. *Woods's Directory,* 1875, pp. 66, 300.

5. United States Census, 1870, Maryland, Baltimore Ward Eleven, 295–99.

6. Folsom, *Our Police,* 380–82; "The New Northwest Police Station," *Baltimore Sun,* Apr. 10, 1874, p. 4.

7. Gilmor, *Four Years in the Saddle,* xi.

8. Folson, *Our Police,* 382.

9. "The Cake-Walk Homicide," *Baltimore Sun,* Nov. 18, 1875, p. 4.

10. "The McDonald Murder Trial," *Baltimore American,* Nov. 17, 1875, p. 4; "The Cake-Walk Homicide," *Baltimore Sun,* Nov. 17, 1875, p. 4; "Court Proceedings," *Baltimore Gazette,* Nov. 17, 1875, p. 4.

11. "A Homicide in Northwest Baltimore," *Baltimore Sun,* Aug. 2, 1875, p. 1. In *Woods's Directory,* 1874, p. 381, McDonald was listed as a laborer.

12. Martin was a flour and feed merchant who had lived in Baltimore for thirty-three years; he owned real estate estimated at $10,000 and personal property valued at $2,000. United States Census, 1870, Maryland, Baltimore City, Ward Eleven, p. 45; *Woods's Directory,* 1875, pp. 372 and 808. The Browns had rented the house owned by Martin for at least two years. *Woods's Directory,* 1873, pp. 668 and 670.

13. The accounts of the killing of Daniel Brown are based on testimony provided at the coroner's inquest as reported in "A Homicide in Northwest Baltimore," *Baltimore Sun,* Aug. 2, 1875, p. 1, and "A Police Murder," *Baltimore American,* Aug. 2, 1875, p. 4.

14. "A Homicide in Northwest Baltimore," *Baltimore Sun,* Aug. 2, 1875, p. 1 (quotation); "A Police Murder," *Baltimore American,* Aug. 2, 1875, p. 4.

15. The Maryland Constitution of 1867 provided for election of a state's attorney in each county and in Baltimore city every four years. Art. V, § 7.

16. Browne, *Proceedings and Acts,* 55, accessible at *Arch. Md. Online,* 1:55.

17. Burney, *Bodies of Evidence,* 4.

18. *Woods's Directory,* 1875, p. 475; United States Census, 1870, Baltimore City, Ward Eleven, 184.

19. Scharf, *History of Baltimore,* 131–32; *Woods's Directory,* 1875, p. 546; United States Census, 1870, Baltimore City, Ward Twelve, 21. Thomas Shryock's father, H. S. Shryock, apparently one of the founders of the firm, held real estate valued at $200,000 and personal property valued at $25,000.

20. United States Census, 1870, Baltimore City, Ward Thirteen, 234.

21. *Woods's Directory,* 1875, pp. 42, 94, 445, and 564.

22. *Woods's Directory,* 1874 and 1875.

23. Dr. Gamble's name was reported as "Gambrill" in the *Baltimore Sun,* Aug. 2, 1875, p. 1, but based on city directory listings, the correct spelling was Gamble. *Woods's Directory,* 1875, p. 846.

24. The accounts of the testimony given at the coroner's inquest are based on detailed reports in "Homicide in Northwest Baltimore," *Baltimore Sun,* Aug. 2, 1875, p. 1; and "A Police Murder," *Baltimore American,* Aug. 2, 1875, p. 4.

25. The blanks are as reported in the newspaper accounts.

26. "Colored People's Mass Meeting," *Baltimore Sun,* Aug. 6, 1875, p. 1.

27. "Letters from the People," *Baltimore American,* Aug. 6, 1875, p. 2.

28. African Methodist Episcopal Church, *Doctrines and Discipline,* 60.

29. Jamison, *Hoedowns, Reels, and Frolics,* 102–3.

30. Long, *Pictures of Slavery,* 18.

31. Woodson, *The Rural Negro,* 140. As late as the 1890s, W. E. B. Du Bois reported many older African Americans in Philadelphia continued to object to dancing, although younger people no longer accepted the prohibition. Du Bois, *Philadelphia Negro,* 320.

32. "Homicide in Northwest Baltimore," *Baltimore Sun,* Aug. 2, 1875, p. 1.

33. Levine, *Black Culture and Black Consciousness,* 38; Jamison, *Hoedowns, Reels, and Frolics,* 106; Lyell, *Second Visit to the United States,* 1:269–70.

34. Emery, *Black Dance,* 210; Malone, *Steppin' on the Blues,* 71.

35. Works Projects Administration, *The Negro in Virginia,* 88–89.

36. Stroyer, *My Life in the South,* 47–48.

37. Levine, *Black Culture,* 16–17; Jamison, *Hoedowns, Reels, and Frolics,* 123–24.

38. Long, *Pictures of Slavery,* 17–21.

39. Du Bois, *Philadelphia Negro,* 320.

40. Du Bois, *Philadelphia Negro,* 320.

41. Long, *Pictures of Slavery,* 13–22.

42. United States Census, 1860, Slave Schedules, Maryland, Prince Georges County, District 7, Collington, 48–50; United States Census, 1860, Free Inhabitants, Maryland, Prince Georges County, District 7, Collington, 119–120; United States Census, 1870, Maryland, Prince Georges County, Queen Anne District, 23; *Woods's Directory,* 1875, p. 439; "Coroner for the Western District," *Baltimore Sun,* Mar. 11, 1875.

43. Scharf, *History of Baltimore,* 131–32.

44. "The Putzel Police Bill," *Baltimore Sun,* Feb. 3, 1898, p. 8; "Democrats for Shryock," *Baltimore Sun,* Feb. 4, 1898, p. 8.

45. "The Governorship of Maryland," *Baltimore Afro-American Ledger,* May 30, 1903, p. 4.

46. The juror's name was reported as Alexander Butcher. The city directory for 1875 lists one man named Alexander Butcher, a confectioner with a store at 189 Madison Avenue. *Woods's Directory,* 1875, p. 94.

47. "Obituary," *Baltimore Sun,* Oct. 6, 1884, p. 4; United States Census, 1860, Maryland, Baltimore, Ward Eight, 858; United States Census, 1870, Maryland, Baltimore, Ward Twelve, 21.

48. "A Police Murder," *Baltimore American,* Aug. 2, 1875, p. 4.

49. "A Police Murder," *Baltimore American,* Aug. 2, 1875, p. 4.

50. For background on the medieval origins of the English institution colonists transplanted in Maryland, see Gross, *Select Cases from the Coroners' Rolls,* xx; Hunnisett, *Medieval Coroner,* 1–2.

51. Browne, *Proceedings and Acts,* 55, accessible at *Arch. Md. Online,* 1:55.

52. Pollock and Maitland, *History of English Law,* 2:553; Hunnisett, *Medieval Coroner,* 1.
53. Brock and Crawford, "Forensic Medicine in Early Colonial Maryland," 25.
54. Browne, *Proceedings and Acts,* 55 and 59, accessible at *Arch. Md. Online,* 1:55 and 1:59.
55. Crocker, *Duties of Sheriffs, Coroners, and Constables.*
56. Crocker, *Duties of Sheriffs, Coroners, and Constables,* 414–15.
57. Some nineteenth-century Baltimore city coroners' inquest records have been preserved, but none in the city archives files are dated after 1867, apparently because after that date coroners received salaries rather than fees for each inquest. Coroners' Inquests, BCA, BRG19-1-29-3.
58. MacDonald and Murphy, *Sleepless Souls,* 114.
59. "The Uses of Inquests," 78–79.
60. Cawthon, "New Life for the Deodand," 137–47.
61. Burney, *Bodies of Evidence,* 5.
62. Coroners' Reports, BCA, BRG19-1-Box 28.
63. "Terrible Case of Ill-Treatment and Death of Wife," *Baltimore Sun,* Dec. 16, 1870, p. 1.
64. "Terrible Tragedy in East Baltimore," *Baltimore Sun,* May 6, 1872, p. 1.
65. "Tragedy in the Penitentiary," *Baltimore Sun,* Mar. 2, 1882, p. 1.
66. "Oldfield Exonerated," *Baltimore Sun,* Aug. 5, 1897, p. 8.
67. "Killed by His Keeper," *Baltimore Sun,* Nov. 9, 1896, p. 10.
68. "Exonerated from Blame," *Baltimore American,* Apr. 21, 1898, p. 12; "Leuba Shot in Self-Defense," *Baltimore Sun,* Feb. 2, 1901, p. 7; "Patrolman Exonerated," *Baltimore Sun,* July 23, 1907, p. 8; "Keeper Murphy Released," *Baltimore Sun,* Dec. 12, 1909, p. 9; "Patrolman Exonerated," *Baltimore Sun,* Sept. 7, 1910.
69. "The South Baltimore Homicide," *Baltimore American,* Sept. 26, 1867, p. 4; Shufelt, "Elusive Justice in Baltimore," 780–81.
70. "Local Matter: Homicide on Federal Hill," *Baltimore Sun,* Sept. 23, 1867, p. 4; "The Federal Hill Homicide," *Baltimore Sun,* Sept. 26, 1867, p. 1; "A Black Woman Killed by a Policeman," *Baltimore American,* Sept. 23, 1867, p. 4; "The South Baltimore Homicide," *Baltimore American,* Sept. 26, 1867, p. 4.
71. Coroners' Inquests, BCA, BRG-19-1-29-3. Gotlieb Frey's first name is spelled Gotleib in the 1850 census reports and Gottleib or Gotleib in some news reports, but Gotlieb is the spelling used by Gotlieb's brother Jacob.
72. Jacob Frey assumed the duties of captain of Baltimore's southern police district in April 1867. Folsom, *Our Police,* 151. Captain Jacob Frey was eight years older than Gotlieb. Jacob and Gotlieb were the children of Gotlieb Frey and Mary Ann Frey. Frey, *Reminiscences,* 47; United States Census, 1850, Maryland, Schedule L, Free Inhabitants, Baltimore Ward Five; "Obituary: Gottleib Frey," *Baltimore Sun,* Apr. 3, 1900, p. 7.
73. Malka, *Men of Mobtown,* 234.
74. "John Carter May Die," *Baltimore Sun,* Apr. 19, 1898, p. 12; "John Carter Is Dead," *Baltimore Sun,* Apr. 20, 1898, p. 7; "Local Items," *Baltimore Afro-American Ledger,* Apr. 23, 1898, p. 1; "Exonerated from Blame," *Baltimore American,* Apr. 21, 1898, p. 12; Shufelt, "Elusive Justice in Baltimore," 781. A few weeks before John Carter's death, Justice Wood had received a threatening letter, allegedly from a gang of black men, after Wood had sentenced an African American defendant to four months in jail for "insulting a lady on the street." "Justice Wood Threatened," *Baltimore Sun,* Mar. 29, 1898, p. 7.
75. "Exonerated from Blame," *Baltimore American,* Apr. 21, 1898, p. 12.
76. Malka, *Men of Mobtown,* 14–15.
77. Monkkonen, *Police in Urban America* (shift to bureaucracies); Harring, *Policing a*

Class Society (capitalist control of labor); Lane, *Violent Death in the City* (loss of personal control).

78. Walker, *Critical History of Police Reform;* Hahn and Jeffries, *Urban America and Its Police;* Holmes and Smith, *Race and Police Brutality.*

79. "For the American," *Baltimore American,* Nov. 4, 1852, p. 2.

80. "For the American," *Baltimore American,* Nov. 4, 1852, p. 2.

81. Observers of slavery and its aftermath from W. E. B. Du Bois and C. Vann Woodward to Eugene Genovese and Eric Foner have noted the role of paternalism in relations between black servants and white employers. Du Bois, *Souls of Black Folk,* 183; Woodward, *Strange Career of Jim Crow,* 12; Genovese, *Roll, Jordan, Roll,* 3–7 and 135; Foner, *Reconstruction,* 130–31.

82. Douglass, *My Bondage and My Freedom; State of Maryland vs. Patrick McDonald,* Oct. Term 1875, folio 29, Baltimore City Criminal Court Trial Docket, MSA, C1849-63.

83. *State v. Patrick McDonald,* no. 486, May Term 1875, folio 61, Baltimore City Criminal Court Grand Jury Docket, MSA T494-22; *State of Maryland v. Patrick McDonald,* Oct. Term 1875, folio 29, Baltimore City Criminal Court Trial Docket, MSA C1849-63.

4. *Black and White Views of Law Enforcement*

1. "A Homicide in Northwest Baltimore," *Baltimore Sun,* Aug. 2, 1875, p. 1.

2. "A Police Murder," *Baltimore American,* Aug. 2, 1875, p. 4.

3. "The Police Murder: Opinions about the Outrage," *Baltimore American,* Aug. 3, 1875, p. 4.

4. "The Use of Firearms by the Police," *Baltimore Sun,* Aug. 3, 1875, p. 2.

5. "The Police Murder: Opinions about the Outrage," *Baltimore American,* Aug. 2, 1875, p. 4, and Aug. 3, 1875, p. 4.

6. "The Killing of Daniel Brown," *Baltimore Daily Gazette,* Aug. 6, 1875, p. 1.

7. "Mordwaffen in den Händen öffentlicher Beamter" [Deadly weapons in the hands of officials], *Baltimore Deutsche Correspondent,* Aug. 4, 1875, p. 2.

8. "The Locust Point Homicide," *Baltimore Sun,* Aug. 12, 1873, p. 1; *Baltimore Deutsche Correspondent,* Aug. 12, 1875, p. 2.

9. "Der Mord auf Locust Point" [The murder at Locust Point], *Baltimore Deutsche Correspondent,* Aug. 14, 1873, p. 2.

10. "Tages Neuigkeit" [The day's news], *Baltimore Deutsche Correspondent,* Aug. 12, 1873, p. 1.

11. "Mordwaffen in den Händen öffentlicher Beamter" [Deadly weapons in the hands of officials], *Baltimore Deutsche Correspondent,* Aug. 4, 1875, p. 2.

12. "The Use of Arms by the Police," *Baltimore Sun,* Aug. 3, 1875, p. 2.

13. "The Use of Arms by the Police," *Baltimore Sun,* Aug. 3, 1875, p. 2.

14. "A Lawless Proceeding," *Baltimore American,* Aug. 4, 1875, p. 2.

15. "A Lawless Proceeding," *Baltimore American,* Aug. 4, 1875, p. 2.

16. "A Lawless Proceeding," *Baltimore American,* Aug. 4, 1875, p. 2.

17. "The Police Murder: Opinions about the Outrage," *Baltimore American,* Aug. 3, 1875, p. 4.

18. "A Lawless Proceeding," *Baltimore American,* Aug. 4, 1875, p. 2.

19. "The Colored People's Meeting," *Baltimore Sun,* Aug. 7, 1875, p. 2.

20. "The Colored People's Meeting," *Baltimore Sun,* Aug. 7, 1875, p. 2.

21. "The Police Murder: Opinions about the Outrage," *Baltimore American,* Aug. 3, 1875, p. 4.

22. "Colored People's Mass Meeting," *Baltimore Sun,* Aug. 6, 1875, p. 1.

23. "The Killing of Daniel Brown," *Baltimore Daily Gazette,* Aug. 6, 1875, p. 1.

24. Brown, *Road to Jim Crow,* 97–98.

25. "Colored People's Mass Meeting," *Baltimore Sun,* Aug. 6, 1875, p. 1.

26. "Colored People's Mass Meeting," *Baltimore Sun,* Aug. 6, 1875, p. 1.

27. "Colored People's Mass Meeting," *Baltimore Sun,* Aug. 6, 1875, p. 1.

28. The magistrates in the police stations had authority to order arrested persons to be held or released on bail to await action in the Baltimore City Criminal Court. They also had authority to issue warrants and, in minor cases, to order payment of fines or sentence offenders to terms in the city jail. Latrobe, *Justices' Practice under the Law of Maryland.*

29. All quotations are from "The Brown Homicide," *Baltimore American,* Aug. 6, 1875, p. 4; "Colored People's Mass Meeting," *Baltimore Sun,* Aug. 6, 1875, p. 1.

30. Baltimore Police Department, Annual Reports, 1874 and 1875, BCA, BMS33-4-1-10.

31. Lane, *Roots of Violence in Black Philadelphia,* 87, contends that there was little or no bias against blacks in Philadelphia's criminal courts. Probably, however, the criminal court trial records do not reflect the experiences of most blacks, whether in Baltimore or Philadelphia.

32. In a sampling of cases brought before Baltimore magistrates from 1873 to 1875, forty-one African Americans were arrested for assaulting whites and eighteen whites were arrested for assaulting blacks. Of the forty-one black arrestees, twenty-two were released on bail, three had their charges dismissed, and sixteen were held in jail. Of the eighteen white arrestees, twelve were released on bail, five had their cases dismissed, and one was held in jail. Baltimore City Police, Eastern Docket Sept. 1873 to Apr. 1874, MSA C2111-12 and Consolidated Dockets, Jan. 1875 to Dec. 1875, MSA C3065-1.

33. The restriction on African American testimony against whites was nullified in Art. III, § 53 of the Maryland Constitution of 1867. Under the pre-1867 statute, African Americans could not provide evidence "where any white person is concerned," but African Americans could testify "for or against any negro or mulatto, slave or free." Scott and M'Cullough, *Maryland Code,* Art. 37, §§ 1–3, accessible at *Arch. Md. Online,* 145:275.

34. O. Howard, *Autobiography,* 2:285.

35. "Local Matters," *Baltimore Sun,* July 9, 1873, p. 1.

36. "An Examination and an Example Needed," *Baltimore American,* July 9, 1873, p. 1.

37. "Are We Barbarians?" *Baltimore American,* July 10, 1873, p. 2.

38. "The Rowdy Attack on the Colored Sunday School—Investigation by the Police," *Baltimore Sun,* July 10, 1873, p. 1; "The Late Riotous Assault—the Investigation by the Police Board," *Baltimore Sun,* July 11, 1873, p. 1.

39. "The Police Investigation," *Baltimore Sun,* July 14, 1873, p. 1.

40. "The Exeter Street Riot," *Baltimore American,* Oct. 30, 1873, p. 2.

41. "The Exeter Street Riot," *Baltimore American,* Oct. 30, 1873, p. 2.

42. "Proceedings of the Court," *Baltimore Sun,* Jan. 6, 1874, p. 3. It was noted in the *Baltimore American* that an African American man, Dennis Johnson, was arrested, but never indicted. Furthermore, according to the *American*'s account, Police Marshal John Gray personally refunded a five-dollar fee Johnson had paid to a station house magistrate to be set free without spending the night in jail. The five-dollar payment, according to the *American,* was not bail or any other payment justified by law. Johnson had been given no hearing before the magistrate, the magistrate had gone home for the evening, and the

money had been sent by messenger to the magistrate's residence to obtain approval of Johnson's release. "Wanted—an Explanation," *Baltimore American,* July 15, 1873, p. 2.

43. Crenson, *Baltimore,* 278–79; Halpin, *Brotherhood of Liberty,* 21–22; Brugger, *Maryland,* 310.

44. "The Civil Rights Law," *Baltimore Sun,* Mar. 4, 1875, p. 1.

45. "The Colored People and the Civil Rights Bill," *Baltimore American,* Mar. 5, 1875, p. 4; "Working of Civil Rights," *Baltimore Sunday Telegram,* Mar. 6, 1875, p. 1. According to the *American*'s account of the incident, two African American men tested the Civil Rights Law. According to the *Sunday Telegram,* the incident involved three African American men. The *American*'s account was unsympathetic to the black men, but the *Telegram*'s version was viciously racist, referring to the incident as a "got-up job" and describing the black men as "worthless, impertinent negroes."

46. "A Colored Man Shot by the Police," *Baltimore Sun,* July 12, 1875, p. 4.

5. Police and Violence in a Divided City

1. "Highly Important News," *Baltimore Sun,* May 26, 1862, p. 2; "Disturbances at Baltimore Yesterday, *Washington Evening Star,* May 26, 1862, p. 2.

2. "Local Matters," *Baltimore Sun,* June 6, 1862, p. 1.

3. Foner, *Reconstruction,* 86; Alexander, "Persistent Whiggery," 305–29.

4. Stampp, *Era of Reconstruction,* 297–98.

5. Higham, *Strangers in the Land,* 13. See also Anbinder, *Nativism and Slavery,* 270–71; Dinnerstein, Nichols, and Reimers, *Natives and Strangers,* 118.

6. Lane, *Roots of Violence in Black Philadelphia,* 9.

7. The demise of the Whig Party scrambled party alliances. The onset of the war added further complications. The term *conservative Democrats* refers to those in the Democratic Party who looked favorably on the culture and politics of the Southern slave states, especially as to white supremacy and states' rights. A faction of Democrats, sometimes referred to as independent Democrats, was less hostile to the Union. During the Civil War and afterward, independent Democrats sometimes aligned with opponents of the conservative Democrats. The opponents of the conservative Democrats were generally Unionists during the war and reform groups in the postwar period. Independent Democrats and reform groups sometimes cooperated with the Republican Party, but Republicans remained a minority party at most times in this era. The faction of Democrats identified as conservative Democrats dominated Maryland politics in the second half of the nineteenth century.

8. *Laws of Maryland Since 1763,* ch. 69, An ACT for the establishment of a night watch, and the erection of lamps, in Baltimore-Town, in Baltimore county, accessible at *Arch. Md. Online,* 203:419.

9. Folsom, *Our Police,* 20.

10. Scharf, *Chronicles of Baltimore,* 209.

11. Malka, *Men of Mobtown,* 30 and 46–47.

12. Phillips, *Freedom's Port,* 13–15 and 29.

13. In 1850, of 28,388 black residents, 25,442 were free and 2,946 were held as slaves. United States Census Office, *Statistical View of the United States,* 1854, p. 397.

14. Malka, *Men of Mobtown,* 23.

15. Fields, *Slavery and Freedom,* 43–45.

16. Rockman, *Scraping By,* 42.

17. "Ruffianism and Crime," *Baltimore Sun,* Nov. 6, 1852, p. 1.

18. Thacher, "Olmsted's Police," 578–79. A growing consensus among social scientists suggests that crime rates in the entire Western world fell throughout the nineteenth century. Tonry, "Why Crime Rates Are Falling," 2. Whether or not the generalization applies to Baltimore, however, matters less than the fact that Baltimoreans perceived an increase in lawlessness.

19. Malka, *Men of Mobtown,* 24.

20. Eric Monkkonen contends that the response to rioting cannot adequately explain the creation of uniformed police forces in the nineteenth century. Monkkonen, *Police in Urban America,* 51. Other studies, however, emphasize riots as a precipitating factor. See, for example, Hahn and Jeffries, *Urban America and Its Police,* 5, and Mitrani, *Rise of the Chicago Police Department,* 14–15.

21. Folsom, *Our Police,* 22–23.

22. Malka, *Men of Mobtown,* 67–68.

23. Maryland Constitution of 1776, Declaration of Rights, Art. 26; Maryland Constitution of 1851, Declaration of Rights, Art. 26.

24. Malka, *Men of Mobtown,* 38. It is noteworthy that reforms of this era included measures to provide better lighting along city streets. See, for example, An Ordinance to extend the limits of direct taxation, §§ 2 and 4, *Ordinances of the Mayor and City Council of Baltimore . . . 1849,* pp. 8–9.

25. Brugger, *Maryland,* 178.

26. Shalhope, *Baltimore Bank Riot,* 1.

27. Harris, *Two Against Lincoln,* 10; Malka, "The Open Violence of Desperate Men," 199–201.

28. Walker, *Critical History of Police Reform,* 5.

29. The homicide rate in New Orleans in the 1850s was roughly ten times the rate in Philadelphia and roughly five times the rate in Boston. Rousey, *Policing the Southern City,* 85.

30. Rousey, *Policing the Southern City,* 85.

31. "Local Matters: And Yet Another," *Baltimore Sun,* Mar. 1, 1850, p. 2.

32. "Local Matters," *Baltimore Sun,* Jan. 2, 1852, p. 2.

33. Monkkonen, *Police in Urban America;* Miller, *Cops and Bobbies;* Richardson, *The New York Police;* Lane, *Policing the City;* Steinberg, *Transformation of Criminal Justice in Philadelphia;* Schneider, *Detroit and the Problem of Order;* Mitrani, *Rise of the Chicago Police Department;* Hindus, *Prison and Plantation;* Rousey, *Policing the Southern City.*

34. As discussions of police reform went on, Baltimore reformers actively sought information from elsewhere in the United States and from Europe. In covering the reform debates, the *Baltimore Sun,* for example, referred to recent lectures about the reorganization of London's police force. "London and Baltimore Police," *Baltimore Sun,* Mar. 31, 1853, p. 2.

35. *Journal of Proceedings, Second Branch of the City Council,* 286–88; Shufelt, "Elusive Justice in Baltimore," 797–99.

36. *Journal of Proceedings, Second Branch of the City Council,* 287.

37. An Act to provide for better security of life and property in the City of Baltimore, by increasing and arming the police thereof, *Laws Made and Passed by the General Assembly, 1853,* ch. 46, p. 43, accessible at *Arch Md. Online,* 403:43.

38. Scharf, *History of Baltimore,* 196–98; An ordinance to establish a Police for the City of Baltimore, *Ordinances of the Mayor and City Council of Baltimore,* 1858, p. 135.

39. "Increased Armed Force and Labor in Jail," *Baltimore Sun,* Mar. 22, 1853, p. 1.

40. "The New Police Bill," *Baltimore Sun*, Feb. 14, 1855, p. 2.

41. An Act for the better security of life and property in the City of Baltimore, by increasing and arming the police thereof, §§ 1 and 2. *Laws Made and Passed by the General Assembly of Maryland, 1853*, p. 43, accessible at *Arch. Md. Online*, 403:43 (emphasis added).

42. An ordinance to establish a Police for the City of Baltimore, § 14, *Ordinances of the Mayor and City Council of Baltimore*, 1858, pp. 140–41.

43. Adam Malka, in *Men of Mobtown*, 67, correctly points out that the wording of the ordinance reflected the city council's intention to limit policemen's use of revolvers. The point here is that there was a counterbalancing concern about the prevalence of weapons already on the streets. In any case, there is no question that by the time Officer McDonald killed Daniel Brown, patrolmen routinely carried revolvers.

44. "Burglary and Arrest," *Baltimore Sun*, Jan. 9, 1857, p. 1.

45. "The Execution," *Baltimore Sun*, Apr. 9, 1859, p. 1.

46. "The Assassination of Officer Rigdon," *Baltimore Sun*, Nov. 6, 1858, p. 2.

47. "The Eighth Ward Murder and Riot Cases," *Baltimore Sun*, Feb. 4, 1859, p. 1.

48. "The South Baltimore Homicide," *Baltimore American*, Sept. 26, 1867, p. 4.

49. "The Veto of the Police Bill, *Baltimore Sun*, July 3, 1853, p. 2; "The Veto of the Police Bill, *Baltimore American*, July 14, 1853, p. 2; "Reorganization of the Police," *Baltimore Sun*, Dec. 12, 1854, p. 2.

50. Argersinger, "From Party Tickets to Secret Ballots," 399; Richter, "Transnational Reform and Democracy," 157–61.

51. Walker, *Critical History of Police Reform*, 3; Anbinder, *Nativism and Slavery*, 145.

52. Maryland General Assembly Report on the Baltimore Board of Police Commissioners 1860, PAM 4108, MHS (hereinafter cited as Md. Gen. Assembly, PAM 4108); Scharf, *History of Baltimore*, 196–97; Towers, "Violence as a Tool of Party Dominance," 15–16; Baker, *Ambivalent Americans*, 28–29; Melton, "The Lost Lives of George Konig," 340–44.

53. Folsom, *Our Police*, 29.

54. Baker, *Politics of Continuity*, 5.

55. Brugger, *Maryland*, 263–64.

56. Steiner, *Citizenship and Suffrage*, 39; "The Election," *Baltimore Sun*, Nov. 5, 1857, p. 1.

57. "City Intelligence: The Mockery of Yesterday," *Baltimore Daily Exchange*, Oct. 14, 1858, p. 1.

58. "The Mayoralty Election," *Baltimore American*, Oct. 14, 1858, p. 1.

59. Towers, "Violence as a Tool of Party Dominance," 15–16.

60. "The Election Today," *Washington Evening Star*, June 1, 1857, p. 3.

61. "The Latest Intelligence," *New York Daily Times*, June 2, 1857, 1.

62. Schmeckebier, *History of the Know Nothing Party*, 100.

63. "Town Meeting: Friends of Law and Order Irrespective of Party," *Baltimore American*, Sept. 9, 1859, p. 1; "Great Gathering of the People," *Baltimore Sun*, Sept. 9, 1859, p. 1.

64. Baker, *Politics of Continuity*, 26–27. The reformers contended they were not a party, but rather the "City Reform Association."

65. "Local Matters: The Election Yesterday," *Baltimore Sun*, Oct. 13, 1859, p. 1.

66. "The Municipal Election," *Baltimore Sun*, Oct. 12, 1859, p. 2.

67. "The Election Yesterday: Scenes at the Polls," *Baltimore American*, Oct. 13, 1859, p. 1; "City Intelligence: The Election Yesterday," *Baltimore Daily Exchange*, Oct. 13, 1859, p. 1.

68. "City Intelligence: The Election Yesterday," *Baltimore Daily Exchange*, Oct. 13, 1859, p. 1. Apparently, the "aged and respected citizen" was the "old citizen" identified in the *Sun* as a citizen whose attackers were not arrested.

69. "The Election Yesterday," *Baltimore American,* Oct. 13, 1859, p. 2.

70. "Reform Town Meeting," *Baltimore American,* Nov. 1, 1859, p. 1; "Large Gathering of the People," *Baltimore Sun,* Nov. 1, 1859, p. 1.

71. Baker, *Ambivalent Americans,* 29. In the Reconstruction era, Davis gained prominence as a Radical Republican.

72. "Baltimore," *Baltimore Daily Exchange,* Oct. 19, 1859, p. 2.

73. *Baltimore Sun,* Nov. 1, 1859, p. 1.

74. Frey, *Reminiscences,* 99.

75. "Baltimore," *Baltimore Daily Exchange,* Oct. 28, 1859, p. 2.

76. "City Affairs: Mass Meeting of the American Party," *Baltimore American,* Oct. 28, 1859, p. 1.

77. "Mass Meeting of the American Party at Monument Square," *Baltimore Daily Exchange,* Oct. 28, 1859, p. 1; "Baltimore," *Baltimore Daily Exchange,* Oct. 28, 1859, p. 2.

78. "Two Elections," *Baltimore American,* Nov. 9, 1859, p. 2.

79. "The Election Yesterday," *Baltimore American,* Nov. 3, 1859, p. 1.

80. "The Fare of Yesterday," *Baltimore Daily Exchange,"* Nov. 3, 1859, p. 1.

81. "Local Matters: Outrages at the Polls," *Baltimore Sun,* Nov. 3, 1859, p. 1.

82. Maryland House of Delegates, *Baltimore City Election: Papers in the Contested Election Case from Baltimore City,* 49 and 93, accessible at *Arch. Md. Online,* 849:1213, 1257.

83. Schmeckebier, *History of the Know Nothing Party,* 103.

84. Scharf, *History of Baltimore,* 126.

85. "The First Fruits," *Baltimore Sun,* Jan. 10, 1860, p. 2.

86. Scott and M'Cullough, *Maryland Code,* Art. 4, §§ 806–22, pp. 312–22, accessible at *Arch. Md. Online,* 145:2:312–22.

87. Frey, *Reminiscences,* 99.

88. Steiner, *Henry Winter Davis,* 147.

89. Scott and M'Cullough, *Maryland Code,* Art. 4, § 809, p. 315, accessible at *Arch. Md. Online,* 145:2:315. The term *black Republican,* although undoubtedly intended to promote a racist ideology, did not refer only to African Americans, but also to white Republicans who favored abolition. The "Helper Book" referred to Hinton R. Helper's *The Impending Crisis of the South,* in which Helper, a native North Carolinian, argued that as a result of slavery, the South remained backward in comparison to the North, and therefore abolition was the correct path.

90. *Mayor and City Council of Baltimore v. Board of Police of the City of Baltimore.*

91. "City Intelligence: Disbanding of the Old Police Force," *Baltimore Daily Exchange,* May 8, 1860, p. 1.

92. "The New and the Old Police," *Baltimore Sun,* May 8, 1860, p. 1.

93. "Appointments by the Police Commissioners," *Baltimore Daily Exchange,* May 7, 1860, p. 1.

94. Baltimore Police Department, Annual Reports, 1861, p. 19. BCA, BMS33-4-1.

95. Scharf, *History of Baltimore,* 788.

96. Brown, *Baltimore and the Nineteenth of April,* 11.

97. "War in Baltimore," *Baltimore American,* Apr. 20, 1861, p. 1.

98. Brown, *Baltimore and the Nineteenth of April,* 53.

99. Crenson, *Baltimore,* 242.

100. Maryland House of Delegates, *Message of the Governor to the General Assembly in Extra Session 1861,* p. 6, accessible at *Arch. Md. Online,* 758:6.

101. Mitchell, "Maryland's Presidential Election of 1860," 323.

102. Brugger, *Maryland,* 278; Crenson, *Baltimore,* 244.

103. Crenson, *Baltimore,* 247.

104. "Military Rule in Baltimore," *Baltimore Sun,* June 28, 1861, p. 1.

105. Crenson, *Baltimore,* 249.

106. F. K. Howard, *Fourteen Months in American Bastilles,* 9.

107. Brown, *Baltimore and the Nineteenth of April,* 102–3.

108. F. K. Howard, *Fourteen Months in American Bastilles,* 8.

109. Gilmor, *Four Years in the Saddle,* 57; "Capture of the Guerilla Harry Gilmor," *Baltimore Sun,* Feb. 9, 1865, p. 1; Goldsborough, *Maryland Line in the Confederate Army,* 245.

110. "Attorney General Randall's Opinion on the Registry Law," *Baltimore American,* Oct. 9, 1866, p. 1; "The Registry Law and the Municipal Election," *Baltimore Sun,* Oct. 9, 1866, p. 2; "Reverdy Johnson and His Opinion Again," *Baltimore American,* Oct. 10, 1866, p. 1; Brugger, *Maryland,* 306.

111. "City Affairs: Meeting of Election Judges," *Baltimore American,* Oct. 10, 1866, p. 4.

112. "Local Matter," *Baltimore Sun,* Oct. 11, 1866, p. 1.

113. Maryland House of Delegates, *Message of Governor Swann . . . 1867,* p. 9, accessible at *Arch. Md. Online,* 133:3083.

114. Schmeckebier, *History of the Know Nothing Party,* 112; Scharf, *History of Baltimore,* 126.

115. "Opinion of the Hon. Reverdy Johnson," *Baltimore Sun,* Oct. 22, 1866, p. 4.

116. "The Baltimore Police Commissioners," *Baltimore Sun,* Nov. 2, 1866, p. 1. The responsibilities of the police commissioners in the elections included the appointment of 240 election judges, 160 clerks, and 400 special policemen. *Record of the Proceedings of the Investigation before His Excellency Thomas Swann,* iii.

117. *Record of the Proceedings of the Investigation before His Excellency Thomas Swann,* iii–iv.

118. "Affidavit of Thomas W. Bobart," *Record of the Proceedings of the Investigation before His Excellency Thomas Swann,* xxix.

119. "Affidavit of Joseph Mace," *Record of the Proceedings of the Investigation before His Excellency Thomas Swann,* xxxi–xxxii.

120. "Affidavit of John Thomas McKeon," *Record of the Proceedings of the Investigation before His Excellency Thomas Swann,* xlv.

121. "Affidavit of John E. Orem," *Record of the Proceedings of the Investigation before His Excellency Thomas Swann,* lvii.

122. "The News," *Baltimore American,* Nov. 1, 1866, p. 1.

123. Bobart was arrested for assaulting William Brennan in 1866. "Local Matters: Assaults," *Baltimore Sun,* Oct. 2, 1866, p. 1. In Baltimore City Criminal Court in 1868 he faced charges of assaulting F. W. Dalton; the charges were compromised on payment of costs. "Proceedings of the Courts," *Baltimore Sun,* Apr. 13, 1868, p. 4. In 1873 Bobart was fined $200 for assaulting Charles O'Neill. "Proceedings of the Courts," *Baltimore Sun,* Feb. 15, 1873, p. 1.

124. *Biographical Sketch of Hon. A. Leo Knot,* 87–88. According to Knott's account, he was arrested by "special police" appointed by the police commissioners to provide extra security on election day; the policemen at the station who harassed him included regular policemen.

125. Both Valiant and Young had served on the Baltimore City Council. Valiant had also held the post of collector of customs of the Port of Baltimore before he was removed during the Lincoln administration. Young served as the head of a group known as the City Conservative Convention, which worked to revive the Democratic Party when the anti-Republican faction broke away from the wartime Unionist coalition. "The Police Commissioner," *Baltimore American,* Nov. 3, 1866, p. 1.

126. Baltimore Police Department, Annual Report, 1867, p. 7. BCA, BMS33-4-1-8.

127. "Police Commissioners: Remarks of Judge Bond," *Baltimore American,* Nov. 5, 1866, p. 1.

128. Baltimore Police Department, Annual Report, 1867, p. 25.

129. "The Registration," *Baltimore American,* Nov. 1, 1866, p. 1.

130. "The Election," *Baltimore American,* Nov. 8, 1866, p. 1.

131. "Letter from Annapolis," *Baltimore Sun,* Jan. 21, 1870, p. 4.

132. Based on their assessment that they were far outnumbered on the voter registration lists, the Republican City Executive Committee adopted a resolution recommending that Baltimore ward organizations make no nominations for city council candidates in the October 1870 elections. "Municipal Elections," *Baltimore American,* Oct. 12, 1870, p. 2. In October 1872, Democrats won seventeen of the twenty seats on the city council First Branch. "Municipal Election," *Baltimore American,* Oct. 24, 1872, p. 1.

133. "The Locust Point Homicide," *Baltimore American,* Aug. 12, 1873, p. 1.

134. "Fatal Shooting," *Wilmington (DE) Daily Commercial,* June 10, 1875, p. 1; "The Use of Firearms by Police, *Wilmington (DE) Daily Gazette,* June 11, 1875, p. 2.

135. "Victim of Carelessness," *Baltimore American,* June 11, 1875, p. 1.

136. "Police and Pistol Shooting," *Baltimore Sun,* June 12, 1875, p. 2.

6. *The Police on Trial*

1. Ammen, "History of Baltimore 1875–1895," 244.

2. "Making a Mayor," *Baltimore American,* June 4, 1875, p. 2.

3. Ammen, "History of Baltimore," 245–46; Kent, *Story of Maryland Politics,* 49.

4. "Municipal Political Movements," *Baltimore Sun,* Aug. 26, 1875, p. 1; "Maryland Politics," *Baltimore Sun,* Aug. 31, 1875, p. 4; Kent, *Story of Maryland Politics,* 49–50.

5. Facts in Connection with the Political Record of Hon. J. Morrison Harris, J. Morrison Harris Papers, box 5.

6. Brown, *Baltimore and the Nineteenth of April,* 63.

7. "A Leader of Men,' *Baltimore Sun,* Apr. 12, 1894, p. 8; "Our First Citizen," *Baltimore Sun,* Apr. 14, 1894, p. 6; Kent, *Story of Maryland Politics,* 33–34.

8. Ammen, "History of Baltimore," 246.

9. "Death of Mr. Warfield," *Baltimore Sun,* Jan. 19, 1885, p. 1; "Death of Mr. Warfield," *Baltimore American,* Jan. 19, 1885, p. 2.

10. Kent, *Story of Maryland Politics,* 50.

11. *Journal of the House of Delegates1876,* p. 1302, accessible at *Arch. Md. Online,* 413:1302.

12. "The Municipal Election," *Baltimore Sun,* Oct. 28, 1875, p. 1.

13. "Free Elections," *Baltimore Sun,* Oct. 29, 1875, p. 2.

14. "The Municipal Election," *Baltimore Sun,* Oct. 28, 1875, p. 1.

15. "Election Arrests," *Baltimore Sun,* Oct. 28, 1875, p. 4.

16. "Excitement in the Streets," *Baltimore Sun,* Oct. 29, 1875, p. 4.

17. "Irregularities at the Late Election," *Baltimore Sun,* Nov. 4, 1875, p. 2.

18. *Journal of Proceedings . . . First Branch of the City Council . . . 1875–76,* p. 403.

19. "Sweeping Democratic Victory," *Baltimore Gazette,* Nov. 3, 1875, p. 4.

20. *Journal of Proceedings . . . First Branch of the City Council . . . 1875–76,* Appendix, Document A, p. 88.

21. *Journal of Proceedings . . . First Branch of the City Council . . . 1875–76,* Appendix, Document A, pp, 96–97.

22. *Journal of Proceedings . . . First Branch of the City Council . . . 1875–76,* Appendix, Document A, pp. 69–71.

23. "End of the Byrn-Donavin Contest," *Baltimore Sun,* Mar. 14, 1876, p. 4.

24. "The Election in Baltimore," *Baltimore Sun,* Nov. 3, 1875, p. 1.

25. "Election Outrages: The Sacking of a House—a Policeman Leads a Mob," *Baltimore American,* Nov. 6, 1875, p. 4.

26. "Third Ward Ruffians," *Baltimore American,* Nov. 6, 1875, p. 4.

27. "Maryland," *New York Times,* Nov. 3, 1875, p. 5.

28. "Maryland: Big Democratic Majority in Baltimore, and Why," *Washington (DC) Evening Star,* Nov. 3, 1875, p. 1.

29. "Plug-Uglyism in Baltimore," *Chicago Daily Tribune,* Nov. 3, 1875, p. 1.

30. Tyson, Brief for the Contestants, 10–11. Quotations are from *Journal of the House of Delegates 1876,* Committee on Elections Minority Report, pp. 1501–2, accessible at *Arch. Md. Online,* 413:1501–2.

31. *Journal of the House of Delegates 1876,* p. 1304, accessible at *Arch. Md. Online,* 413:1304.

32. Scharf, *History of Baltimore,* 166.

33. Wallis, *The Spoils and the Spoilers . . . in Maryland.*

34. "Our Police Force," *Baltimore American,* Nov. 15, 1875, p. 1.

35. "Letters from the People," *Baltimore American,* Nov. 19, 1875, p. 2.

36. "Court Proceedings," *Baltimore Gazette,* Nov. 23, 1875, p. 4.

37. "Sweeping Democratic Victory," *Baltimore Gazette,* Nov. 3, 1875, p. 4.

38. Folsom, *Our Police,* 73; "Local Matters: The New Police Board," *Baltimore Sun,* Mar. 16, 1867, p. 1.

39. Baltimore City Police Department, Annual Reports, 1874–75.

40. "Southern Rights Convention," *Baltimore Sun,* Apr. 18, 1861, p. 1; "Local Matters: The Conservative Mayoralty Convention," *Baltimore Sun,* Jan. 25, 1867, p. 1.

41. In the rare instances where blacks joined Southern police forces, their duties were restricted by white resistance to allowing blacks to arrest whites. Nashville, for example, added black special detectives to the force for the purpose of arresting blacks. In Montgomery, black policemen won authorization to arrest whites only after a confrontation between a black leader and a prominent white Republican. Rabinowitz, *Race Relations in the Urban South,* 42–43 and 266.

42. "The New Police," *Raleigh Weekly North-Carolina Standard,* July 29, 1868, p. 3.

43. "Long Fight Won First Police Badge," *Baltimore Afro-American Ledger,* Dec. 18, 1937, p. 16; "Lawson Picks 4 Policemen," *Baltimore Afro-American Ledger,* July 16, 1938, p. 12.

44. *State of Maryland v. Patrick McDonald,* Oct. Term 1875, folio 29, Baltimore City Criminal Court Trial Docket.

45. Scharf, *History of Baltimore,* 720–21; *Biographical Sketch of Hon. A. Leo Knot,* 11.

46. Lambert, *Arthur Pue Gorman,* 117–18.

47. Mayer, Fisher, and Cross, *Revised Code . . . 1878,* Title 26, Art. 62, §§ 1 and 2, pp. 558–59, accessible at *Arch. Md. Online,* 388:558–59. The reference to "county clerks" included the clerk of Baltimore City. Title 1, Art. 1, § 11, p. 22, accessible at *Arch. Md. Online,* 388:22.

48. The Baltimore City Criminal Court was part of the state court system. In the 1870s, African Americans served as jurors in federal courts in Baltimore, but the Supreme Bench of Baltimore, the administrative unit of the state courts in Baltimore, did not consider integrating juries until the US Supreme Court, in *Strauder v. West Virginia,* 100 US 303 (1880), briefly forced them to consider the possibility. "The Colored Jury Question," *Baltimore Sun,* Mar. 18, 1880, p. 1.

49. "Civil Rights to the Colored Man," *Baltimore Sun,* Sept. 2, 1875, p. 1; Brackett, *Notes on the Progress of the Colored People,* 414.

50. "More on the Colored Juror in Garrett County," *Baltimore Sun,* Sept. 6, 1875, p. 1.

51. *Strauder v. West Virginia,* 100 US 303 (1880); *Virginia v. Rives,* 100 US 313 (1880).

52. Wiecek, *Liberty under Law,* 103.

53. In response to the Supreme Court's decision in the Strauder case, the judges of the Supreme Bench of Baltimore discussed the possibility of allowing African Americans to sit on juries in the Criminal Court, "where so many colored persons are tried," and in the course of the discussion they assumed they had the discretion to choose "some of the best qualified colored men in Baltimore." "The Colored Jury Question," *Baltimore Sun,* Mar. 18, 1880, p. 1.

54. *Laws Made and Passed . . . 1832,* ch. 62, accessible at *Arch. Md. Online,* 213:336. When the General Assembly revised the provisions for admission to the practice of law in 1876, the whites-only provision was retained, despite the ratification of the Fourteenth Amendment in 1868. Mayer, Fisher, and Cross, *Revised Code . . . 1878,* Title 26, Art. 11, § 3, p. 542, accessible at *Arch. Md. Online,* 388:542.

55. "The Supreme Bench of Maryland, *Cecil (Maryland) Whig,* Mar. 21, 1885, p. 2; "Admission of Colored Lawyers to the Bar," *Baltimore Sun,* Mar. 20, 1885, p. 2. The persistent efforts of an African American minister, Harvey Johnson, apparently played a major role in the success of Charles Wilson's claim. James Wolff, one of the two lawyers who failed to gain admission in 1877, wrote to Johnson to thank him for his efforts in Wilson's successful claim in 1885. Halpin, "'For My Race against All Political Parties,'" 93; Johnson, *The Nations,* 22.

56. The University of Maryland's law school excluded African Americans throughout the nineteenth century except for a brief period in the late 1880s. In 1887, two African American students, Harry S. Cummings and Charles W. Johnson, began studies in the University of Maryland's law program, and both men graduated in 1889. Two more African American students, W. Ashbie Hawkins and John L. Dozier, started classes in 1889, but segregationists denied them a chance to complete the program. Conservative Democrats voiced opposition to integration of the university, and the law school dean joined forces with the law school's white students to force out the black students. In September 1890, after they had completed one year of study, Hawkins and Dozier were expelled. Hawkins and Dozier completed their law studies, but they had to leave Maryland to do so. Both men graduated from Howard University's law school. The University of Maryland School of Law remained a segregated institution until 1935, when the NAACP, represented by Thurgood Marshall and Charles H. Houston, convinced the Maryland Court of Appeals that the Maryland School of Law had an obligation to accept African American students because the state had provided no separate, equal law school. Bogen, "The First Integration of the University of Maryland School of Law," 39–44; Kuebler, "The Desegregation of the University of Maryland," 37–49.

57. Gilmor Family, Dielman-Hayward Files. Judge Gilmor's father, Robert Gilmor III, owned a Baltimore shipping firm. Ruffner, *Maryland's Blue and Gray,* 191.

58. Ruffner, "'More Trouble Than a Brigade,'" 391 and 406n11.

59. "Local Matters: The Vote of the City," *Baltimore Sun,* Oct. 25, 1867, p. 1.

60. "Ex-Judge Gilmor Dead," *Baltimore Sun,* Apr. 20, 1906, p. 7.

61. "A Bright Light Gone Out," *Baltimore American,* Mar. 12, 1895, p. 2; Malka, *Men of Mobtown,* 207–8.

62. *Debates of the Constitutional Convention of the State of Maryland, 1864,* p. 1589, accessible at *Arch. Md. Online,* 102:1589.

63. Fuke, *Imperfect Equality,* 78–81; Low, "The Freedmen's Bureau and Civil Rights in Maryland," 221–47; Malka, *Men of Mobtown,* 207–8.

64. Thomas, "A Nineteenth Century Black Operated Shipyard," 10.

65. Clark, "Politics in Maryland during the Civil War," 183.

66. Bogen, "The First Integration of the University of Maryland School of Law," 39–44.

67. Arthur P. Gorman Diary, Jan. 3, 1904, Arthur P. Gorman Papers; Crooks, *Politics and Progress,* 58; Callcott, *Negro in Maryland Politics,* 107–20. The Poe amendment was defeated in a statewide vote in 1905. Poe's account book does not reveal who paid McDonald's defense attorneys. John Prentiss Poe Account Book, 1860–78.

68. Hall, *Baltimore: Its History and Its People,* 2:159; "Death of Thomas E. Hambleton," *Baltimore Sun,* Aug. 19, 1876, p. 4.

69. "Letter from Talbot County, Md.," *Baltimore Sun,* Oct. 22, 1869, p. 4.

70. "Democratic Meetings," *Baltimore Sun,* Oct. 1, 1875, p. 1; "Legislative Election Contested Cases," *Baltimore Sun,* Feb. 22, 1876, p. 1.

71. "Obituary: Joseph S. Heuisler," *Baltimore Sun,* Oct. 19, 1899, p. 7.

72. "The Municipal Election, "*Baltimore Sun,* Oct. 28, 1875, p. 1.

73. "Democratic Demonstration," *Baltimore Sun,* Oct. 9, 1875, p. 1.

74. J. Douglass Hambleton to F. C. Latrobe, Feb. 5, 1876. Mayor's Correspondence, BRG9-2-40-2.

75. John Prentiss Poe Account Book, 1860–78.

76. "Ex Officer McKenna," *Baltimore American,* Oct. 13, 1876, p. 4; "Sentence of Ex-Officer McKenna," *Baltimore American,* Oct. 24, 1876, p. 4.

77. *Journal of Proceedings, First Branch of the City Council . . . 1875–76,* Appendix, Document A, p. 18.

78. "The Weidner Homicide," *Baltimore American,* Jan. 12, 1878, p. 4; "Acquittal of Freeze," *Baltimore Gazette,* Jan. 12, 1878, p. 4.

79. Although the testimony presented at the coroner's inquest in August, as well as the evidence presented in the trial in November, made it very clear that the social event at Brown's home was not a so-called cakewalk or party at which guests paid an admission fee, the *Sun* repeatedly printed headlines referring to the matter as the "Cake-Walk Homicide." The *American* generally referred to the matter as the McDonald trial.

80. "Cake-Walk Homicide," *Baltimore Sun,* Nov. 16, 1875, p. 4.

81. "Trial of M'Donald," *Baltimore American,* Nov. 16, 1875, p. 4.

82. "The Cake-Walk Homicide," *Baltimore Sun,* Nov. 17, 1875, p. 4.

83. *Woods's Directory,* 1875, pp. 215, 485, 545, and 590. The complete list of jurors seated was: Robert Williams, J. Hanson Thomas Jr., John M. Getz, Duncan M. Robb, William S. Tyler, R. Lewis Whiteford, Andrew Hankof, H. C. Mayner, Josiah Kinsey, Albert H. Shook, James Boyle, and Soloman Brown. Baltimore City Criminal Trial Docket. Oct. 1875, folio 29, MSA C1849-63.

84. "The Cake-Walk Homicide," *Baltimore Sun,* Nov. 17, 1875, p. 4.

85. Because the defendant's counsel filed an appeal, officers of the Baltimore City Criminal Court were required to prepare records of the trial for review by the Maryland Court of Appeals. The transcript or other records should have been returned to the Baltimore City Criminal Court after the appeal was decided. However, the collection of Criminal Court papers at the Maryland State Archives does not include transcripts or other records prepared for the appeal of the McDonald trial. Baltimore City Criminal Court, Criminal Papers, 1872–1982. MSA T495. Special Collections in the Maryland State Archives include papers of the Baltimore City Supreme Bench, Appeals 1871–96, but no

papers from the McDonald trial have been preserved in that collection. Baltimore City Circuit Court/Baltimore Courthouse and Law Museum Collection of Papers Relating to the Supreme Bench of Baltimore City, series 3, box 2. MSA SC5603-3-2. The *Baltimore Sun* and the *Baltimore American* carried detailed accounts of the trial in their issues dated November 16–25, 1875; these provide the best available sources for details of the proceedings.

86. "The Cake-Walk Homicide," *Baltimore Sun,* Nov. 17, 1875, p. 4.

87. *Supplement to the Maryland Code, 1861 . . . 1867,* Public General Laws, Art. 37, § 3, p. 109, accessible at *Arch. Md. Online,* 384:109.

88. The law was amended shortly after the McDonald trial to allow a criminal defendant, "at his own request, but not otherwise, be deemed a competent witness; but the neglect or refusal of any such person to testify shall not create a presumption against him." Mayer, Fisher, and Cross, *Revised Code . . . 1878,* Title 26, Art. 70, § 3, pp. 750–51, accessible at *Arch. Md. Online,* 388:750–51.

89. "The Cake-Walk Homicide," *Baltimore Sun,* Nov. 17, 1875, p. 4.

90. "The Cake-Walk Homicide," *Baltimore Sun,* Nov. 18, 1875, p. 4.

91. "The M'Donald Trial," *Baltimore American,* Nov. 17, 1875, p. 4.

92. "The M'Donald Trial," *Baltimore American,* Nov. 17, 1875, p. 4.

93. "The Cake-Walk Homicide," *Baltimore Sun,* Nov. 17, 1875, p. 4; The *American* reported Gresham's statement as "All right, sir." "The M'Donald Murder Trial," *Baltimore American,* Nov. 17, 1875, p. 4.

94. "The Cake-Walk Homicide," *Baltimore Sun,* Nov. 17, 1875, p. 4; "The M'Donald Murder Trial," *Baltimore American,* Nov. 17, 1875, p. 4.

95. Mayer, Fisher, and Cross, *Revised Code . . . 1878,* Title 27, Art. 72, § 1, 785, accessible at *Arch. Md. Online,* 388:785.

96. "The M'Donald Murder Trial," *Baltimore American,* Nov. 17, 1875, p. 4.

97. The blanks in the testimony are as reported in "The Cake-Walk Homicide," *Baltimore Sun,* Nov. 17, 1875, p. 4, and "The M'Donald Murder Trial," *Baltimore American,* Nov. 17, 1875, p. 4.

98. "The Cake-Walk Homicide," *Baltimore Sun,* Nov. 17, 1875, p. 4.

99. "The M'Donald Murder Trial," *Baltimore American,* Nov. 17, 1875, p. 4. According to the *Sun*'s account, "Mr." Brown asked Gresham to go for a doctor. The *American*'s report that it was "Mrs." Brown seems more likely.

100. "The Cake-Walk Homicide," *Baltimore Sun,* Nov. 17, 1875, p. 4.

101. "The Cake-Walk Homicide," *Baltimore Sun,* Nov. 17, 1875, p. 4.

102. "The M'Donald Murder Trial," *Baltimore American,* Nov. 17, 1875, p. 4.

103. "The M'Donald Murder Trial," *Baltimore American,* Nov. 17, 1875, p. 4; "The Cake-Walk Homicide," *Baltimore Sun,* Nov. 19, 1875, p. 4.

104. "Trial of M'Donald," *Baltimore American,* Nov. 18, 1875, p. 4.

105. "The Cake-Walk Homicide," *Baltimore Sun,* Nov. 17, 1875, p. 1; "Trial of M'Donald," *Baltimore American,* Nov. 18, 1875, p. 4.

106. "The Cake-Walk Homicide," *Baltimore Sun,* Nov. 18, 1875, p. 4.

107. "The M'Donald Trial," *Baltimore American,* Nov. 17, 1875, p. 4; "The Cake-Walk Homicide," *Baltimore Sun,* Nov. 17, 1875, p. 4.

108. "The Cake-Walk Homicide," *Baltimore Sun,* Nov. 18, 1875, p. 4.

109. "Trial of M'Donald," *Baltimore American,* Nov. 18, 1875, p. 4.

110. "Trial of M'Donald," *Baltimore American,* Nov. 18, 1875, p. 4.

111. Baltimore City Criminal Court, Grand Jury Docket, May term 1875, folio 61. MSA T494-22.

112. "Trial of M'Donald," *Baltimore American,* Nov. 18, 1875, p. 4. "The Cake-Walk Homicide," *Baltimore Sun,* Nov. 18, 1875, p. 4.

113. "Trial of M'Donald," *Baltimore American,* Nov. 18, 1875, p. 4.

114. "The Cake-Walk Homicide," *Baltimore Sun,* Nov. 18, 1875, p. 4.

115. "Trial of M'Donald," *Baltimore American,* Nov. 18, 1875, p. 4.

116. "The Cake-Walk Homicide," *Baltimore Sun,* Nov. 18, 1875, p. 4.

117. "Trial of M'Donald," *Baltimore American,* Nov. 18, 1875, p. 4; *Woods's Directory,* 1875, pp. 252 and 852.

118. In one unbroken paragraph, with no mention of Abraham Trusty, the *Baltimore Sun*'s coverage seems to attribute some of Trusty's statements to Joseph Boston. The *Baltimore American*'s report, however, is clearer, and it indicates a clear separation between the testimony of Boston and Trusty.

119. "Trial of M'Donald," *Baltimore American,* Nov. 18, 1875, p. 4.

120. "Trial of M'Donald," *Baltimore American,* Nov. 18, 1875, p. 4.

121. "The Cake-Walk Homicide," *Baltimore Sun,* Nov. 18, 1875, p. 4.

122. "The Cake-Walk Homicide," *Baltimore Sun,* Nov. 19, 1875, p. 4. According to the *Baltimore Gazette*'s reporter, McDonald's demeanor remained the same, and he showed "no sign of feeling" even when a guilty verdict was finally announced. "Court Proceedings," *Baltimore Gazette,* Nov. 23, 1875, p. 4.

123. "The M'Donald Trial," *Baltimore American,* Nov. 19, 1875, p. 4.

124. "The Cake-Walk Homicide," *Baltimore Sun,* Nov. 19, 1875, p. 4.

125. "The M'Donald Trial," *Baltimore American,* Nov. 19, 1875, p. 4.

126. "The Cake-Walk Homicide," *Baltimore Sun,* Nov. 19, 1875, p. 4; "The M'Donald Trial," *Baltimore American,* Nov. 19, 1875, p. 4.

127. "The M'Donald Trial," *Baltimore American,* Nov. 19, 1875, p. 4.

128. "The M'Donald Trial," *Baltimore American,* Nov. 19, 1875, p. 4.

129. "The Cake-Walk Homicide," *Baltimore Sun,* Nov. 19, 1875, p. 4.

130. "The M'Donald Trial," *Baltimore American,* Nov. 19, 1875, p. 4.

131. "The Cake-Walk Homicide," *Baltimore Sun,* Nov. 19, 1875, p. 4.

132. "The Cake-Walk Homicide," *Baltimore Sun,* Nov. 19, 1875, p. 4.

133. "The Cake-Walk Homicide," *Baltimore Sun,* Nov. 20, 1875, p. 4.

134. "The Cake-Walk Homicide," *Baltimore Sun,* Nov. 19, 1875, p. 4.

135. "The Cake-Walk Homicide," *Baltimore Sun,* Nov. 22, 1875, p. 4.

136. "The Cake-Walk Homicide," *Baltimore Sun,* Nov. 20, 1875, p. 1 supplement.

137. "The Cake-Walk Homicide," *Baltimore Sun,* Nov. 20, 1875, p. 1 supplement.

138. "The Cake-Walk Homicide," *Baltimore Sun,* Nov. 20, 1875, p. 1 supplement. By statute, Maryland divided the common-law offense of murder into degrees for purposes of determining the applicable penalty. First-degree murder required a "deliberate and premeditated killing," or a killing in specified circumstances, such as, for example, "by means of poison, or lying in wait." In the absence of premeditation or one of the specified circumstances, the penalty for second degree applied. The penalty for first-degree murder was death; the penalty for second-degree murder was five to eighteen years in the penitentiary. Mayer, Fisher, and Cross, *Revised Code . . . 1879,* Art. 72, Offenses against the Person, §§ 1–8, pp. 785–86, accessible at *Arch. Md. Online,* 388:785–86. Thus, in a murder trial, the jury's first duty was to decide the question of guilt or innocence of murder; if the verdict was guilty of murder, the jury was required to ascertain whether it was murder in the first or second degree. *Davis v. State of Maryland* 39 Md. 355 (1874).

139. "The Cake-Walk Homicide," *Baltimore Sun,* Nov. 20, 1875, p. 1 supplement.

140. "The Cake-Walk Homicide," *Baltimore Sun,* Nov. 22, 1875, p. 4.
141. "The Cake-Walk Homicide," *Baltimore Sun,* Nov. 22, 1875, p. 4.
142. "The Cake-Walk Homicide," *Baltimore Sun,* Nov. 25, 1875, p. 4.

Conclusion

1. Maryland's 1864 Constitution in Art. I, § 1, limited voting to "white male" citizens; the provision was retained in Maryland's 1867 Constitution in Art. I, § 1.

2. Callcott, *Negro in Maryland Politics,* 94–95. On the development of Maryland's segregated schools, see Fuke, "The Baltimore Association for the Moral and Educational Improvement of the Colored People," 369–404.

3. "Dissatisfied Republicans," *Baltimore American,* Nov. 9, 1874, p. 4.

4. Halpin, *Brotherhood of Liberty,* 25.

5. Mayer, Fisher, and Cross, *Revised Code . . . 1878,* Title 27, Art. 72, § 9, p. 786, accessible at *Arch. Md. Online,* 388:786.

6. *McDonald v. State,* 45 Md. 90 (1876), at 91.

7. *McDonald v. State,* note following the decision.

8. "McDonald's Release," *Baltimore American,* July 17, 1876, p. 2.

9. Judge Gilmor presided over many manslaughter trials before he sentenced Officer McDonald. Although it can never be known with certainty why Judge Gilmor erred in sentencing Officer McDonald, examples of cases in which he sentenced defendants convicted of manslaughter to the city jail or the state penitentiary with terms appropriate under the statute are not hard to find. In 1868 he sentenced Thomas Murray and Thomas Farrell each to six years in the penitentiary ("Sentence of Murray and Farrell," *Baltimore Sun,* Nov. 19, 1868, p. 1). In 1873 he sentenced John A. Curtis to six years in the penitentiary ("Proceedings of the Courts," *Baltimore Sun,* July 4, 1873). In 1868 he sentenced Stephen T. Denny to the city jail for one year ("Local Matters," *Baltimore Sun,* Dec. 18, 1868, p. 1). In 1869 he sentenced Samuel Smith to one year in jail ("Proceedings of the Courts," *Baltimore Sun,* Nov. 30, 1869, p. 4).

10. *McDonald v. State,* at 97. In the note appended to Judge Miller's decision, the Court suggested the legislature could empower the Court to remand criminal cases for correction of sentencing errors. At the first legislative session following McDonald's release, the Maryland General Assembly added a new section to the law of appeals making it the "duty" of the Court of Appeals in cases of erroneous sentencing to remit the record to the court below for resentencing. Mayer, Fisher, and Cross, *Revised Code . . . 1878,* Title 26, Art. 71, § 38 (added Jan. 1878 session), accessible at *Arch. Md. Online,* 388:770.

11. "An Act relative to the jurisdiction of the court of appeals, passed 19th December 1800," *Laws of Maryland Made and Passed,* 1800, ch. 69, p. 44, accessible at *Arch. Md. Online,* 94:44. This provision was codified in 1860: Scott and M'Cullough, *Maryland Code,* 1860, "Appeals" Art. 5, §14, p. 22, accessible at *Arch. Md. Online,* 145:22.

12. 14 Md. 412 (1859), at 417.

13. *McDonald v. State,* at 97.

14. *Isaacs v. State,* 23 Md. 410 (1865), at 413. Although the issue was argued by counsel, the Court of Appeals in this case did not rule on the question of whether the statute applied because the Court found no error in the appellant's sentence.

Bibliography

Abbreviations

Arch. Md. Online	*Archives of Maryland Online* (http://aomol.msa.maryland.gov)
BCA	Baltimore City Archives
MHM	*Maryland Historical Magazine*
MHS	Maryland Historical Society, Baltimore
MSA	Maryland State Archives, Annapolis

Archival Sources

Arthur P. Gorman Papers. MS706. MHS.

Baltimore City Circuit Court/Baltimore Courthouse and Law Museum Foundation Collection of Papers Relating to the Supreme Bench of Baltimore City. Appeals 1871–96. SC5603-3. MSA.

Baltimore City Court of Common Pleas, Marriage Index, Male, 1851–85. CM-205. MSA.

Baltimore City Criminal Court Grand Jury Docket. T494-22. MSA.

Baltimore City Criminal Court Trial Docket. C1849-63. MSA.

Baltimore City Health Department, Bureau of Vital Statistics, Death Record, 1875–1972, Index. CM1132. MSA.

Baltimore City Jail Assault and Battery Docket. C2058-5. MSA.

Baltimore City Police, Consolidated Dockets, Jan. 1875 to Dec. 1875, MSA C3065-1.

Baltimore City Police, Eastern Docket, Sept. 1873 to Apr. 1874. C2111-12. MSA.

Bradbury, Mary Elizabeth. Mary Elizabeth Bradbury Papers. Collection No. 88–91. Univ. of Maryland Library, College Park, MD.

Coroners' Inquests. BRG19-1. BSA

Dodson, Leonidas. Leonidas Dodson Papers. Collection No. 85–86. Univ. of Maryland Library, College Park, MD.

Gilmor Family. Dielman-Hayward Files. MHS.

Harris, J. Morrison. J. Morrison Harris Papers. MS2739. MHS.

John Prentiss Poe Account Book, 1860–1878. MS2576. MHS.

Maryland General Assembly Report on the Baltimore Board of Police Commissioners, 1860. PAM4108. MHS.

Mayor's Correspondence, 1797–1923. Applications for Positions. BRG9-2, BCA.

Sinn, William E., letter to John Ford, Mar. 4, 1875. Vertical File. MHS.

Tyson, J. S. Brief for the Contestants, before the Committee of Elections of the House of Delegates of Maryland in the Matter of the Contested Election for the 2nd Legislative District of Baltimore. H. Furlong Baldwin Library, MHS.

Wallis, S. Teakle. *The Spoils and the Spoilers: Papers on the Political Situation in Maryland, 1887.* PAM3594. MHS.

Government Reports and Publications

Baltimore City Code: Comprising the Laws of Maryland Relating to Baltimore and the Ordinances of the Mayor and City Council, with an Appendix to the End of the Session of 1877–78. Baltimore: John Cox, 1879.

Baltimore Police Department Annual Report 1874 and 1875. Electronic Baltimore City Police Records. BMS33-4-1-10. BCA. http://guide.msa.maryland.gov/pages/series.aspx?ID=BMS33-4-1.

Bureau of Refugees, Freedmen and Abandoned Lands. *First Semi-annual Report on Schools and Finances of Freedmen, 1866.* Washington, DC: Government Printing Office, 1868.

Davis v. State of Maryland. 39 Md. 355 (1874).

Isaacs v. State of Maryland. 23 Md. 410 (1865).

Journal of Proceedings of the First Branch of the City Council of Baltimore, Sessions 1875–76. Baltimore: John Cox, 1876.

Journal of the Proceedings of the Second Branch of the City Council of Baltimore, January Session—Extra Sessions 1852. Baltimore: Jos. Robinson, 1853.

Laws Made and Passed by the General Assembly of the State of Maryland, 1832. Annapolis: J. Hughes, 1832. *Arch. Md. Online,* vol. 213.

Laws Made and Passed by the General Assembly of the State of Maryland, 1853. Annapolis: B. H. Richardson, 1853. *Arch. Md. Online,* vol. 403.

Laws of Maryland Made Since 1763, Consisting of Acts of Assembly under the Proprietary Government . . . and Acts of Assembly since the Revolution. Annapolis: Frederick Green, 1787. *Arch. Md. Online,* vol. 203.

Laws of Maryland Made and Passed at a Session of Assembly . . . in the Year of Our Lord One Thousand Eight Hundred. Annapolis: Frederick Green, n.d. *Arch. Md. Online,* vol. 94.

Laws of the State of Maryland, Made and Passed, 1867. Annapolis: Henry A. Lucas, 1867. *Arch. Md. Online,* vol. 133.

Maryland Bureau of Industrial Statistics and Information. *First Biennial Report of the Bureau of Industrial Statistics and Information, 1884–1885.* Baltimore: Guggenheimer, Weil and Co., 1886.

Maryland House of Delegates. *Baltimore City Election: Papers in the Contested Election Case from Baltimore City.* Annapolis: B. H. Richardson, 1860. *Arch. Md. Online,* vol. 849.

———. *Journal of the Proceedings of the House of Delegates, 1858.* Annapolis: Thomas J. Wilson, 1858. *Arch. Md. Online,* vol. 665.

———. *Journal of the Proceedings of the House of Delegates, 1865.* Document EE, Report of the Select Committee Appointed to Prepare a Statement in Relation to the Resources of Maryland. Annapolis: Richard P. Bayly, 1865. *Arch. Md. Online*, vol. 753.

———. *Journal of the Proceedings of the House of Delegates of Maryland, January Session 1876*. Annapolis: John F. Wiley, 1876. *Arch. Md. Online*, vol. 413.

———. *Message of Governor Swann to the General Assembly at Its Regular Session, 1867.* Annapolis: Henry A. Lucas, 1867. *Arch. Md. Online*, vol. 133: 3083.

———. *Message of the Governor to the General Assembly in Extra Session 1861*. Frederick, MD: E. S. Riley, 1861. *Arch. Md. Online*, vol. 758.

Mayer, Lewis, Louis C. Fisher, and E. J. D. Cross, comps. *Revised Code of the Public General Laws of the State of Maryland, with the Constitution of the State. Legalized by the General Assembly of 1878*. Baltimore: John Murphy and Co., 1879. *Arch. Md. Online*, vol. 388.

Mayor and City Council of Baltimore v. Board of Police of the City of Baltimore. 15 Maryland Reports 376 (1860).

McDonald v. State of Maryland. 45 Md. 90 (1876).

Ordinances of the Mayor and City Council of Baltimore. Baltimore: George W. Bowen and Co., 1858.

Ordinances of the Mayor and City Council of Baltimore Passed at a December Session 1849. Baltimore: James Lucas, 1850.

Record of the Proceedings of the Investigation before His Excellency Thomas Swann Governor of Maryland, in the Case of Samuel Hindes and Nicholas L. Wood, Commissioners of the Board of Police of the City of Baltimore, upon Charges against Them for Official Misconduct. Copy in H. Furlong Baldwin Library, MHS.

Register of the Corporation Officers of Baltimore City for the Year 1874. Baltimore: King Brothers Printers, 1874.

Register of the Corporation Officers of Baltimore City for the Year 1876. Baltimore: King Brothers Printers, 1876.

Register of the Corporation Officers of Baltimore City for the Year 1887. Baltimore: Stephen Tongue, City Printer, 1887.

Scott, Otho, and Hiram M'Cullough, comps. *Maryland Code*. Vol. 1, *Public General Laws*. Baltimore: John Murphy and Co., 1860. *Arch. Md. Online*, vol. 145.

Strauder v. West Virginia. 100 US 303 (1880).

Supplement to the Maryland Code, Containing the Acts of the General Assembly Passed at Sessions of 1861, 1861–62, 1864, 1865, 1866 and 1867. Baltimore: John Murphy and Co., 1868. *Arch. Md. Online*, vol. 384.

United States Census, 1850, Maryland, Schedule L, Free Inhabitants.

United States Census, 1860, Population Schedules, Maryland.

United States Census, 1860, Slave Schedules, Maryland.

United States Census, 1870, Population Schedules, Maryland.

United States Census, 1880, Maryland, Baltimore City.

United States Census Office. *Compendium of the Ninth Census, 1870*. Washington, DC: Government Printing Office, 1872.

———. *Population of the United States in 1860*. Washington, DC: Government Printing Office, 1864.

———. *Statistical View of the United States, Being a Compendium of the Seventh Census*. Washington, DC: A. O. P. Nicholson, 1854.

Virginia v. Rives. 100 US 313 (1880).

Watkins v. State of Maryland. 14 Md. 412 (1859).

Works Projects Administration, Virginia Writers' Project. *The Negro in Virginia.* New York: Hastings House, 1940.

Young, Edward. *The Cost of Labor in the United States for the Year 1869, as Compared with Previous Years.* Washington, DC: Government Printing Office, 1870. https://www.hathitrust.org/.

Newspapers

Baltimore Afro-American Ledger
Baltimore American and Commercial Advertiser
Baltimore Daily Exchange
Baltimore Daily Gazette
Baltimore Deutsche Correspondent
Baltimore Gazette
Baltimore Sun
Baltimore Sunday Telegram
Cecil (MD) Whig
Chicago Daily Tribune
New York Daily Times
New York Times
Raleigh Weekly North Carolina Standard
Washington Evening Star
Washington Post
Wilmington (DE) Daily Commercial
Wilmington (DE) Daily Gazette

Published Primary Sources

African Methodist Episcopal Church. *Doctrines and Discipline of the African Methodist Episcopal Church.* Philadelphia: AME Book Concern, 1878. https://www.hathitrust.org/.

Baltimore Citizens. *Proceedings of the Great Meeting of the Friends of Civil and Religious Liberty, Held at the Baltimore Exchange, October 23, 1837. . . .* Baltimore: Bull and Tuttle, 1837. https://www.hathitrust.org/.

A Biographical Sketch of Hon. A. Leo Knot with a Relation of Some Political Transactions in Maryland, 1861–1867, Being the History of the Redemption of the State. Baltimore: N.p., 1898. (Copy in MHS.)

Brown, George William. *Baltimore and the Nineteenth of April, 1861: A Study of the War.* Baltimore: Johns Hopkins Univ., 1887.

Browne, William Hand, ed. *Archives of Maryland: Proceedings and Acts of the General Assembly of Maryland, January 25, 1637–September 1664.* Baltimore: Maryland Historical Society, 1883. *Arch. Md. Online,* vol. 1.

"The Course of Maryland." *Douglass' Monthly* 4 (June 1861): 468.

Crocker, John G. *The Duties of Sheriffs, Coroners, and Constables, with Practical Forms.* 2nd ed. New York: Banks and Brothers, Law Publishers, 1871.

Davis, Noah. *A Narrative of the Life of Rev. Noah Davis: A Colored Man.* Baltimore: J. F. Weishampel Jr., 1859.

Debates of the Constitutional Convention of the State of Maryland, 1864. 3 vols. Annapolis: Richard P. Bayly. *Arch. Md. Online*, vol. 102.

Douglass, Frederick. *Life and Times of Frederick Douglass.* With a new introduction by Rayford W. Logan. 1892. Reprint, London: Collier Books, 1962.

———. *My Bondage and My Freedom.* With an introduction by James M'Cune Smith. New York and Auburn: Miller, Orton and Mulligan, 1855.

Dufferin, Lord, and the Honorable G. F. Boyle. *Narrative of a Journey from Oxford to Skibereen during the Year of the Irish Famine.* Oxford: John Henry Parker, 1847. https://www.hathitrust.org/.

Gilmor, Harry. *Four Years in the Saddle.* New York: Harper and Brothers, 1866.

Helper, Hinton Rowan. *The Impending Crisis of the South: How to Meet It.* New York: Burdick Brothers, 1857. https://www.hathitrust.org/.

Howard, Frank Key. *Fourteen Months in American Bastilles.* Baltimore: Kelly, Hedian and Piet, 1863. https://www.hathitrust.org/.

Howard, O. O. *Autobiography of Oliver Otis Howard, Major General, United States Army.* 2 vols. New York: Baker and Taylor Co., 1908. https://www.hathitrust.org/.

Johnson, Harvey. *The Nations from a New Point of View.* Nashville: National Baptist Publishing Board, 1903. https://www.hathitrust.org/.

Johnson, Reverdy. [A Marylander, pseudonym] *A Further Consideration of the Dangerous Condition of the Country, the Causes of It, and the Duty of the People.* Baltimore: Sun Printing Establishment, 1867.

Kemp, Janet. *Housing Conditions in Baltimore: Report of a Special Committee of the Association for the Improvement of the Poor and Charity Organization Society.* Baltimore: Baltimore Association for the Improvement of the Poor, 1907.

Latrobe, John H. B. *The Justices' Practice under the Law of Maryland, Including the Duties of a Constable and Also of a Coroner.* 8th ed. Baltimore: Lucas Brothers, 1889.

Long, John Dixon. *Pictures of Slavery in Church and State, Including Personal Reminiscences, Biographical Sketches, Anecdotes.* 3rd ed. Philadelphia: By the author, 1857. https://www.hathitrust.org/.

Lyell, Charles. *A Second Visit to the United States of North America.* Vol. 1. New York: Harper and Brothers, 1849. https://www.hathitrust.org/.

Matchett's Baltimore Directory for 1847–1848.

Niccol, Robert. *Essay on Sugar and General Treatise on Sugar Refining as Practiced in the Clyde Refineries: Embracing the Latest Improvements.* Greenock, UK: Mackenzie and Co., 1864. https://www.hathitrust.org/.

O'Donovan, Jeremiah. *A Brief Account of the Author's Interviews with His Countrymen, and of the Emerald Isle Whence They Came. . . .* Pittsburgh: By the author, 1864. https://www.hathitrust.org/.

O'Rourke, John. *The History of the Great Irish Famine of 1847.* 3rd ed. Dublin: James Duffy and Co., 1902. https://www.hathitrust.org/.

Pim, Jonathan. *The Conditions and Prospects of Ireland and the Evils Arising from the Present Distribution of Landed Property.* Dublin: Hodges and Smith, 1848. https://www.hathitrust.org/.

Society of Friends. *Transactions of the Central Relief Committee of the Society of Friends during the Famine in Ireland in 1846 and 1847.* Dublin: Hodges and Smith, 1852. https://www.hathitrust.org/.

Stroyer, Jacob. *My Life in the South.* 3rd ed. Salem, MA: Salem Observer Book and Job Printer, 1885. https://www.hathitrust.org/.

Trevelyan, C. E. *The Irish Crisis*. London: Longman, Brown, Green and Longmans, 1848. https://www.hathitrust.org/.
"The Uses of Inquests." *Spectator* 56 (Jan. 20, 1883): 78–79.
Wallis, Severn Teakle. *Writings of Severn Teakle Wallis*. Vol. 1, *Addresses and Poems*. Baltimore: John Murphy and Co., 1896.
Woods's Baltimore City Directory, 1860, 1870, 1871, 1872, 1873, 1874, 1875, 1876.

Secondary Sources

Adler, Jeffrey S. "Shoot to Kill: The Use of Deadly Force by the Chicago Police Force, 1875–1920." *Journal of Interdisciplinary History* 38 (Autumn 2007): 233–54.
Alexander, Thomas B. "Persistent Whiggery in the Confederate South, 1860–1877." *Journal of Southern History* 27 (Aug. 1961): 305–29.
Ammen, S. Z. "History of Baltimore 1875–1895." In *Baltimore: Its History and Its People*, vol. 1, *History*, edited by Clayton Colman Hall, 241–88. New York: Lewis Historical Publishing Co., 1912.
Anbinder, Tyler. *Nativism and Slavery: The Northern Know Nothings and the Politics of the 1850s*. New York: Oxford Univ. Press, 1992.
———. "'We Will Dirk Every Mother's Son of Y': Five Points and the Irish Conquest of New York." In *New Directions in Irish-American History*, edited by Kevin Kenny, 105–21. Madison: Univ. of Wisconsin Press, 2003.
Argersinger, Peter H. "From Party Tickets to Secret Ballots: The Evolution of the Electoral Process in Maryland during the Gilded Age." *MHM* 82 (Fall 1987): 214–39.
Baker, Jean H. *Ambivalent Americans: The Know Nothing Party in Maryland*. Baltimore: Johns Hopkins Univ. Press, 1977.
———. *The Politics of Continuity: Maryland Political Parties from 1858 to 1870*. Baltimore: Johns Hopkins Univ. Press, 1973.
Baltimore City Archives. *Suspicious Deaths in Mid-19th Century Baltimore*. Silver Spring, MD: Family Line Publications, 1986.
Berlin, Ira. *Slaves without Masters: The Free Negro in the Antebellum South*. Oxford: Oxford Univ. Press, 1974.
Bernasconi, Robert. "When Police Violence Is More Than Violent Policing." *New Centennial Review* 14 (Fall 2014): 145–52.
Bogen, David Skillen. "The First Integration of the University of Maryland School of Law." *MHM* 84 (Spring 1989): 39–49.
Brackett, Jeffrey Richardson. *The Negro in Maryland: A Study of the Institution of Slavery*. Baltimore: John Murphy and Co., 1889.
———. *Notes on the Progress of the Colored People of Maryland Since the War*. Baltimore: John Murphy and Co., 1890.
Brock, Helen, and Catherine Crawford. "Forensic Medicine in Early Colonial Maryland." In *Legal Medicine in History*, edited by Michael Clark and Catherine Crawford, 25–44. Cambridge: Cambridge Univ. Press, 1994.
Brown, C. Christopher. *The Road to Jim Crow: The African American Struggle On Maryland's Eastern Shore, 1860–1915*. Baltimore: Maryland Historical Society, 2016.
Browne, Joseph L. "'The Expenses Are Borne by the Parents': Freedmen's Schools in Southern Maryland." *MHM* 86 (Winter 1991): 407–22.
Brugger, Robert J. *Maryland: A Middle Temperament, 1634–1980*. Baltimore: Johns Hopkins Univ. Press, 1988.

Burney, Ian A. *Bodies of Evidence: Medicine and the Politics of the English Inquest 1830–1926*. Baltimore: Johns Hopkins Univ. Press, 2000.
Calderhead, William. "Slavery in the Age of Revolution." *MHM* 98 (Fall 2003): 303–24.
Callcott, Margaret Law. *The Negro in Maryland Politics 1870–1912*. Baltimore: Johns Hopkins Univ. Press, 1969.
Cawthon, Elisabeth. "New Life for the Deodand: Coroners' Inquests and Occupational Deaths in England, 1830–46." *American Journal of Legal History* 33 (Apr. 1989): 137–47.
Clark, Charles Branch. "Politics in Maryland during the Civil War." *MHM* 37 (June 1942): 171–92.
Crenson, Matthew A. *Baltimore: A Political History*. Baltimore: Johns Hopkins Univ. Press, 2017.
Crooks, James B. *Politics and Progress: The Rise of Urban Progressivism in Baltimore*. Baton Rouge: Louisiana State Univ. Press, 1968.
Della, Ray M., Jr. "The Problems of Negro Labor in the 1850's." *MHM* 66 (Spring 1971): 14–32.
Diner, Hasia. *Erin's Daughters in America: Irish Immigrant Women in the Nineteenth Century*. Baltimore: Johns Hopkins Univ. Press, 1983.
Dinnerstein, Leonard, Roger L. Nichols, and David M. Reimers. *Natives and Strangers: A Multicultural History of Americans*. New York: Oxford Univ. Press, 1996.
Doyle, David Noel. "The Remaking of Irish America, 1845–1880." In *Making the Irish American: History and Heritage of the Irish in the United States*, edited by J. J. Lee and Marion R. Casey, 213–52. New York: New York Univ. Press, 2006.
Du Bois, W. E. B. *The Philadelphia Negro: A Social Study*. Philadelphia: Univ. of Pennsylvania, 1899.
———. *The Souls of Black Folk: Essays and Sketches*. 2nd ed. Chicago: A. C. McClurg and Co., 1903.
Emery, Lynne Fauley. *Black Dance from 1619 to Today*. 2nd ed. With a foreword by Katherine Dunham. Hightstown, NJ: Princeton Book Co., 1988.
Euchner, Charles C. "The Politics of Urban Expansion: Baltimore and the Sewerage Question, 1859–1905." *MHM* 86 (Fall 1991): 270–91.
Fields, Barbara Jeanne. *Slavery and Freedom on the Middle Ground: Maryland during the Nineteenth Century*. New Haven, CT: Yale Univ. Press, 1985.
Fisher, R. S. *Gazetteer of the State of Maryland Compiled from the Seventh Census of the United States*. Baltimore: James S. Waters, 1852. https://www.hathitrust.org/.
Folsom, de Francias, ed. *Our Police: A History of the Baltimore Force from the First Watchman to the Latest Appointee*. Baltimore: J. D. Ehlers and Co., 1888.
Foner, Eric. *Reconstruction: America's Unfinished Revolution, 1863–1877*. New York: Harper and Row, 1988.
Frey, Jacob. *Reminiscences of Baltimore*. Baltimore: Maryland Book Exchange, 1893. https://www.hathitrust.org/.
Fuke, Richard P. "The Baltimore Association for the Moral and Educational Improvement of the Colored People 1864–1870." *MHM* 66 (Winter 1971): 369–404.
———. *Imperfect Equality: African Americans and the Confines of White Racial Attitudes in Post-Emancipation Maryland*. New York: Fordham Univ. Press, 1999.
Garonzik, Joseph. "The Racial and Ethnic Make-up of Baltimore Neighborhoods, 1850–1870." *MHM* 71 (Fall 1976): 392–402.
Genovese, Eugene D. *Roll, Jordan, Roll: The World the Slaves Made*. New York: Random House, 1972; Vintage Books, 1976.
Goldsborough, W. W. *The Maryland Line in the Confederate Army, 1861–1865*. Baltimore: Guggenheimer, Weil and Co., 1900.

Gray, Peter. *Famine, Land and Politics: British Government and Irish Society, 1843–50*. Dublin: Irish Academic Press, 1999.

Greenberg, Amy Sophia. "Mayhem in Mobtown: Firefighting in Antebellum Baltimore." *MHM* 90 (Summer 1995): 165–79.

Gross, Charles, ed. *Select Cases from the Coroners' Rolls A.D. 1265–1413, with a Brief History of the Office of Coroner*. London: Bernard Quaritch, 1896. https://www.hathitrust.org/.

Groves, Paul A., and Edward K. Muller. "The Evolution of Black Residential Areas in Late Nineteenth-Century Cities." *Journal of Historical Geography* 1 (Apr. 1975): 169–91.

Hahn, Harlan, and Judson L. Jeffries. *Urban America and Its Police: From the Postcolonial Era through the Turbulent 1960s*. Boulder: Univ. Press of Colorado, 2003.

Hall, Clayton Colman, ed. *Baltimore: Its History and Its People*. Vol. 2, *Biography*. New York: Lewis Historical Publishing Co., 1912.

Halpin, Dennis P. *A Brotherhood of Liberty: Black Reconstruction and Its Legacies in Baltimore, 1865–1920*. Philadelphia: Univ. of Pennsylvania Press, 2019.

———. "'For My Race against All Political Parties': Building a Radical Activist Foundation, 1870–1885." *MHM* 111 (Spring/Summer 2016): 86–107.

Harring, Sidney L. *Policing a Class Society: The Experience of American Cities, 1865–1915*. New Brunswick, NJ: Rutgers Univ. Press, 1983.

Harris, William C. *Two against Lincoln: Reverdy Johnson and Horatio Seymour, Champions of the Loyal Opposition*. Lawrence: Univ. Press of Kansas, 2017.

Higham, John. *Strangers in the Land: Patterns of American Nativism, 1860–1925*. New Brunswick, NJ: Rutgers Univ. Press, 1988.

Hindus, Michael Stephen. *Prison and Plantation: Crime Justice and Authority in Massachusetts and South Carolina*. Chapel Hill: Univ. of North Carolina Press, 1980.

Holmes, Malcolm D., and Brad W. Smith. *Race and Police Brutality: Roots of an Urban Dilemma*. Albany: State Univ. of New York Press, 2008.

Hunnisett, R. F. *The Medieval Coroner*. Cambridge: Cambridge Univ. Press, 1961.

Hyman, Harold M., and William M. Wiecek. *Equal Justice under the Law: Constitutional Development 1835–1875*. New York: Harper Torchbooks, 1982.

Ignatiev, Noel. *How the Irish Became White*. New York: Routledge, 1995.

Jamison, Phil. *Hoedowns, Reels, and Frolics: Roots and Branches of Southern Appalachian Dance*. Urbana: Univ. of Illinois Press, 2015.

Jones, Jacqueline. *Labor of Love, Labor of Sorrow: Black Women, Work and the Family, from Slavery to the Present*. New York: Vintage Books, 1986.

Jones, Martha. *Birthright Citizens: A History of Race and Rights in Antebellum America*. Cambridge: Cambridge Univ. Press, 2018.

Jordan, Winthrop D. *White over Black: American Attitudes toward the Negro 1550–1812*. Baltimore: Penguin Books, Inc., 1969.

Kenny, Kevin, ed. *New Directions in Irish-American History*. Madison: Univ. of Wisconsin Press, 2003.

Kent, Frank Richardson. *The Story of Maryland Politics*. Baltimore: Thomas and Evans, 1911.

Kuebler, Edward J. "The Desegregation of the University of Maryland." *MHM* 71 (Spring 1976): 37–49.

Lambert, John R. *Arthur Pue Gorman*. Baton Rouge: Louisiana State Univ. Press, 1953.

Lane, Roger. *Policing the City: Boston, 1822–1885*. Cambridge: Harvard Univ. Press, 1967.

———. *Roots of Violence in Black Philadelphia, 1860–1900*. Cambridge: Harvard Univ. Press, 1986.

———. *Violent Death in the City: Suicide, Accident, and Murder in Nineteenth-Century Philadelphia*. Cambridge: Harvard Univ. Press, 1979.

Lee, J. J. "Introduction: Interpreting Irish America." In *Making the Irish American: History and Heritage of the Irish in the United States,* edited by J. J. Lee and Marion R. Casey, 1–60. New York: New York Univ. Press, 2006.

Levine, Lawrence W. *Black Culture and Black Consciousness: Afro-American Folk Thought from Slavery to Freedom.* New York: Oxford Univ. Press, 1977.

Low, W. A. "The Freedmen's Bureau and Civil Rights in Maryland." *Journal of Negro History* 37 (July 1952): 221–47.

———. "The Freedmen's Bureau and Education in Maryland." *MHM* 47 (Mar. 1952): 29–39.

MacDonald, Michael, and Terence R. Murphy. *Sleepless Souls: Suicide in Early Modern England.* Oxford: Clarendon Press, 1990.

Malka, Adam. *The Men of Mobtown: Policing Baltimore in the Age of Slavery and Emancipation.* Chapel Hill: Univ. of North Carolina Press, 2018.

———. "The Open Violence of Desperate Men: Rethinking Property and Power in the 1835 Baltimore Bank Riot." *Journal of the Early Republic* 37 (Summer 2017): 193–223.

Malone, Jacqui. *Steppin'on the Blues: Rhytms of African American Dance.* Urbana:Univ. of Illinois Press, 1996.

Melton, Tracy Matthew. "The Case of the Catholic Know-Nothings." *MHM* 109 (Fall 2014): 351–71.

———. "The Lost Lives of George Konig Sr., and Jr., a Father-Son Tale of Old Fells Point." *MHM* 101 (Fall 2006): 332–61.

———. "Michael J. Redding and Irish-American Patriotism." *MHM* 107 (Fall 2012): 321–58.

Miller, Kerby A. *Emigrants and Exiles: Ireland and the Irish Exodus to North America.* New York: Oxford Univ. Press, 1985.

Miller, Wilbur. *Cops and Bobbies: Police Authority in New York and London, 1830–1870.* Chicago: Univ. of Chicago Press, 1977.

Mitchell, Charles W. "Maryland's Presidential Election of 1860." *MHM* 109 (Fall 2014): 307–27.

Mitrani, Sam. *The Rise of the Chicago Police Department: Class and Conflict 1850–1894.* Urbana: Univ. of Illinois Press, 2013.

Mohr, James. *Doctors and the Law: Medical Jurisprudence in Nineteenth-Century America.* New York: Oxford Univ. Press, 1993.

Monkkonen, Eric H. *The Dangerous Class: Crime and Poverty in Columbus, Ohio, 1860–1885.* Cambridge: Harvard Univ. Press, 1975.

———. *Police in Urban America 1860–1920.* Cambridge: Cambridge Univ. Press, 1981.

Phillips, Christopher. *Freedom's Port: The African American Community of Baltimore, 1790–1860.* Urbana: Univ. of Illinois Press, 1997.

Pollock, Frederick, and Frederic William Maitland. *The History of English Law before the Time of Edward I.* 2 vols. 2nd ed. Cambridge: Cambridge Univ. Press, 1923.

Potter, David M. *The Impending Crisis of the South.* Completed and edited by Don E. Fehrenbacher. New York: Harper and Row, 1976.

Power, Garrett. "Apartheid Baltimore Style: The Residential Segregation Ordinances of 1910–1913." *Maryland Law Review* 42 (Nov. 1983): 294–328.

Rabinowitz, Howard N. *Race Relations in the Urban South, 1865–1890.* Urbana: Univ. of Illinois Press, 1978.

Reilly, Eileen. "Modern Ireland: An Introductory Survey." In *Making the Irish American: History and Heritage of the Irish in the United States,* edited by J. J. Lee and Marion R. Casey, 63–147. New York: New York Univ. Press, 2006.

Richardson, James F. *The New York Police: Colonial Times to 1901.* New York: Oxford Univ. Press, 1970.

Richter, Hedwig. "Transnational Reform and Democracy: Election Reforms in New York City and Berlin around 1900." *Journal of the Gilded Age and the Progressive Era* 15 (Apr. 2016): 147–75.

Rockman, Seth. *Scraping By: Wage Labor, Slavery, and Survival in Early Baltimore.* Baltimore: Johns Hopkins Univ. Press, 2009.

Roediger, David R. *The Wages of Whiteness: Race and the Making of the American Working Class.* London: Verso, 1991.

Rohr, Clyde C. "Charities and Charitable Institutions." In *Baltimore: Its History and Its People.* Vol. 1, *History,* edited by Clayton Colman Hall, 657–77. New York: Lewis Historical Publishing Co., 1912.

Ross, Michael A. *The Great New Orleans Kidnapping Case: Race, Law, and Justice in the Reconstruction Era.* New York: Oxford Univ. Press, 2015.

Rousey, Dennis C. *Policing the Southern City—New Orleans, 1805–1889.* Baton Rouge: Louisiana State Univ. Press, 1997.

Ruffner, Kevin Conley. *Maryland's Blue and Gray: A Border State's Union and Confederate Junior Officer Corps.* Baton Rouge: Louisiana State Univ. Press, 1997.

———. "'More Trouble Than a Brigade': Harry Gilmor's 2d Maryland Cavalry in the Shenandoah Valley." *MHM* 89 (Winter 1994): 389–411.

Scharf, J. Thomas. *Chronicles of Baltimore, Being a Complete History of "Baltimore Town" and Baltimore City from the Earliest Period to the Present Time.* Baltimore: Turnbull Brothers, 1874.

———. *History of Baltimore City and County.* Philadelphia: Louis H. Everts, 1881.

Schmeckebier, Laurence Frederick. *History of the Know Nothing Party in Maryland.* Baltimore: Johns Hopkins Univ. Press, 1899.

Schneider, John C. *Detroit and the Problem of Order, 1830–1880: A Geography of Crime, Riot, and Policing.* Lincoln: Univ. of Nebraska Press, 1980.

Shalhope, Robert E. *The Baltimore Bank Riot: Political Upheaval in Antebellum Maryland.* Urbana: Univ. of Illinois Press, 2009.

Shufelt, Gordon H. "Elusive Justice in Baltimore: The Conviction of a White Policeman for Killing a Black Man in 1875." *Journal of Southern History* 83 (Nov. 2017): 773–814.

Spalding, Thomas W. *The Premier See: A History of the Archdiocese of Baltimore.* Baltimore: Johns Hopkins Univ. Press, 1989.

Stampp, Kenneth M. *The Era of Reconstruction, 1865–1877.* New York: Vintage Books, 1965.

Steinberg, Allen. *The Transformation of Criminal Justice in Philadelphia, 1800–1880.* Chapel Hill: Univ. of North Carolina Press, 1989.

Steiner, Bernard C. *Citizenship and Suffrage in Maryland.* Baltimore: Cushing and Co., 1895.

———. *Life of Henry Winter Davis.* Baltimore: Norman, Remington Co., 1914.

Thacher, David. "Olmsted's Police." *Law and History Review.* 33 (Aug. 2015): 577–620.

Thomas, Bettye C. "A Nineteenth Century Black Operated Shipyard, 1866–1884: Reflections on Its Inception and Operation." *Journal of Negro History* 59 (Jan. 1974): 1–12.

Tóibín, Colm. "The Irish Famine." In *The Irish Famine: A Documentary,* edited by Colm Tóibín and Diarmaid Ferriter, 1–36. New York: St. Martin's Press, 2002.

Tonry, Michael. "Why Crime Rates Are Falling throughout the Western World." *Crime and Justice* 43 (Sept. 2014): 1–63.

Towers, Frank. "Job Busting at Baltimore Shipyards: Racial Violence in the Civil War South." *Journal of Southern History* 66 (May 2000): 221–56.

———. "Violence as a Tool of Party Dominance: Election Riots and the Baltimore Know Nothings, 1854–1860." *MHM* 93 (Spring 1998): 5–38.

Wade, Richard C. *Slavery in the Cities: The South 1820–1860.* London: Oxford Univ. Press, 1964.

Walker, Samuel. *A Critical History of Police Reform: The Emergence of Professionalism.* Lexington, MA: D. C. Heath and Co., 1977.

Wiecek, William M. *Liberty under Law: The Supreme Court in American Life.* Baltimore: Johns Hopkins Univ. Press, 1988.

Whitman, T. Stephen. *Challenging Slavery in the Chesapeake: Black and White Resistance to Human Bondage.* Baltimore: Maryland Historical Society, 2007.

———. "Manumission and Apprenticeship in Maryland, 1770–1870." *MHM* 101 (Spring 2006): 55–72.

Woodson, Carter G. *The Rural Negro.* Washington, DC: Association for the Study of Negro Life and History, 1930.

Woodward, C. Vann. *The Strange Career of Jim Crow.* 2nd ed. London: Oxford Univ. Press, 1966.

Wright, James M. *The Free Negro in Maryland, 1634–1860.* New York: Columbia Univ. Press, 1921.

Index